"Thoroughly researched and clearly written, *Autism Spectrum Disorder, Developmental Disabilities, and the Criminal Justice System* explores in depth all aspects of the interface between the autism spectrum and the criminal justice system. Based upon both personal experiences and scholarly inquiries, this encyclopedic book will be extremely helpful in selecting an attorney to defend a person on the spectrum facing criminal charges, finding the right experts to bolster the defense, and confronting the draconian sex offender registries. This book should be required reading for those grappling with and seeking to understand these extremely difficult and complicated issues. A monumental achievement."

—David Thomas, criminal defense attorney, Clinical Professor of Law, IIT Chicago-Kent College of Law, and Executive Director, Illinois Torture Inquiry and Relief Commission

"All levels of the criminal justice system need to accommodate the characteristics of autism to ensure justice and the prevention of future crimes. With Nick's book, we now have a primary source of information on autism for those in the legal profession and law enforcement agencies, as well as for families and autistic adults. The explanations and recommendations are based on an extensive review of the research literature, and well-illustrated by case studies and conversations with those who have direct experience of the criminal justice system. This book will contribute to the ending of injustice and inappropriate incarceration."

—Tony Attwood, PhD, Adjunct Professor, Griffith University, Queensland, author of The Complete Guide to Asperger's Syndrome *and* Asperger's Syndrome: A Guide for Parents and Professionals

"In *Autism Spectrum Disorder, Developmental Disabilities, and the Criminal Justice System*, Nick Dubin turns the nightmare of his criminal conviction into an opportunity to educate the public about the nexus between the unique qualities of ASD and criminal conduct. But more importantly, Nick offers tangible strategies to prevent people with ASD and developmental disabilities from becoming ensnared in the criminal justice system in the first place. This book is scholarly yet readable, brutally honest but rational and realistic."

—Elizabeth Kelley, criminal defense lawyer, editor of Representing People with Autism Spectrum Disorders: A Practical Guide for Criminal Defense Lawyers

"Nick Dubin's book is one of a kind. Through his personal experience, he provides practical strategies and guidance to families and adults. Sexuality, the internet and social media need to be addressed and recognized as an essential topic when it comes to teaching autistic adolescents and adults. This also acts as powerful prevention. I definitely support Nick's recommendations and I encourage every professional in the field to read this unique book."

—*Isabelle Hénault, psychologist and sexologist, Director of the Autism & Asperger's Clinic, Canada*

Autism Spectrum Disorder, Developmental Disabilities, and the Criminal Justice System

by the same author

The Autism Spectrum, Sexuality and the Law
What Every Parent and Professional Needs to Know
Tony Attwood, Isabelle Hénault and Nick Dubin
ISBN 978 1 84905 919 0
eISBN 978 0 85700 679 0

The Autism Spectrum and Depression
Nick Dubin
ISBN 978 1 84905 814 8
eISBN 978 0 85700 242 6

Asperger Syndrome and Anxiety
A Guide to Successful Stress Management
Nick Dubin
ISBN 978 1 84310 895 5
eISBN 978 1 84642 922 4

Asperger Syndrome and Bullying
Strategies and Solutions
Nick Dubin
ISBN 978 1 84310 846 7
eISBN 978 1 84642 635 3

of related interest

Caught in the Web of the Criminal Justice System
Autism, Developmental Disabilities, and Sex Offenses
Edited by Lawrence A. Dubin, J.D. and Emily Horowitz, Ph.D.
Foreword by Alan Gershel, J.D.
ISBN 978 1 78592 713 3
eISBN 978 1 78450 298 0

Autism and the Police
Practical Advice for Officers and Other First Responders
Andy Buchan
ISBN 978 1 78775 284 9
eISBN 978 1 78775 285 6

Autism Spectrum Disorder, Developmental Disabilities, and the Criminal Justice System

Breaking the Cycle

Nick Dubin

Foreword by Dr. Clare Allely

Jessica Kingsley Publishers
London and Philadelphia

First published in Great Britain in 2021 by Jessica Kingsley Publishers
An Hachette Company

1

Copyright © Nick Dubin 2021
Foreword copyright © Dr. Clare Allely 2021

A CIP catalogue record for this title is available from the
British Library and the Library of Congress

ISBN 978 1 78775 361 7
eISBN 978 1 78775 362 4

Printed and bound in Great Britain by CPI Group

Jessica Kingsley Publishers' policy is to use papers that are natural, renewable
and recyclable products and made from wood grown in sustainable
forests. The logging and manufacturing processes are expected to conform
to the environmental regulations of the country of origin.

Jessica Kingsley Publishers
Carmelite House
50 Victoria Embankment
London EC4Y 0DZ

www.jkp.com

To my parents, who have always been there for me.

Huge thanks to my editor, Elizabeth Katz.

Contents

Foreword

A number of years ago as I sat on a bustling Glasgow bus on the way home from work, I realized with a jolt that I had missed my stop to catch the second bus on my journey. No, I had not missed my stop because darkness had fallen and I could not see where I was, nor had I fallen into a deep, dribble-inducing slumber; instead I had been too deeply engrossed in a book to realize where I was or have any awareness of anything going on around me. The book in question was *The Autism Spectrum, Sexuality and the Law: What Every Parent and Professional Needs to Know*. It was in this book that I first encountered the brave and inspirational young autistic man, Nick Dubin. In collaboration with Isabelle Hénault and Tony Attwood, Nick gave a deeply insightful, personal, and groundbreaking account of his experiences when he found himself suddenly caught up in the criminal justice system following an arrest for possession of child pornography. Despite my psychological qualifications coupled with my understanding and research in the field of autism, when I first grasped this book, I have to be honest, I was somewhat skeptical. Could some of the key symptomology of autism really provide the context for vulnerability to engaging in the possession of child pornography? If so, to what extent? Can an autistic individual who downloads child pornography really have no appreciation that what they are doing is wrong?

After reading this book, I gained such a deep appreciation and understanding into the various ways in which the symptomology of autism can provide the context for vulnerability to engaging in the possession of child pornography, at least in a subgroup of autistic individuals who are charged with such an offense. Since reading this book, I am often found saying to my students who show an interest in the field of autism and offending behavior or the criminal justice system that even if they have to eat beans for a week, they need to purchase this book. So you can probably imagine my joy when Nick approached me to write this foreword for a new book he had written on the topic, which really builds on his previous book, particularly focusing on prevention. Since reading Nick's account, I have been propelled to research in this field and have published a number of papers with various colleagues across the world including the United States and Australia. One of the key things that struck me during this time was the lack of understanding, even amongst many clinical professionals, of how the symptomology of autism can provide the context for vulnerability to engaging in the possession of child pornography. Such a varied or lack of understanding really underscores the very real and urgent need for resources in this area that really aim to equip professionals and families with the knowledge and information that is so desperately needed. This new book by Nick addresses this worrying gap and will prove an excellent and invaluable resource to support an unimaginable number of autistic individuals and their families who find themselves in a similar position to the one Nick found himself in all those years ago.

Autistic individuals may explore the internet for sexual education or to satisfy sexual needs due to a lack of sexual outlets with peers/friends. Many autistic people will have average or above average intelligence while their social maturity is that of someone much younger. Regarding the viewing of child pornography, issues occur when autistic individuals are unaware that what they have done is a criminal offense. One explanation for the lack of awareness that they have committed a crime is their inability to recognize the facial expressions in the images of the children. Such an inability to recognize facial expressions (such as fear) is supported by a large amount of studies. Another issue that needs to be considered is that many autistic individuals may inadvertently view child pornography as a result of their inability to guess correctly the age of the individuals in the images, and sometimes the boundaries/distinction between an adult and a child is blurry. This is important to understand given that the legality and severity of the offense is determined by the age of the victims in the images being viewed by the defendant.

For autistic people, exploring sexuality on the internet through child pornography is one way for them to try to understand relationships and sexuality as opposed to being a precursor to any sexual offending towards a minor. As with many things that interest them, the desire for this material can end up being particularly excessive and compulsive. The internet coupled with sexuality can result in what Mark Mahoney, a noted criminal defense attorney who has experience in defending autistic individuals charged with criminal offenses, calls a "lethal combination" for autistic individuals. There are numerous cases where an autistic individual has been found to have large collections of pornographic material (e.g., involving children) (as part of the ritualistic nature of autism) with thousands of files not even opened. They may not be aware of the broader issues like where and how they got those files, who else might be able to access them, and what the consequences are for (and impact is on) the minors in the images they are viewing. Because of their literal view of the world, they would not consider that something that is illegal could be so freely available on the internet. The media is fraught with marketing materials with risqué images of teenage models or images where older models have been made to look "barely legal." Such images can be confusing for some autistic individuals, making it more difficult for them to determine what is illegal pornography.

Another issue is the assumption that the level of risk is associated with the number of images that the individual has accumulated or the nature of the content. This is because some believe that the more images the greater the obsession and that someone is more at risk of acting on these urges as a result. However, studies do not support this. This is even more inappropriate for autistic individuals because it ignores the relationship between the volume of collected pornography and the compulsive and obsessive features of autism. There is also no research which indicates that extreme sexual content is predictive of dangerousness. Looking at extreme sexual material is not always a reflection of the presence of deviant sexuality. Instead, it can be what is referred to as "counterfeit deviance," in other words a naive curiosity, in individuals with a diagnosis of autism.

Crucially, the majority of autistic people never become involved with the criminal justice system. However, there is a small subgroup who do. For those who find themselves faced with a criminal charge, it is imperative that there is research and understanding of how their characteristics or features of autism may have contributed to their behavior (the charge that they are faced with). Such knowledge and information can be used to ensure a fair trial. This could lead to a number of possibilities in some cases, including: reduced sentencing, diversionary measures (with psychoeducation), or suspended sentences. This book delves into these various areas in great depth and will no doubt find me yet again advocating a week of eating beans to my interested students.

Dr. Clare Allely
Reader in Forensic Psychology at the University of Salford in Manchester,
England. Affiliate member of the Gillberg Neuropsychiatry Centre at the
University of Gothenburg, Sweden. Honorary Research Fellow in the College
of Medical, Veterinary and Life Sciences affiliated to the Institute of Health
and Wellbeing at the University of Glasgow, Scotland. Associate of the Centre
for Youth and Criminal Justice at the University of Strathclyde, Scotland.

Introduction

This is a book I never wanted to write but felt needed to be written.

I am an autistic individual. In 2010, I was arrested for possession of child pornography and pleaded guilty in federal court. I have been angry at myself since that day but, more importantly, I wanted to try to understand what happened. So, in collaboration with Isabelle Hénault and Tony Attwood (2014), I wrote about the experience in great detail and how it interacted with my life story. Writing the book did have an effect of heightening my own self-awareness, as well as helping other parents and autistic individuals going through similar situations.

However, this book is not that. In this book, I attempt to explore why autistic people get caught up in the criminal justice system and what we as a community can do to prevent that from happening. It should be pointed out that autistic people are far more likely to be the victims of crime than the victimizers (Copenhaver & Tewksbury, 2019). This book does not look to further stigmatize autistic people but lift them up from an oppressive system that might misunderstand them. It looks to hold accountable those autistic people who will not take responsibility for their actions. Sexual crimes are traumatic, damaging for life, and should not be minimized. I am not writing this book to minimize sex crimes or any other type of crime where harm is done and someone needs to be made whole. Instead, I want to examine why autistic people might commit certain crimes. I also want to explore alternative ways of handling these situations for first-time offenders, individuals who have taken responsibility for their actions, those with less criminal responsibility, and low-risk individuals.

Chapter 1 focuses on the prevention of autistic people committing crimes, and it is the most important chapter of the book as far as I am concerned. If we cannot prevent more autistic people from entering the criminal justice system, we will continue to see more systemic tragedies and more victims. Nobody wants that.

Chapter 2 focuses on autistic individuals and their interactions with the police and how systematic policies need to be put in place to make sure these encounters don't escalate and end in violence or even death.

Chapter 3 describes what to expect once the autistic defendant has crossed the point of no return and entered the criminal justice system. I look in depth at what the adjudication process is like, what strategies might want to be considered for judges, law enforcement officials, and lawyers, and what I would like to see changed on a large-scale basis in the future.

And finally, Chapter 4 discusses the aftermath of sentencing. I talk about what usually happens to autistic people and what I would like to see happen instead.

It should be noted that while all types of crime are covered throughout this book, sex crimes are mentioned the most, because they appear most in the literature in relation to autism spectrum disorders (ASD) and feature most prominently in my interactions with other parents whose children have gone through the criminal justice system.

CHAPTER 1

Prevention

Prevention is power. If we can help prevent autistic people from ending up in the criminal justice system, we give them a chance at life they wouldn't otherwise have. Autistic people already have disadvantages to face in society simply because of their atypicality. Facing the stigma of a criminal conviction, possible sex offender registration, and the trauma of incarceration is too much for most neurotypical people to bear. It is much harder for autistic people and those with disabilities.

A book about autism and crime that doesn't focus on prevention falls short. I am writing this book so there will be fewer perpetrators and fewer victims. This chapter focuses on that very topic before we move on to how we can help autistic people if it is too late and they are already engulfed in the system.

Much of this book will focus on autistic individuals across all thresholds of functionality. It is important to underscore, however, the sheer importance and magnitude of providing quality sex education tailored specifically for the needs and abilities of individuals with cognitive disabilities, as well as autistic individuals who have no intellectual impairment (Craft, 1994; Dewinter *et al.*, 2013; Gerouki, 2007; Gilmour, Schalomon & Smith, 2012; Gougeon, 2010; Hénault, 2006; Howard-Barr *et al.*, 2005; Kellaher, 2015; McCabe, 1993; Steutel & Spiecker, 2004).

While there is plenty of literature focused on intellectual disabilities and cognitive impairments (most of the research focuses on this with regards to sex education), for this discussion I am concerned about individuals with higher levels of cognitive functioning who might be susceptible or vulnerable to becoming involved with the criminal justice system. While we know autistic people can be extremely law abiding due to their rule-following nature (Stout, 2016), we are also aware that autistic people are vulnerable to committing many kinds of crimes (Haskins & Silva, 2006). First, we will focus on sex education and its vital role in preventing autistic people with significant cognitive ability from ending up in the criminal justice system.

Unfortunately, when it comes to crimes that autistic people are vulnerable to committing, crimes of a sexual nature are mentioned most often (Bleil Walters *et al.*, 2013; Mogavero, 2016; Sevlever, Roth & Gillis, 2013; Søndenaa *et al.*, 2014). This, however, is not because they have a greater tendency for true sexual deviancy (Gilmour *et al.*, 2012; Murrie *et al.*, 2002; Payne *et al.*, 2019b). To help us explain why crimes of a sexual nature are mentioned most often, let's look at a recent study.

Payne *et al.* (2019a) interviewed nine autistic adults who had been convicted of sex offenses in the United Kingdom. The five major themes cited by the participants were misunderstanding of the transgression or law that they had broken, inadequate control, disequilibrium, social difficulties, and sex and relationship deficits. Most individuals in the study reported wanting to have appropriate relationships but had a lack of appropriate opportunities to do so (*ibid.*). The literature backs this up (Hénault & Attwood, 2002; Mehzabin & Stokes, 2011). Indeed, lack of appropriate sexual outlets or relationship deficits can underlie some sex offenses in autistic men (Fabian, 2011). One study showed that autistic men who did not have an intellectual disability had less sexual experience than the group with an intellectual disability (Gougeon, 2013). In other words, those without autism but with a lower intellectual quotient (IQ) found it easier to have sexual experiences than the non-intellectually impaired autistics. Hancock, Stokes and Mesibov (2020) recruited 459 individuals, with 232 being autistic and the remaining number typically developing. The ASD group overwhelmingly felt that they had fewer opportunities to meet new partners, shorter relationship durations, and greater concern about their future relationships.

Disequilibrium was also mentioned in Payne *et al.*'s (2019a) study. This is not a surprising feature when we consider that most participants in the study felt that they lacked professional support in their social and sexual development. Lack of emotional control was reported in Payne *et al.*'s (*ibid.*) study where participants stated they felt younger than their chronological age and had an admitted immaturity. It is well known in the literature that autistic people can lag behind their chronological age, with their subjective or social age being considerably younger (Anderson *et al.*, 2016). Klin *et al.* (2007) found that in a sample of children and adolescents with an average or above average IQ and a mean chronological age of 12.4 years, their mean interpersonal social age was 3.2 years.

And finally, the subjects in Payne *et al.*'s (2019a) study not understanding their transgressions is also not surprising because many autistic people do not intuitively pick up on rules, codes, and established behaviors of a given society. Once they know what they are, they follow them to a tee. Fesmire (2003) calls autism a condition of "moral rehearsal" and notes that if morality was merely reducible to following memorized codes and rules, autistic people would be the moral ideal (De Vignemont & Frith, 2008). I hope it is becoming clear that traditional sexual education classes cannot possibly address these issues early on in an autistic person's development as a means of preventing these tragic outcomes (Hannah & Stagg, 2016). One-sized curriculums do not work. Autistic people require curriculums tailored to their own specific needs. I will delve into how to accomplish this later in this chapter.

A Starting Place

Autistic individuals are sexual beings with the same needs, desires, and sex drives as their neurotypical peers (Postorino et al., 2018). The notion that autistic individuals are asexual was debunked a long time ago (Kellaher, 2015). As I explained in my own book (Attwood, Hénault & Dubin, 2014), I did not want to acknowledge that I was a sexual being for the majority of my life. I remember having one brief sexual education course in high school that taught us about our anatomical body parts and the course was completely meaningless to me. I had sexual longings, desires, and feelings I didn't understand, and they went unacknowledged by my family and myself because there were so many other issues on my plate. Sexuality literally took a back seat. I believe this was extremely detrimental to the course of my life.

Acknowledging autistic people as sexual beings, just like everyone else, is the crucial first step towards providing the sexual education they need to have pleasurable and safe relationships. These relationships must be free of coercion, discrimination, violence, or the possibility of becoming involved in the justice system (Loftin & Hartlage, 2015). Consider that peer-reviewed articles not long ago were suggesting that sex was not relevant for autistic people (Torisky, 1985) and therefore sex education was not important. Even as recently as 2002 (Aunos & Feldman, 2002), many parents supported sterilizing their intellectually disabled children. This kind of misinformed literature and bigoted attitude has contributed to the problem we are seeing today. In this regard, we have a lot to overcome.

Many parents report difficulty in having conversations with their children about sex-related topics (Dewinter et al., 2017). Because parents are the primary educators of their children regarding sexual matters, their underestimation of their child's interest and/or ability to participate diminishes important conversations between them (Ballan, 2012). It is extremely important that social-skills training precedes sexual education and that conversations about sex in the home begin as early as they would for neurotypicals.

Invisible Fencing

Once we acknowledge that autistic people are sexual beings, we can face any warning signs that might be present without fearing them. For example, we know that hypersexuality is one of the problematic sexual behaviors in which young autistic people can become involved. In a meta-analysis of 5241 studies, it was found that hyper-masturbation, public masturbation, inappropriate romantic gestures, and exhibitionism were among the most common issues that adolescent autistic people display (Beddows & Brooks, 2016). This is predictable because autistic individuals can have tactile hypersensitivities, preoccupations, and a certain amount of compulsiveness (Dewinter *et al.*, 2015). Turner, Briken and Schöttle (2019) caution that these hypo or hypersensitivities help to explain why certain men with ASD may develop unwanted sexual behaviors, which can lead to encounters with law enforcement. Knowing this, the natural temptation when an adult witnesses some of these behaviors would be to get the autistic person to stop immediately. Perhaps some of the behaviors might force caregivers to punish the person in certain ways. This is actually appropriate and sometimes absolutely necessary. Certain behaviors cannot be tolerated for the child or adolescent's own good. In taking these precautionary measures though, one has to be careful that the caregiver isn't unintentionally sending the message that "sex is bad." Parents are rightly concerned that their ASD child's non-sexual actions will be misinterpreted by others as sexual (Ballan & Freyer, 2017; Mackin *et al.*, 2016), further adding to the fear surrounding sex and autism.

This unconscious "sex is bad" attitude that gets transmitted is what I will call "invisible fencing." I call it that because it is almost like a dog that tries to exceed the boundaries of the yard and gets shocked each time it tries to leave. Gradually, the dog learns that leaving the yard is not a very good idea because it will experience pain. In our analogy, sometimes the wiring of the fencing glitches from time to time, leading to confusing shocks for the "dog," or autistic individual. A good example of this is an outrageous story that made headlines in the United States (Slisco, 2019). In September 2019, an autistic five-year-old's mother received a rather shocking call from her son's school. She was sick to her stomach when they told her that young Nathan's hugging and kissing another student was tantamount to "sexual activity." The school denied taking formal disciplinary matters against Nathan but nevertheless insinuated that his motivations were sexual: a five-year-old. It is very likely that Nathan will internalize negative feelings regarding showing affection for others because of this confusing situation. While he should have been taught appropriate boundaries and to ask permission before touching someone else, he was instead looked upon as a sexual deviant. Day (1997) suggests that autistic people and those with intellectual impairments are often punished for what would otherwise be considered normative behavior that has no sexual connotations.

This sounds extreme but the lengths to which we used to go to treat public displays of sexual behavior in autistic people is horrifying. Restricting the sexuality of developmentally disabled individuals is part of our history. There have historically been institutional and legal restrictions on the intimate contact of people with developmental disabilities (Siebers, 2008), which Goodley, Runswick-Cole and Liddiard (2016) see as a basic denial of human rights. Prior to the 1970s, public displays of sexual behavior among those with autism were handled with institutionalization (Griffiths, Quinsey & Hingsburger, 1989). As far as society was concerned, it was out of sight and out of mind (Realmuto & Ruble, 1999). But prior to the days of institutionalization, which began even earlier in the 1930s and 1940s, people with developmental disabilities were seen as either purely sexually innocent or sexually dangerous, promiscuous, and in need of legal sanctioning (Griffiths *et al.*, 2002). According to Griffiths *et al.* (2002), the developmentally disabled were congregated and separated from other populations who had committed crimes and were seen as sexually promiscuous and poverty stricken. The end game was forced sterilization and controlled marriage of the "genetically inferior" through a rigorous scientific "eugenic" campaign. It was feared that more crime would be forced upon future generations if the developmentally disabled could have children. Other arguments, along the line of "disabled people are sexually innocent," were that disabled people needed to be protected from the knowledge of sexuality or engagement in sex (Daly, Heah & Liddiard, 2019). It was almost as if it was a laudable goal to keep the disabled in a perpetual state of sexual innocence, far away from the Tree of the Knowledge of Good and Evil in the Garden of Eden. Hingsburger (1992) observed that, as a result of this collective trauma inflicted on these autistic individuals over the years, many of the developmentally disabled from that era had erotophobia, which is a fear of anything sexual including one's own private parts. Erotophobia also involves what Hingsburger (1992) calls a "conspiracy of denial and anger" over the development of one's own sexuality. I interpret this to mean that one wants to disavow the sexual aspects of one's being but can't. The literature has not yet explored whether erotophobia still exists among autistic people at large.

To bring this all down to earth, one example of erotophobia comes from Craig, Lindsay and Browne (2010). A man named Ron who had a developmental disability was living in a group home. He was enrolled in sex education classes and the instructors noticed that Ron became very angry and aggressive after each class. This was not a characteristic behavior for him in general. It was discovered that Ron used to receive corporal punishment from his father when he was caught masturbating in front of him and thus experienced negative emotions when faced with attending these classes.

I admit that this "invisible fencing" and erotophobia applied to me throughout much of my life. For the longest time I had internalized feelings of homophobia that began in middle school, but it was not clear whether these feelings were related to my overall differences or my true sexual orientation. When I was around 19 or 20, I attempted to "come out" to my parents. They felt I couldn't possibly know if I was gay because I did not yet have sexual experiences with the opposite sex. My parents felt that, because I had so many other issues on my plate due to my disability, identifying as "gay" would make my life that much harder. This was well intentioned, but the end result was that after this conversation, the issue of sex was never talked about between me and my parents until my arrest. As a result, I tried to bury all of my sexual feelings. I didn't see myself as a sexual being capable of having a relationship, much less with someone of the same sex. If I was asked by parents of autistic children if I ever planned to get married, I tried shirking the question but deep down it did produce a "denial and anger over one's developing sexuality" in me that Hingsburger (Griffiths *et al.*, 2002, p.427) discusses. What I didn't know at the time was that adults dismissing the self-assessment of an autistic person's sexual orientation is not uncommon (Strang, 2018). I also didn't know that ASD individuals report increased feelings of being gay, lesbian, bisexual, or transgender in comparison with neurotypicals (George & Stokes, 2018). Indeed, it appears that ASD individuals display greater gender fluidity than their typically developing peers (Strang *et al.*, 2018).

Of course, buried feelings don't go away. They come out in unexpected and tragic ways, which is one of the reasons why they shouldn't be allowed to go underground. Autistic people deserve to be in relationships. They also deserve to have their feelings addressed so they can live a fully self-determined life, free from victimization by others or becoming involved in the criminal justice system.

If the autistic person is able to "leave the yard" without the threat of "invisible fencing," the good news is that autistic individuals, by and large, want to be involved in romantic relationships (Hellemans *et al.*, 2007). This is promising and hopeful because our focus is prevention. The goal is prosocial behavior that avoids encounters with law enforcement. Yet the biggest obstacles for ASD individuals when entering healthy relationships are negative attitudes and feelings that they may have about sexuality (Byers, Nichols & Voyer, 2013). This was certainly true for me.

The Hidden Curriculum

Part of the reason that sex is such a daunting topic to teach in schools is that it is quite hard to cover everything. Unlike chemistry and biology, where the real-world applications can be fully explored in the textbook through classroom experiments, students in sex education classes are already expected to intuitively know and understand the underlying codes and rituals that define courtship in a given culture. These things that autistic people don't know, but most neurotypicals do, all fall within a hidden curriculum. This curriculum needs to be taught explicitly to autistic individuals. A "hidden curriculum" is essentially "everything a learner learns that goes above and beyond the planned curriculum" (Murphy, Mufti & Kossem, 2009, p.164). In other words, hidden curriculums tend to be remedial. They are not taught unless educators feel that students need to know them and wouldn't learn the information on their own.

Part of the reason that teaching a hidden curriculum on sex and healthy relationships is difficult is because social rules of engagement are prerequisites for them. To further complicate matters, the rules of social engagement are very broad and aren't easily generalizable from situation to situation. In other words, autistic people don't easily learn the rules of proper social engagement. For example, eye contact may be appropriate with one's boss or during a job interview but not in a men's bathroom when you're next to another guy in a stall. Swearing may be inappropriate in most formal social contexts but expected among peers to experience the benefits of "in-group membership" (Myles, Trautman & Schelvan, 2004). Hewitt (2011) aptly compares social learning for an ASD individual to an adult learning a second language. By the time the average high-school graduate completes their education, they know about 60,000 words. It would be difficult to teach even the most fluent second-language learner that many words simply because babies are naturally wired to learn language and adults are not. Fluency in a second language as an adult doesn't require the same vocabulary as the native tongue speakers. Individuals on the spectrum and their caregivers face the same challenge. It may not be possible to learn every social skill imaginable because contexts vary infinitely. Generalizability would be impossible without flexibility of social thinking from situation to situation. A person has to acquire broad social knowledge. Just as babies are wired for language, Grandin and Barron (2005) believe that neurotypicals are born with a broad "social sense" that ASD individuals simply don't have. Hewitt (2011) notes that lack of attention to these broad areas of social learning can end up causing legal problems for ASD individuals.

Yet even straightforward, broad-stroke instruction of social skills to remediate this can fall short. The English language is filled with so many inconsistencies and double meanings that it can be difficult for an autistic person with a literal mind to instinctively learn proper cues in a social setting. Take the phrase, "Don't talk to strangers." Most neurotypical young children who are taught this maxim will instinctively know what it means and need no further instruction. It, of course, means that if you are approached by a stranger, you mustn't speak to them. But as Myles and Simpson (2001) point out, there are actually many ways to interpret this phrase. A new school bus driver is a stranger. Is it okay to talk to them? What about a cashier in a store? Or a flight attendant?

To mitigate against such misunderstandings, social learning activities like The Incredible 5-Point Scale™ have been used to help ASD individuals categorize acceptable and unacceptable behaviors. It does this incrementally, using a Likert scale with visual prompts (Buron & Curtis, 2003). A five on the scale might indicate a behavior that is clearly against the law (such as touching a stranger), while a one might describe a social faux pas (such as picking one's nose). The problem is that even this kind of categorization can be misinterpreted.

Take John (pseudonym) as an example. John is a smart autistic young man who graduated near the top of his high-school class. He got a bachelor's degree from a well-respected university and had a promising career ahead of him. He likes the feel of different types of silky clothing. He also wears spandex himself and is gender fluid. John also has delayed social skills.

John's problem related to the fact that he had the habit of walking up to women, striking up friendly conversations with them, and then asking if he could touch their clothing. Most of the time women agreed, but on one occasion, John touched the wrong woman. She immediately went to the police and John was detained. Not realizing what he had done wrong, John sat and waited for almost a year in the county jail while his fate was being decided. Eventually, he pleaded to a misdemeanor offense, but it put him on the sex offender registry. John insists today that the touch was non-sexual and tactile-sensory seeking.

Where would this example fall on the five-point scale for an intelligent individual like John? Certainly, he must have known that touching people without their consent is wrong. And he likely knew that touching someone sexually upon meeting them is something one shouldn't do. Likely, both of these things would have been a "five" in John's mind. Yet, he assumed that it was socially appropriate to touch a stranger near or around the waist upon meeting them as long as it was non-sexual in nature, even with their consent. No one actually taught him explicitly that although this behavior may, on the surface, seem appropriate since the woman gave her consent, you should never do this to an unfamiliar person. The broad-stroke instruction he received was clearly not enough and failed him.

Not only did John lack a proper sexual education curriculum, he also wasn't taught emotional regulation skills or given proper sensory integration tools. He also lacked central coherence or the ability to see the big picture. These are crucial components for leading a sexually satisfying life and not violating the consent of another human being. I will speak to emotional regulation now and how it ties into the broader subject of sex and the law.

Emotional Regulation

So far, I have established that both social skills, or what I might call the hidden curriculum, and the ability to regulate one's emotions should precede the teaching of healthy sexuality to ASD students: they are basic prerequisites. So, let's delve into this further.

Emotional regulation is a complex interaction of many different areas. It probably lies at the core of most human behavior, but the explanations for it go into many different areas. Simply put, our ability to regulate emotion has to do with how we internally appraise it and then control the extent to which we deal with it in real time. It is how we consciously modify our emotions to achieve external goals (Mazefsky et al., 2013). If a person feels an overabundance of emotions at an extremely deep level but can't process these emotions, this can lead to confusion, panic, and possible impulsive behavior. After all, we couldn't go around actively showing all of our emotions without suppressing ones that may not be appropriate in a given context, such as laughing at a funeral. Our goal at a funeral is to mourn and act in a socially appropriate way. Laughing would impede this goal.

For some people, emotional regulation doesn't come easily. If one is cognitively rigid and perseverates, sees only their own perspective in a given situation, or has a hard time with the basic pragmatics of everyday life, their emotional responses to these cognitions will be reflected outwardly. If information processing is different in a person, such as not being able to filter out certain kinds of information or misreading social cues, the emotional responses to this information will be different from what most people are accustomed to. If emotion for a particular individual is less goal directed and is based more on their internal states, the emotional reactions that the person has will be less likely to help the individual achieve their goals. If the neural circuitry differs in an individual and they have an enlarged amygdala and different cortical activities in the prefrontal area of the brain, this too will affect emotional regulation. All of these characteristics are typically found in individuals on the autism spectrum (Mazefsky et al., 2013). This is to say, emotional regulation is a difficulty for people on the spectrum.

Lerner et al. (2012) believe that lack of emotional regulation in autistic individuals is a contributing factor to these individuals committing certain violent crimes, while also acknowledging that autistic people are less prone to crime in general. Kaartinen *et al.* (2014) have observed that ASD boys have fewer inhibitory tools to use when they receive gender-related cues from the opposite sex and are therefore more likely to respond to girls with aggression than their typically developing peers. Hans Asperger in his original paper from 1944 (Asperger, 1991) used the phrase "autistic malice" to describe certain behaviors he found troublesome, but this was clarified decades later by Uta Frith who suggested that such behavior was usually derived from eliciting an emotional reaction in another person in order to make more sense of the social world (Jones *et al.*, 2009). This, of course, implies that the emotional reactions of other people often don't make sense to autistic people, so to correspond them to their own experiences, autistic people act a certain way to elicit more predictable responses. Unfortunately, this can sometimes backfire, resulting in the opposite of a predictable reaction, including encounters with law enforcement and the criminal justice system.

Emotional regulation also requires basic emotional awareness. One must be able to know what one is feeling and put words to those emotions. Sometimes this skill is lacking for ASD individuals; this is known clinically as alexithymia (Samson, Huber & Gross, 2012), which is estimated to affect 85 percent of people on the autism spectrum (Hill, Berthoz & Frith, 2004). Research indicates/suggests that alexithymic individuals display more disruptive behavior at times. One study compared reform-school adolescents with a control group using an instrument designed to measure alexithymia. Study results found that the reform-school group was significantly more alexithymic (Manninen *et al.*, 2011). Payne and Hollin (2014) also found that offender populations were higher in alexithymic individuals when compared with others. And Strickland *et al.* (2017) also found this to be true when studying the issue in Australia. This makes sense. If someone has a hard time identifying emotions within themselves, their behavior might be out of kilter with how that person is truly feeling. This incongruent behavior might not only be out of sync with the person themselves but also with society's norms, rules, and expectations.

This strongly suggests that teaching ASD individuals feeling states and their corresponding physiological accompanying sensations might be crucial in helping them to avoid the criminal justice system. Music therapy can help autistic individuals who are also alexithymic to identify their own feelings (Allen & Heaton, 2010). Most people, including those with autism, experience positive and negative reactions to music. Music evokes certain emotions in most of us, which is why it is often referred to as a universal language. Music therapy has been shown to be superior to the placebo effect as an intervention for children with ASD in interactions within therapy, generalized social interaction outside the therapy context, social adaptation, and relationships (Geretsegger *et al.*, 2014). In the case of alexithymia, and for individuals with more expressive language problems and those who have greater inability to track their feelings, this might work more unconventionally. Because music evolved as a cohesive structure to keep unity within a society, autistic and alexithymic individuals who don't share a common language with the rest of the culture are at a disadvantage. According to Allen and Heaton (2010), if asked how a person is feeling, an autistic person could say "like a James Brown song" and we might assume they are feeling energetic or full of life. If they said they felt like a Chopin nocturne, perhaps it would tell us they are a little melancholy. And even if the music doesn't evoke the same emotion in the alexithymic group as it usually would for others, it could be useful to track their own internal emotions. Apps with visible musical icons could assist in this process for nonverbal individuals.

Knowing how one is feeling can help to regulate one's emotions more effectively. Once a person is able to have some awareness of their emotions (even if they continue to be mildly alexithymic), assistive technology can be hugely effective. If distressing states make it hard for a person to identify their emotions, smartwatches with the appropriate apps can sense the heart rate going up and alert the wearer through a form of biofeedback (Torrado, Montoro & Gomez, 2016). A person with autism can be taught that when this happens, "Don't do anything impulsive or without thinking twice." This alone could help certain individuals to avoid encounters with the criminal justice system. It could also teach individuals about what to do in distressing situations by preparing a text, image, or audio recording. These could help the individual avoid the circumstance or learn how to cope with it. The programming icons can guess or anticipate the circumstances that the individual reacts to the most strongly the most often. The smartwatch can also develop a scale of emotional intensity using visual icons and by assigning names to different emotional states such as a sunny day (for happiness) or a tornado (for an emotionally troubling situation). Torrado *et al.* (2016) give an example of the wearer seeing a big dog such as a pit bull. The smartwatch, triggered by an elevated heart rate, could question what the issue is and the user could be presented with a number of visual prompts as answers. In other words, with this particular example, the smartwatch would try to catch the wearer's attention through sound or vibration, tell the user where to go, or direct him to shelter where he is less likely to get hurt by the dog (assuming this is programmed into the app). With advances in artificial intelligence (AI), we may get to the point where this kind of assistive technology becomes much more advanced than it is today.

Cognitive behavioral therapy (CBT) has been shown to be effective for remediating difficulties with emotional regulation in ASD individuals (Scarpa, White & Attwood, 2013). CBT begins with the premise that thoughts influence feelings, as well as actions. Metacognition over one's thoughts can help someone manage their emotions. In other words, all people (neurotypicals and autistics, alike) make a number of "thinking errors" every day that we don't always correct because we lack personal objectivity about ourselves. We may think that a person hates us when, in fact, we simply misread their nonverbal communication towards us. Or we may believe everyone is out to get us when there is no evidence to support that. Thus, our emotions flow from our initial thoughts. Studies show that emotion and cognition are not separate entities but rather are highly interdependent (Storbeck & Clore, 2007). If a person can modify their thoughts by reframing them as more realistic appraisals of their situations, not only will they experience a healthier emotional life, but their alexithymia will decrease as well.

Mindfulness is another option. The idea of mindfulness is to bring our attention to our experiences in the present moment through deep breathing, a quieting of the mind, and a non-judgmental attitude towards ourself. If we can, without judgment, observe our thoughts and feelings from moment to moment in a trained way through guided meditations, it is expected that our emotional awareness will increase (Brown & Kasser, 2005). Mindfulness has also been clinically shown to reduce stress. This could reduce instances where autistic people have trouble containing their emotions in public, thus becoming the focus of attention from police and bystanders (Feldman *et al.*, 2007). Mindfulness is also shown to help individuals who perseverate or overengage their thoughts (Baer *et al.*, 2006) and to decrease this obsessive tendency, which, if combined with restlessness, could lead to impulsivity and acting out. And mindfulness tends to decrease stress levels in individuals (Christopher & Gilbert, 2010), which can contribute to an overall higher quality of life. Research has already shown that mindfulness is effective for other disorders or mental illnesses when dealing with emotional regulation issues (Gu *et al.*, 2015; Wupperman *et al.*, 2015). But is it effective for the autistic population? The answer seems to be yes. In a study by Conner *et al.* (2019), researchers found that medium to large effects or improvements were seen by ASD adolescents who had undergone a comprehensive mindfulness curriculum. This curriculum included helping with depression, anxiety, and problem behaviors. Future research needs to focus on how to incorporate both CBT and mindfulness into a sexuality curriculum for autistic adolescents to help them achieve lasting relationships and avoid potential conflicts with law enforcement.

Emotional regulation helps one from acting impulsively. This is perhaps the most important reason that emotional regulation is pertinent to our discussion. It not only helps with self-monitoring one's own internal state, but it can also guide one to act in accordance with the emotional demands of a situation (i.e., not laughing at a funeral or yelling an obscenity to a police officer if triggered). For example, if I know I like a woman and that makes me feel excited, I can cognitively appraise whether I am in the appropriate setting to go over and talk to her. But if I am just feeling a mixture of emotions that I can't name yet physiological responses that correspond to excitement are still present, I won't have the luxury of making the cognitive appraisal of whether this is the appropriate time or place. If one knows that a funeral is probably not the most appropriate time to talk to a woman one is excited to see, one can use internal self-talk and perhaps call her later. In the context of a sexual offense, sexual excitement without impulse control is a dangerous combination. It is essential for a person to know what settings are appropriate for flirting and to act accordingly.

Notwithstanding executive functioning difficulties and issues with global processing, which will probably always be present in an individual to some extent, the ability to emotionally regulate and pick up the hidden curriculum at even a minimal level are prerequisites for a sex education program. And, of course, our focus is helping this program to be successful in keeping ASD individuals out of the criminal justice system for unintended sex-related offenses.

Prevention and Sex Education

In addition to the potential benefit of avoiding involvement with the criminal justice system, there are, of course, other benefits too. Proponents of sex education for autistic people say that it helps to decrease misinformation, decreases the risk of catching a sexually transmitted disease (STD), increases self-advocacy skills in general, decreases the risk that someone may be abused or exploited themselves, and increases overall social inclusion (Craft, 1994; Demetral, 1981; Di Giulio, 2003; Donovan, 1998; Gerhardt, 2006; Gougeon, 2009; Griffiths, 2003; Kirby, Laris & Rolleri, 2007; Sobsey, 1994).

It may seem like ableism to acquaint parents of children with assessments like the Autism Social Skills Profile (Bellini & Hopf, 2007), but it is recommended by Catherine Davies and Melissa Dubie (2011) in their fantastic sex education curriculum for autistic people as a starting point for ascertaining current abilities on certain prerequisites for relationships and dating. Although it is not a diagnostic tool, it can give a baseline estimate to clinicians and even caregivers as to where an ASD person's social strengths and weaknesses lie before formally beginning a sex-ed curriculum. The test measures a person's impulse control in social situations, social reciprocity, hygiene, empathy, understanding humor, conflict resolution, and many other interpersonal milestones. While the test measures may not naturally play to the strengths of most ASD individuals, virtually all of these skills are intermeshed with relationships and sexuality, which make them an essential learning tool. Therefore, it's unwise to approach sexuality and relationships in a vacuum. As is and has been our mantra, teaching social skills precedes a sexual education curriculum for this population. Indeed, even when a sexual education curriculum has been formally introduced to students, social skills will need to be continually monitored and reinforced.

According to Davies and Dubie (2011), whose curriculum is among the most comprehensive for ASD individuals, a good sexual education class should teach the following subjects to ASD students. Incidentally, most of these are also adopted by the *National Sexuality Education Standards: Content and Skills, K-12* (Greiert, 2016).

- Changes in one's body during puberty

- Sexual anatomy

- Reproductive health

- Sexual responses and partnered sex

- Contraception and STDs

- An introduction to dating

- A more focused lesson on the dating world and all that it entails

- The stages of relationships and maintaining them

- Attitudes, values, and differences (facts about age of consent and internet dangers)

- Sexual intimidation: harassment, aggression, and abuse

- Personal safety.

Not knowing any of these subjects is problematic and can get an ASD individual into trouble with the law. For example, if someone has HIV, it is illegal in some states to have sex without disclosing that fact to their partner (Weill-Greenberg, 2019). Not disclosing this information can land the person on the sex offender registry. Lacking knowledge of contraception can result in an unwanted pregnancy, which can be of huge concern if the relationship is statutory (meaning an 18-year-old or above autistic person dating someone who is underage). Teaching an autistic individual the stages of relationships is necessary to temper what may be too enthusiastic a response at the beginning of a courtship by the ASD person towards the object of their affection so that they don't fall into the "love is blind" trap. This can turn into stalking if there are no reciprocal feelings from the other person. Some studies suggest that courting behavior can turn into stalking for ASD individuals who may only be aware of their own feelings towards the other person and disregard rejections because they are difficult to socially interpret (Hannah & Stagg, 2016; Post *et al.*, 2014; Stokes, Newton & Kaur, 2007). As I will show in Chapter 2 of this book, women on the autism spectrum are much more at risk of being sexually abused throughout the course of their lives than autistic and/or neurotypical men, and this is where being taught about personal safety, boundaries, and how to get help in a crisis is essential. Autistic author Lola Phoenix (2017) speaks openly about how difficult the concept of consent has been for them in saying "no" to unwanted sexual advances. They note that life is difficult enough with having their boundaries ignored, trampled, and ridiculed, so providing consent in sexual situations seems downright overwhelming to them.

Teaching consent is crucial for so many reasons. Aside from violating someone else's boundaries and causing harm, it can result in arrest, conviction, and placement on a sex offender registry. Consent can be a potentially tricky subject for ASD individuals to grasp because it involves difficulty with understanding the notion of it being a fluid process, perhaps a resistance to change, and possible lack of impulse control. Any person can revoke consent in the middle of a sexual encounter, and if a person doesn't stop, they can be charged with any number of sexual crimes (Mooney, 2017). The revocation of consent doesn't even have to be verbal. It can be as simple as a woman holding her hand up to communicate "stop" and the man must recognize that he is being told to go no further. I am familiar with a couple of cases where this very thing occurred. In one instance, a teenage boy on the autism spectrum and his high-school girlfriend had been dating for a considerable length of time. The boy invited the girl back to his place for what was going to be a night of just "hanging out." Eventually, the two made their way to the bedroom where it seemed as if the girl was interested in a sexual encounter. According to the girl's version of events, she nonverbally gestured to the boy to stop...that she had enough. She said that physically she wasn't in a position to verbalize her request and therefore didn't say it. But the boy didn't hear or even notice anything. To cut a long story short, he was convicted of a sexual crime, served three years in prison, and will have to register as a sex offender for the rest of his life. To this day, he maintains his innocence and the girl maintains that she revoked consent. It is extremely possible that the autistic boy had trouble conceiving that consent is a fluid process: it is not contractual and can be reversed and revoked at any stage of the encounter. All teenage boys and girls need to learn this fact, but it is absolutely crucial for individuals on the autism spectrum to know it.

Where Are Autistic People Learning About Sex?

When we were growing up, most of us learned about sex from our peers. Most neurotypicals take this fact for granted. It is almost a rite of passage for males to talk about other girls with same-aged peers or brag about having sexual activity with girls. Boys will typically ask questions involving "what base" an individual got to with a girl. To even understand this question, one has to know what that phrase means and what sexual activity each base refers to. It can easily be argued that adolescents learn from peers rather than any formal curriculum.

This was not true for me and it is also not true for a majority of individuals on the autism spectrum. An obvious question and concern then becomes immediately apparent: if autistic people are not obtaining sexual knowledge by means of their peer group, where is it coming from? Back when I was in middle school and high school, there was no internet as we know it today. The only way one could truly attain some understanding of anatomy for sexual arousal or knowledge was to buy a *Playboy* magazine or perhaps watch one's parents' pornography VHS cassettes. Today, the landscape has opened up unfortunate vistas that are simply too easy to access. With just a few clicks of the mouse, territory that was uncharted 25 or 30 years ago is easily reachable today.

The literature indicates that, since they are left to do it alone, ASD individuals are learning more about sex on their own. Mehzabin and Stokes (2011) noted that ASD individuals frequently reported television as a source of their learning about sex. This makes sense with the concept of "scripting," where ASD individuals often quote television or movie references in conversation as a way of interjecting a statement (Tonge & Brereton, 2011). Hénault (2006) says that limited peer interaction may lead ASD individuals to misunderstand important sexual knowledge-gaining opportunities and sources of information. And as I alluded to earlier in our discussion on "invisible fencing," many parents are afraid to broach the topic of sex with their children out of a fear that it will increase the autistic person's sexual interests and problematic behaviors that parents may worry about (Konstantareas & Lunsky, 1997; Meister *et al.*, 1994). A typical father is probably less likely to have "the important talk" with their autistic son than a neurotypical son. Thus, another source of information that the parent can convey is absent from the picture.

One study looked at this in detail. Brown-Lavoie, Viecili and Weiss (2014) compared 95 participants with "high-functioning autism" with 117 neurotypical matched controls and found that the ASD group was 2.53–3.35 times less likely than the control group to report obtaining information related to sexually transmitted infections (STIs) from their parents, teachers, and peers. They also found that the ASD group was 1.76–4.13 times more likely to report learning about sex from religious figures, educational brochures, the internet, pornography, and television/radio than the matched non-ASD controls. Lastly, they found that with regards to contraceptives, the ASD group was alarmingly 2.96–4.70 times less likely to report obtaining this knowledge from parents, teachers, and peers than the neurotypicals.

Indeed, as ASD adults come of age and enter into adulthood, many find online dating preferable because of lack of success with traditional face-to-face dating (Roth & Gills, 2015). This too can present safety concerns when total strangers meet each other. This issue was reported amongst the ASD participants in Roth and Gills' (2015) study. In another study that compared 232 ASD individuals with 227 neurotypicals, the ASD adults reported the same level of sexual interest as their counterparts but fewer opportunities to meet potential partners (Hancock *et al.*, 2020). The ASD group also had shorter relationship duration, had more anxiety about relationships, and learned less from their peers about sex than their counterparts.

The problem with learning about sex from television and pornography instead of appropriate sources may be immediately apparent to most readers. Television shows or movies do not informatively teach about important matters related to sexual development. Pornography will not teach a person about STIs or contraceptives other than sometimes seeing adult actors using them on screen. The important life lessons that come from learning about the birds and the bees are missed in these superficial mediums.

What remains essential is that autistic people and others with developmental disabilities not be hindered from learning about sex through normal channels: a tailored curriculum designed specifically for their needs is essential. The literature finds that this is lacking and it may be one reason autistic people are vulnerable for ending up in the criminal justice system for a sexual offense.

Self-Advocacy

Researchers have suggested that self-advocates on the autism spectrum should have a role in the creation of a curriculum for the younger ASD population (Wehmeyer, 2002). I agree with this. Who better to know the specific challenges, hurdles, potential pitfalls, and possibilities that lie ahead for the ASD population than other adult autistics? One study (Friedman *et al.*, 2014) interviewed autistic self-advocates along with others who had intellectual and/or developmental disabilities. The themes that emerged as being important to them were the ability to make their own choices (or autonomy), communication skills, and having their independence respected.

Allison Fleming (2015) did her master's thesis on this topic and I recommend that you read this accessible and important work (you can find it by looking up the article cited in the reference on Google Scholar). Fleming asked ASD self-advocates what they wanted in a sex education curriculum and a few salient findings are relevant here. The self-advocates in this study, ranging in age from their 20s to their 40s, with just a few exceptions, believed that it was important for them to have sex education but felt it was lacking for them personally. Some astutely remarked that there is a misconception that autistic people are asexual and perhaps are not given an adequate education on the matter. One recognized social skills acquisition as being intrinsically important to foster an effective curriculum. They wanted to be taught about sex with a "neutral tone," which is referred to in the literature as a "sex-positive" approach (Harden, 2014) in that it does not focus only on abstinence but instead encourages the healthy development and exploration of one's sexuality. They didn't want to be told all of the "negatives" in terms of what they shouldn't do. Instead, they wanted to know what the options were and be told about positive things they could do to help them in their relationships. Neutrality of content was a huge theme for these self-advocates: they wanted a non-preachy message. Many of the participants wanted to learn specifically about dating and how to handle this murky terrain where eye contact, making conversation, and social skills come into play. Some male participants wanted to be taught about what constitutes harassment and specifically expressed a fear of being labeled a sexual deviant. One individual felt that teaching about consent and the consequences was imperative so that he could stay out of trouble. Corroborating research previously cited in this chapter found that when participants were asked where they learned the most about their sexuality, most said they taught themselves. Many individuals felt that they had questions that their curriculums didn't address, and they wanted to answer their own questions using blogs and books. One participant said that instead of asking peers, teachers, or family questions, she would research the information on her own. I have already established how problematic this can be if not augmented by peer support and direct instruction.

Barnett and Maticka-Tyndale (2015) similarly conducted a qualitative study asking adults with ages ranging from 19 to 61 about their sexual experiences as a way to understand how to design an appropriate sexual education curriculum for students. Among the common concerns of this group were learning about courtship, sensory dysregulation, how uncomfortable sensations related to touch could interfere with their relationships, and a lack of adequate sexual education. Some participants reported never having been taught about reproductive sex and some of their parents objected to them receiving sex education out of fear that it was "inappropriate." One participant nicknamed Dragonfly reported that since no one would answer his questions about sex, he turned to books. Some participants in this study also criticized their sexual education as taking on too negative a tone and making sex seem off limits for them. Many felt that they should be taught about exploitation and grooming techniques, recognizing their own susceptibility to being sexually abused by others.

Another study recruited both high-school individuals with ASD and neurotypical high schoolers around the same age (McNaughtan, 2017). Fifty percent of the neurotypical population had been on a date, whereas only 18.2 percent of the autistic group had. Sixty percent of neurotypicals knew that one way to tell if someone likes you is by how much attention they bestow upon you, whereas only 5 percent of the autistics (one person) recognized this. When asked how you show someone that you like them, 50 percent of the neurotypicals answered that you give them your time and energy, whereas no one in the autism group answered that way. One autistic person said that one way to show a person you are interested in them is by demonstrating how smart you are. When asked how they would move past rejection, 60 percent of the neurotypicals believed that they could get over it, while only 14 percent of the autistic group responded this way. Furthermore, 55 percent of the autistic group said that they would ask again or try to reschedule the date with the person who rejected them.

I took the liberty of visiting the Wrong Planet Autism Community Forum (2010) to see how people responded to the question "Did your parents talk to you about sex?" Wrong Planet[1] is an online resource and chat forum where autistic adults talk to each other about various aspects of life. Very few people reported that their parents informed them adequately about sex, which comports with the research I have reviewed. On another Wrong Planet post called "Should high schools teach how to date?" (2012), the vast majority of the autistic people said absolutely not, while some felt that it would be necessary to help them in social situations where dating and the hidden curriculum intersect. I suspect that this highly negative reaction to sexual education and dating instruction in the schools is for the same reasons that were reported in the other studies: they felt that sex education

---

1   wrongplanet.net

was too negative and not neutral enough, and that everything seemed off limits to them.

This scenario presents us with a bit of a quandary. This whole chapter has been about helping autistic people to avoid the criminal justice system by helping them understand what can land them in trouble. We have seen that they do not want a sexual education that tells them what they can't do or seems limiting to them. We can infer that many autistic individuals are put off by the idea of sexual education because many of the adults have been disengaged or seem uncomfortable teaching this subject to them. Yet we have also seen in one of the studies that some autistic people do not handle rejection well and may ask for another date, even when the other person has made it clear that they are not interested. So how can we help autistic people with their sexuality while not being too prescriptive? How can we deliver a "neutral" tone in a sex education curriculum while also being very clear about what is and isn't acceptable or even legal behavior?

Peer-Mediated Intervention

Given that we know that social isolation is common for ASD individuals throughout adolescence and young adulthood, it makes sense that peer-mediated intervention (PMI) could be multipurpose. PMI involves training neurotypical, same-aged (or older) peers in behavioral or social strategies that they can then use to assist the ASD individual in learning. The idea behind it is that this mediation is coming from someone who seems more like a "friend" to the student than an authority figure. According to Chang and Locke (2016), there are several benefits of this type of intervention for autistic adolescents. First, peers can acquire new social behaviors by learning from their mentors. Second, peers can act as agents of intervention when challenges arise. And finally, having a mentor gives the ASD individual a chance to practice their skills in a safe and non-judgmental setting. PMI has been shown to work more effectively with trained peers and students than with untrained strangers (Schlieder, Maldonado & Baltes, 2014). PMI has been shown to fill in the gaps where a lack of friendships exists. One study (Shattuck *et al.*, 2012) showed that nearly half of ASD adolescents were never called by friends, never invited to social activities, and had an overall lower rate of social participation. Płatos and Wojaczek (2018) highlight the importance of PMI generalizing beyond the classroom into out-of-school activities to truly be a successful intervention. Płatos and Wojaczek say that the intervention should be related to friendship, social participation, and well-being, which is a holistic approach. In other words, the goal of PMI is not to make someone seem indistinguishable from their peers. Not only is this not usually possible (Gibson & Douglas, 2018), but it can also inflict trauma and negatively affect the self-esteem and self-worth of the ASD individual (Milton, 2014). I would argue that mentoring should also help to augment sex education and I would like to see future research on this subject occur. Indeed, Connolly, Furman and Konarski (2000), along with scores of other researchers, see friendship and intimacy as a prerequisite for relationships. The problem, as of this writing, is that studies of PMI are generally limited to individuals under the age of 13, other than a few select studies regarding undergraduate college students, making what I am proposing here somewhat uncharted territory (Płatos & Wojaczek, 2018).

But all is not lost. For starters, there are two kinds of PMI in use. It used to be that PMI was primarily thought of as a way to teach social skills, help autistic people assimilate, and make them act as neurotypical as possible. This would be classified as a "mentoring" approach, which is valuable. But there is also the "befriending" approach (which has existed for other populations of mentally ill individuals for decades) (Cassidy *et al.*, 2019), where the emphasis is on building supportive relationships, developing true friendships, discovering mutual areas of interest between peer and mentor, and helping to facilitate disclosure and emotional support (Thompson *et al.*, 2016). While the acquisition of social skills is a necessary part of this intervention because of inherent weaknesses in that area for the ASD population (Laugeson & Frankel, 2010), it's hardly complete unless the skills are used organically and can be generalized to other situations. We have to ensure that ASD individuals gain a sense of happiness and joy from these relationships so they can experience these same emotions in romantic relationships later. Interventionists tend to have a bias against modalities that target anything other than thoughts and behavior in autism: rarely do we care about the emotional well-being of the autistic individual (Wong *et al.*, 2015). But sexual education that looks to inform, provide a better quality of life, and help ASD individuals avoid encounters with law enforcement must address the emotional needs of the developing autistic individual. We cannot rely on teaching behavior alone, as has been indicated by autistic people themselves. What they want out of sex education and befriending seems to help fill that emotional need. In some cases, however, long-term friendship between mentor and the peer with ASD may prove difficult, as it blurs boundaries and creates unrealistic expectations (Sims *et al.*, 2016). In that case, time-limited, goal-oriented tasks and the mentoring approach can be more appropriate. But no matter whether it is the mentoring or befriending approach that is chosen, based on the ASD person's needs, it is important that the relationship is one of reciprocal partnership instead of a "helper-helpee" relationship (Kluth, 2003).

We can take a cue as to how we might proceed in the future with one particularly compelling and interesting study (Bertilsdotter-Rosqvist, 2019).

The author's goal was to find out from autistic individuals themselves how peer support might be helpful to them. In her literature review on the topic, she noted the importance of establishing positive self-identities within mentoring without the nature of the relationship being seen as limiting independence or stigmatizing in some way. She also notes correctly (and some research backs this up) that support coming from other autistics can be more effective than if it comes from neurotypical mentors because autistic people know the experience of being autistic better than neurotypicals (Macleod, 2010). Indeed, it makes sense that many neurodiverse populations seek help amongst themselves because there is a built-in level of trust already present at the outset of the relationship (Stevenson, Cornell & Hinchcliffe, 2016). A brief look on Twitter, Facebook, and Wrong Planet, and at in-person meetups all over the world where autistic people get together to socialize, shows just how true this has become.

Bertilsdotter-Rosqvist (2019) ran a group for seven autistic adults, aged in their 20s–50s. She saw herself as a "critical friend" to the group, having autistic traits herself but not being formally diagnosed. In other words, she was acting in the capacity of a mentor. She conducted a series of group interviews that were later transcribed word for word. Her analysis showed two very distinct themes: autistic peer support and non-autistic professional support. The group felt strongly that autistics and non-autistics inhabit almost two different worlds. They saw the neurotypical support as being there to focus on hardships and difficulties, including what not to do, and they felt more understood by the autistic group. They felt strongly that there couldn't be any hint of condemnation because this could increase a person's self-questioning and doubt. They described non-autistic support for them as being "locked in a bubble," which they saw as the opposite of development. They felt misunderstood by their neurotypical peer supports, feeling blamed for being either lazy or too high functioning.

This presents us with another quandary. We have seen previously that autistic people do not respond well to sex education curriculums that remind them of what they can't do, focus on the negative, and do not respect their self-determination. Here, we are also seeing that many autistics value peer support that comes from other autistics rather than their neurotypical counterparts. Other research backs this up. A large subset of autistic people feel that they are the experts of their own lives and some even resent intrusion from neurotypicals who think they know better (Griffith et al., 2012). Indeed, some autistics felt that only other autistics could truly understand autism (Jones, Huws & Beck, 2013). Our question now becomes: how do we help augment a sexual education curriculum with peer support in schools that includes older autistic individuals who may have had experiences in dating and relationships and can serve as mentors?

Autistic Peer Mentoring

The task before us is complex. In such a program, we need built-in structures that respect autistic individuals and do not condescend to them. We need to teach them that certain inappropriate behaviors can land them in the criminal justice system and cause harm to others, without shutting them down before they have a chance to take in the message. We need a top-down approach that works horizontally as well as vertically.

There are certain aspects of life that only another autistic can truly understand. Neurotypicals who have received appropriate training can understand autistic life in an academic, if not wholly experiential, sense. But there will always be a slight barrier. For example, an autistic person will understand that eye contact is difficult because it requires two forms of sensory processing simultaneously, whereas a neurotypical might need to consult experts or the internet to answer that question. Only another autistic will truly understand the role and importance that "stims" (repetitive motor movements) play in one's life and not see it as a pathology initially.

At the college level, there is evidence of success using autistic peer mentoring. Three nonverbal autistic college students discussed the gratification and success they had at being peer mentors towards other autistics and the overall success of the program (Capozzi *et al.*, 2019). The Mentoring and Befriending Foundation (2010) also found that co-equal mentoring (where there was a reciprocal partnership) had 80 percent of the mentees report feeling positive about their mentor, while 90 percent of the mentors had a positive experience with their mentee. One new model of peer mentoring for autistic individuals emerges from the dissertation of Bradley (2017), which he calls an autism-friendly model of The New Peer Mentoring. This model grew out of the Autism Education Trust Outcomes Report (*ibid.*, p.53), which sought the opinions of autistic people themselves and their families to establish priorities. A few of the aims central to the program that Bradley (*ibid.*) lists are as follows.

- Consultation with autistic students before, during, and after the program to promote agency and self-determination

- Include personal, social, and health education more broadly, going beyond the normal school curriculum

- Using autistic peer mentors themselves

- Utilizing the mentor-peer relationship outside of the classroom

- Staff giving more authority to the students themselves to discuss what is relevant to them

- Eliminate hierarchy from the program (mentor to peer), which reinforces a deficit model, and instead focus on the development of the relationships

- Having a knowledgeable staff person on hand to guide discussions and help with problem solving

- Give clear guidelines for autistic mentors on what being a peer mentor meant and what the program entailed.

For the topic I have been dealing with in this chapter, it's been important to try to find the right balance between student autonomy and imposing the right amount of structure necessary to drive home important points that need reinforcement. As an experiment, I would like to see the use of older autistic adults as mentors for a subject as complex as sexuality. Autistic adult mentors who could pass a criminal background check and express a willingness to share what they have learned in relationships might be invaluable to augment the sex education curriculum. Additionally, for lesbian, gay, bisexual, transgender, or questioning autistic individuals who need a type of mentoring that isn't cisgender, it is important to find autistic sexual minority community members who could fill this crucial gap. To my knowledge, no such program exists for autistic individuals. I am calling for research to be conducted in this area so we can assess whether this is an effective method for the delivery of a sex education that helps to avoid contact with the criminal justice system. Given that we know that autistic people want a sex-positive approach, don't like being talked down to, and want some agency and autonomy over the process, this may be a good model.

It isn't a perfect model, however. It leaves too much open to chance. Adults, such as teachers, parents, and social workers, do need to provide some structure to sex education and any possible mentorships. This is important, especially because we're dealing with a subject that autistic young people may find uncomfortable but need to know about. I would recommend a blended approach that combines and integrates formal and informal channels of instruction: combining autistic adult peer mentoring with an academically provided sex education curriculum that focuses on the sexuality of oneself and others. Somewhere along the line, certain "dos" and "don'ts" need to be spelled out very clearly but in such a way that the autistic person doesn't perceive them a slight or commentary on who they are. Rather, we need to covey that there are traps out there that can have life-altering repercussions for the autistic person and possibly others. The literature clearly tells us that such traps exist. I would like to review them while keeping in mind that these lessons are important touchstones in the mentoring setting and in the classroom.

Important Touchstones in a Prevention-Based Education Curriculum

Earlier in the chapter, we saw in one study that some autistic individuals handled rejection less adaptively than neurotypicals. This corroborates not only my own personal experience, but also what I have observed anecdotally in other spectrumites. If one is not aware of rejection and violates the boundaries of others as a result, one lacks privacy awareness. The literature confirms that autistic individuals have less awareness of privacy than neurotypical people, as has been self-reported by adolescents on the spectrum, parents, and young adults (Ginevra, Nota & Stokes, 2016; Mehzabin & Stokes, 2011; Stokes & Kaur, 2005). Pathways into the criminal justice system that can arise from poor boundaries and/or less privacy awareness are exhibitionism, stalking, making threats over the internet, hacking into a government or corporate database, sexting, and internet behavior such as downloading child pornography that might seem private to the user. When the line between private and public behavior blurs, people act in ways that they normally wouldn't. Let us delve into this more, because it's important to understand how this can happen.

Neurotypicals who are aware of how their behavior might be perceived in public can restrain themselves appropriately before letting things fly once they are in private. But with the advent of the internet, this is less true for neurotypicals than it used to be. The reason for this is the "disinhibition effect" (Suler, 2004), and it plays a destructive role in how people interact with each other today. The internet allows us to have less impulse control because we have the illusion of privacy when we are sitting behind a keyboard in our own room. So, we may confront people on Twitter and/or say more hurtful things than we would say face to face.

Many individuals (neurotypicals and autistics, alike) find comfort in forming relationships from behind a computer screen as opposed to the face-to-face demands of an in-person relationship. It can be argued that the social experience of the internet is a good thing, as it allows autistic people to compensate for their offline social challenges (Finkenauer et al., 2012). Yet autism spectrum disorders go beyond mere social difficulties and also encompass restrictive and repetitive behavior (American Psychiatric Association, 2013). Reports in the literature also suggest that individuals sometimes use the internet to investigate their highly focused special interests that might not necessarily have a social component to them (MacMullin, Lunsky, & Weiss, 2015; Mazurek *et al.*, 2012; Mazurek & Wenstrup, 2013). Furthermore, Romano *et al.* (2014) found that compulsive use of the internet was more prevalent in a sample of higher functioning autistic individuals than in those with more challenges or who were lower functioning. Some researchers attribute this to the generalized anxiety that autistic individuals face in the real world, which can often mirror social anxiety, shyness, or loneliness (Shane-Simpson *et al.*, 2016). It can also be related to high intelligence and the desire to investigate.

Shane-Simpson *et al.* (2016) list three main reasons for compulsive internet use in ASD individuals.

- Social compensation

- Offline social difficulties are recapitulated or exacerbated

- Focused interests.

Although unrelated to sexual development, some research (Palermo, 2013) suggests that online radicalization for possible terrorist activities, extremism, or ideological violence for the ASD population can take place through both social compensation and past trauma that gets reenacted online. This is an extremely rare event for ASD individuals. One study that examined 153 lone wolves (who carry out these acts as individuals as opposed to being part of a group) found that 3.3 percent had ASD, and it was unknown what comorbidities existed (Corner, Gill & Mason, 2016). But because this type of recruitment happens, even rarely, we must discuss it. Though this study investigated lone wolves, we can understand this happening within the context of forming relationships with a radicalized mentor who might take an impressionable ASD young man under his wing and give him the social acceptance he so badly craves (Allely & Faccini, 2017). Combining this desired social acceptance with a sense of alienation he might already feel can cause the young man to recapitulate his past trauma and transform it into the form of a hostile ideology that is antagonistic to mankind (The University of Manchester, 2019). As Allely (2019) argues, feeling defective, seeing the world as a threat, social isolation, heightened agitation, and a downward spiral can all be risk factors towards a pathway to violence for young people with ASD. Mentoring programs should be rooted in keeping children and adolescents socially engaged, decreasing isolation, and broadening interests. Peers should be free to talk about any material they are discovering online without feeling judged. Simultaneously, any content promoting radicalization or violence should immediately be flagged and talked about with the ASD individual.

Let's focus on that last bullet point in Shane-Simpson *et al.*'s (2016) list: focused interests. It is important to point out that the majority of the time, autistic individuals *do* use social media to connect with others in a prosocial way (Mazurek, 2013). But I must note that when the interests are nonsocial in nature (and outside of traditional areas of interest like science, mechanics, history, etc.), the internet can open up a Pandora's box, with lifelong consequences. ASD individuals may become fixated on body parts or pornography (Higgs & Carter, 2015). The collection of pornography and storage of it on a computer can then take place rather easily (Haskins & Silva, 2006). Defense attorney Mark Mahoney (2009) goes so far as to call the recipe of computer access, ASD, and pornography a "lethal combination." Indeed, another defense attorney named Elizabeth Kelley (2020) also notes that autistic individuals are often implicated in sexual offenses involving the internet. Pornography offenses for ASD individuals combine both the disinhibition effect and repetitive or obsessive behavior specifically exhibited by some individuals with ASD (Mogavero, 2016). Most autistic people would never look at any kind of pornography on a park bench (whether illegal or legal pornography) or in a restaurant. The isolation of the computer and the illusion of privacy, however, makes viewing pornography easier in private. This, combined with a propensity to build a collection (Haskins & Silva, 2006), can cause an autistic individual to venture into illegal pornography. Mesibov and Sreckovic (2017) point out that many autistic people would have trouble differentiating between someone of legal age and someone who is not, particularly if the person is slightly under the age of 18. We would expect any peer-mentoring program to redirect curiosity regarding learning about sex from the internet to real-world experience where autistic participants could ask their mentors any questions they desired. Mentors should discourage the use of the internet for sexual gratification and enforce the legal consequences for venturing into illicit territory, even if done in private. In other words, autistic people should note that if they engage in this behavior, they could end up spending over a decade (or more) in prison and with a lifetime placement on the sex offender registry. This could foreclose most of life's important opportunities for them. The danger of this trap cannot be overstated enough.

Another interest I have seen develop in autistic people is manga or anime (Rozema, 2015). Many autistic people love anime and manga. As an autistic person myself, I personally do not, but I know from firsthand experience of meeting other autistic people that it appeals to them. It is an image-rich medium that appeals to visual learners, and emotions are more clearly expressed on the cartoon-like figures than in regular photographs or drawings. But anime, and, more specifically, hentai pornography, can be a gateway for ASD individuals to view actual pornography, including child pornography (Fabian, 2011). Hentai pornography and manga figures depict very young-looking individuals, certainly below the age of 18. Manga can be beneficial for ASD learners, but it can also turn dangerous if left unchecked. Parents, schools, and mentors should actively monitor the type of manga content an autistic person is viewing to make sure it is for educational and enjoyment purposes rather than a way to learn about sexuality.

Sexting is also a potential issue for neurotypicals and autistics alike. Of all the videos and images that are sent among teenagers and adolescents, 25 percent will be of sexual content (Rice *et al.*, 2014). It is a little-known fact that if an underage person takes a picture of his or herself and sends it to someone, this act can be charged as dissemination of child pornography in some jurisdictions. Sexting is the result of the disinhibition effect (Dir, Cyders & Coskunpinar, 2013). Psychologically, it is easier to send a picture of oneself on a mobile phone in private than doing something inappropriate in public, because the illusion of privacy makes one believe that the act has no real-world consequences. There can also be instances of coaxing, where autistic people are set up to take the blame. An article in *The Atlantic* (Rosin, 2014) describes a scenario where two teenage girls persuaded an autistic boy to sext a picture of his penis to them, which they then proceeded to circulate among classmates at school. The district attorney was planning to file charges against the boy when the American Civil Liberties Union (ACLU) in Pennsylvania intervened in the case. Sexting is rampant among teenagers and adolescents in society. It can be used for blackmailing and extortion purposes, making autistic people especially vulnerable to becoming a victim of this crime. As a means of preventing students from committing these crimes, some schools bring in local prosecutors and sheriffs to warn students of sexting and the criminal penalties they may incur if they engage in the behavior (Marshall Independent, 2019). Regardless of the method chosen, the dangers of sexting need to be emphasized repeatedly to prevent autistic people from being victimized and to prevent unnecessary encounters with the criminal justice system and the sex offender registry. Mentors may choose to discuss with their peers alternatives to sexting, so students can learn about sex in appropriate ways rather than doing so through the ease of 21st-century technology.

Lack of privacy awareness makes it extremely important to have a sex education curriculum in place to teach ASD individuals the issue of maintaining boundaries and using restraint. If this is not addressed, the end result can lead to stalking behavior. Stalking involves repeated or persistent attempts to communicate with another person, even when the desire for attention is unreciprocated or unwanted (Mullen *et al.*, 1999). Several articles have suggested that ASD individuals are vulnerable to committing acts of stalking when seeking out friendships or intimacy (Church, Alisanski & Amanullah, 2000; Clements & Zarkowska, 2000; Green *et al.*, 2000; Howlin, 1997; Myles & Simpson, 2002; Stokes & Newton, 2004). Stokes *et al.* (2007) attribute stalking behavior in ASD to difficulties in making small talk, blurring the lines between platonic friendship and romantic relationships, lacking understanding of the social context (related to central coherence), and difficulty reading the social cues of others displaying rejection. Stokes *et al.* also note, as confirmed earlier in the chapter, that many ASD individuals pursue relationships for longer than their typically developing peers when there is either no response or a negative response. To help counteract this, mentors who feel that the ASD individuals are violating their boundaries could use the opportunity to address the issue of boundary violations. If the person on the spectrum became too attached to their mentor or contacted them too frequently, the mentor could explain objectively how the behavior is affecting the mentor and also why the boundary violations are not acceptable. And a curriculum in schools geared towards individuals on the spectrum needs to explain that stalking is a criminal offense, often punishable by imprisonment and a criminal record.

Though we must acknowledge that autistic people are typically law abiding and have low rates of criminality across the board (Ghaziuddin, Tsai & Ghaziuddin, 1991; Heeramun *et al.*, 2017; Hippler *et al.*, 2010; Howlin, 2007; Murrie *et al.*, 2002; Wing, 1981; Woodbury-Smith *et al.*, 2005, 2006), they may be more inclined to commit certain types of cybercrime. Studies have suggested that competence shown through online relationships is key to progressing in these circles (Brosnan & Gavin 2015; Gillespie-Lynch *et al.*, 2014; van der Aa *et al.*, 2016).

One study tried to find out whether there was an association between ASD and cybercrime (Payne *et al.*, 2019a). The authors found that a higher score on the Autism Quotient (AQ) correlated with a propensity for cybercrime but cautiously reported that a diagnosis of autism actually seemed to mitigate against that. In other words, if someone was diagnosed with autism, it lowered the chances that they would be engaged in cybercrime. Payne *et al.* (2019a) attributed this decrease to a layer of protection that might be added with a diagnosis (more support, education, etc.) and the autistic individual's strength of honesty, which accompanies self-awareness once they have received their diagnosis. This underscores the importance of education in developing self-awareness, mindfulness, and an awareness of boundaries, which may improve with a diagnosis and early intervention.

Another online crime we need to be mindful of is child luring. Rankin (2017) notes a developmentally disabled 21-year-old individual who talked online with someone who he believed was a 14-year-old girl. According to the article, the man was encouraged by a buddy to use a dating app since he was lonely. Right away, a woman going by the name of Ashley approached him online. Her profile said she was 19, but then she disclosed to him that she was 14. "Ashley" asked the man where he worked, and he told her. He recalls her asking him on a date, and he replied "Okay." When he arrived at his place of work, where they'd agreed to meet, an online vigilante group was waiting for him. They confronted him aggressively at his workplace, filmed him, and put this encounter on social media. As a result, the man lost his job and everything he had worked for.

As horrible as this encounter was, it could have ended in a much worse way. If this was a real girl, he could have encountered this girl's parents—and who knows how bad the outcome of that scenario would have been. The parents might have called the police or used violence to protect their daughter. Or it could have been a police sting operation in which the individual in question would have been charged.

Child luring does not end well for perpetrators, and it can cause lifelong trauma for victims. It is important to teach autistic youngsters not only to avoid strangers on the internet, but also never to talk to individuals who are younger than them. Being lonely or not understanding boundaries can cause someone to not grasp the seriousness of the situation if they engage in talk with a child, or, worse, go to meet them. That kind of encounter can ruin a child's life and the autistic adult's life too. The stakes could not be higher.

To help prevent potential online criminal behavior, mentors could check in with the ASD individual's peers and ask them who their friends are online. Are they people they just met recently? Are they asking them to do things that seem odd or highly out of sync with anything they are usually asked to do? Are the people online from other parts of the world? Are autistic people curious about finding top secret information that might bring about hacking into a government or corporate database? These are important questions to ask, not so that the mentor can report the ASD person to the police but so that the behavior can be stopped in its tracks. It would also help the autistic peer to understand why their actions could be wrong and/or illegal and the potential consequences they may face if they continue.

There is one last area of prevention I must cover, and indeed, it was a surprise to me to come across this when I began writing this chapter. That issue is arson, which is unrelated to sexual development and the internet, but necessary to talk about. Barry-Walsh and Mullen (2004) wrote a paper that included a report of an ASD man who had engaged in arson, setting fire to a hedge and causing significant damage. The man was identified as Mr. BD. At the time of the incident, he was aged 26 and his IQ was within the normal range. One might think any act of arson is done out of malice, but this does not seem to be the case for Mr. BD. As a youth, Mr. BD developed a fascination for flickering flames. He would watch a gas heater's pilot flame for hours on end. In this instance, the act of setting property on fire seemed more tied to a fixed interest of watching fire burn than hurting other people and the destruction of property. Unfortunately for him and everyone else, destruction of property and harm of others are natural consequences of arson. Allely (2019) states in a literature review that, based on previous studies, the sole interest in watching flames or seeing fire burn just for its own sake was the most prevalent reason for ASD individuals committing arson. Setting fires can be used as an alternative outlet for letting out frustrations, instead of solving real-world problems. Indeed, Freckelton and List (2009) note that some ASD individuals who commit arson have preoccupations with flames, cinders, colors, and heat, as opposed to reasons of malice for engaging in arson (McEwan & Freckelton, 2011). On Gillberg's blog (Allely, 2019), she states that conventional punishment and retribution would not be effective with these types of offenders since their motivation was a psychological curiosity for fire rather than a desire to hurt other people. There is a small amount of empirical evidence to support the contention that this behavior occurs with more frequency among ASD individuals. One study (Siponmaa *et al.*, 2001) examined 126 individuals who had been referred for forensic psychiatric examination, presumably because each of them had broken the law. Among the arsonists in the group, 10 out of 16 of them (63%) were on the autism spectrum. Furthermore, when speaking about learning-disabled arsonists, Hall, Clayton and Johnson (2005) identified a number of characteristics often found in young arsonists including poor self-esteem and social isolation, poor ability to communicate one's needs to others, feelings of frustration, and a need to be heard.

The high-profile case of John Elder Robison's son is an example of this. Many individuals in the autism community are familiar with this case concerning arson and explosives. Jack "Cubby" Robison was a bright child with an interest in rockets and mixing chemicals (Donaldson, 2013). Cubby dropped out of high school and began experimenting with chemical explosions, which he filmed and posted on YouTube. He acquired his materials legally and his interests lay purely within the realm of science. Something about his activities caught the eye of law enforcement. Though Cubby's state of mind was entirely innocent, the prosecutor in his case showed no mercy and took the case to trial. Had Cubby been convicted, he would have been looking at many years in prison. Fortunately (at least in the eyes of this author), he was found not guilty.

Things did not work out so well for Darius McCollum, however. Darius is an African American man from New York City who is on the autism spectrum. As a boy, Darius developed an interest in trains, planes, and buses. Untrained, he taught himself how to man Manhattan subway cars and conducted rides successfully, never harming anyone. Yet he commandeered them under false pretenses and wasn't an employee of the New York City Transit Authority (MTA) with the legal right to conduct the subways. It became a lifelong habit for him, and after a series of arrests, Darius was committed to a mental institution. The forensic experts in Darius's case said he was not a threat or a danger and that the deviant behavior here stemmed from his special fixated interests and obsessions, while emphasizing that he had injured no one on these occasions (Wallace, 2018).

A documentary of his struggle through the criminal justice system, titled *Off the Rails*, was created to humanize Darius and show that his behavior was unrelated to true criminal intent or a guilty state of mind. Filmmaker Adam Irving called Darius a "Shakespearian figure" and a "tragic figure" who had his fate sealed at an early age because of tragic life circumstances and his neurological wiring. As a result of driving the E train at age 15, Darius destroyed his chances of ever obtaining a job with the MTA. Dropping out of school at the age of 12 due to bullying seemed to be his trigger incident. Darius took refuge in the underground world of the subways. He was quoted as saying that the subway became his "new school." He made friends with transit workers who showed him acceptance for the first time in his life. For Darius, conducting the subway was his chance to act like a hero. In one incident where he saw a train come to a halt, he raced over to the station to lead passengers through the train cars to safety (Rivoli, 2016). This fixation with public transportation would eventually cost him everything. All sources indicated that Darius was not a bad or evil man. He was someone who needed his interests channeled in productive ways. He also needed a lot of outpatient professional help, which his legal defense team requested but didn't get. Furthermore, I have a personal source who knows Darius very well and tells me he is one of the sweetest and kindest individuals on the planet who would never hurt a soul. The source told me that the last place Darius belongs is in a prison or a mental institution. Unfortunately, unless something dramatic happens, it appears that Darius will remain in a mental institution for the rest of his life.

If pyromania or obsessive interests lead to boundary violations and are comorbid with ASD, we must have prevention strategies in place to ensure that there are no more Dariuses or Cubbys. Arson sometimes stems from a low locus of external control (Doley, Dickens & Gannon, 2015), which means that someone believes they have very little control of their life. We saw that Darius most likely believed this when his chance for a job with the MTA was permanently eliminated at a young age. As we have seen, when it comes to an external locus of control, ASD students sometimes take to arson, or crimes related to special interests, as a way to feel productive, gain self-determination, and master a craft outside of traditional learning methods. Unfortunately, these behaviors end up backfiring because they are done outside of legally and socially acceptable channels. Hall *et al.* (2005) explain that young arsonists who are neurotypical should have a "psychotherapy file" that helps the person keep track of their triggers. They also recommend cognitive analytic therapy, which is a combination of cognitive behavioral therapy and psychoanalysis. Hall *et al.* mention that young arsonists with learning disabilities can get caught up in "traps," "dilemmas," and "snags." Traps are negative assumptions about oneself that produce negative consequences, which then reinforce the assumption. In other words, they are self-fulfilling prophecies. In Darius's case, he was probably aware that he would never attain a job with the MTA after his incident at age 15, but his drive to help others became a basis for his sustained behavior. At the same time, and after several arrests conducting subways under false pretenses, it is likely that he knew he was going to be caught, reinforcing all of the problems he previously had to deal with. Dilemmas (Hall *et al.*, 2005) are "either/or" choices or false dichotomies that people unconsciously make in an effort to solve a problem. When Cubby dropped out of school and started making videos on YouTube showing him mixing chemicals and using explosives, instead of turning that interest into a scholastic career, he might have felt he had an either/or choice to make. He either pursued his interests in explosives and chemicals outside of an academic setting or not at all. Unfortunately, the lack of an external locus of control, of feeling like he could not control his destiny through the proper channels, led to him being the center of a law enforcement investigation and trial. Finally, Hall *et al.* identify snags as the abandonment of goals with the belief that others will oppose them. This typically happens when a person feels hopeless, depressed, and undeserving of anything good in life. Hall *et al.* suggest that these concepts can be transformed into a visual format for learners who would find it easier to digest the information with pictures. After this instruction has taken place and students have listed their traps, dilemmas, and snags, they can reframe and reformulate their newly acquired insights through drawings, writings, or any other means of expression that play to their strengths.

The interventions described above should be undertaken with a trusted therapist. Peer mentors can also gain insight into an ASD student's possible interests in these matters and help to prevent problematic behavior from arising in the first place. Though a simple interest in fire, embers, and the like wouldn't necessarily be a red flag, mentors should ask follow-up questions if a student mentions those interests. They should discuss what it is about fire that interests them. Would they like to do anything with fire themselves or simply observe it? If students bring up certain fascinations, mentors would be aware of a potential pathway into the criminal justice system and take appropriate professional interventions.

Conclusion

I was recently interviewed by a major media outlet. The reporter wanted to know what could have helped me as a youngster to avoid the criminal justice system. I had to pause a moment to think about it. Growing up, I was taught to obey the law. I was an inherent rule follower, as most autistic people are. Frith and De Vignemont (2005) note that ASD individuals are extremely sensitive to normative rules and consider them a way to cope with their lack of social limitations. This was certainly true for me. I never thought for a minute that I was someone who would ever have contact with law enforcement other than possibly receiving a traffic ticket.

Perhaps this was the problem all along. It is counterintuitive to think that one needs to spend more time explaining the traps of the criminal justice system to inherent rule followers but less so when one counterbalances that by considering the social deficits that are part of the ASD profile. My parents viewed me as the quintessential rule follower and a very ethical person, which I also consider myself to be. No one ever thought my traits were a recipe for landing me in the criminal justice system. There was no prevention in my education because no one thought I needed it. I suspect that this is true for a lot of autistic people who grew up in my generation—Generation X. Many of us were either "invisibly fenced" and not given a comprehensive sexual education program or uninformed of the hidden dangers that awaited many of us due to our vulnerabilities, which could land us in the criminal justice system.

What was my answer to the reporter's question? I told her that more than anything, I believe an older peer mentor would have helped me. I would have had a lot of questions for that mentor. I never got a chance to ask anyone about my sexual orientation. As a young adult, I was not able to come to terms with my sexual orientation, mistaking being gay for perhaps a "bug" of autism or a temporary phase. This was simply internalized homophobia on my part, and it made a lot of my sexual feelings go underground, where I buried them. This was, of course, a huge mistake on my part. One's sexuality does not go away simply because one doesn't want to address it. I certainly did not want to address my sexuality. Yet I had no one I could talk to about it. So instead of asking questions of a peer mentor and learning about appropriate and inappropriate ways of gaining knowledge of sex, I inadvertently did so outside of legally permissible channels. As I have come into contact with the hundreds of ASD individuals who have suffered a similar fate to my own, I've seen that this is one of the common denominators between us. Most of us had few friends, no access to dating with either the opposite sex or the same sex, and a lack of sexual education growing up. Many of these individuals were very academically accomplished and intellectually bright but had significant social deficits and an uneven developmental profile. Over the last nine years, when I have met parents and individuals on the spectrum with similar situations to mine, I have been struck by our commonalities. It was those similarities and tragic outcomes that drove me to write this book. If we can prevent a generation of autistic people from involvement in a system that only looks to punish and leave a scarlet letter[2] on one's chest without hope of redemption, I feel I will help to right my wrongs.

Because most parents of autistic children never suspect that their children will ever have contact with the criminal justice system, they most likely have never had a discussion with their kids as to how to handle an encounter with the police. I turn my attention to that issue in the next chapter.

---

2   The letter "A" that was left on the fictional Hester Prynne's dress for her crime of adultery in Nathaniel Hawthorne's classic 19th-century novel exploring stigma and shame, *The Scarlet Letter*.

Encounters with the Police

Picture this: a young autistic adolescent has struggled all his life. Since he was a small child he has taken four or five different medications and he has been hospitalized numerous times. He has a hard time academically and in handling practical matters, like counting money or telling time. Persistent issues include personal hygiene and his attachment to his mother. He has comorbid diagnoses as well as his autism.

According to a report, another student sitting opposite him on the school bus begins talking and the autistic boy repeats inappropriate sexual phrases that others were saying at school. The other student allegedly asks him to show him what color his undershorts are, and he obliges. After the conversation stops, he scratches his groin area when he thinks no one is looking. Bus surveillance video confirms that he looked around to make sure that no one saw him do it. The bus driver contacts school administrators who end up referring this case to the local district attorney's office. The young man maintains that he was not masturbating but his charge is the following: "Felony child molestation in the presence of minors." The young autistic boy didn't touch anyone. As of the date of this writing, if he is found "guilty" he will end up on the sex offender registry and will have to move out of his mother's home, because he has siblings and cannot live in the presence of other minors (Szilagyi, 2019).

Also consider the case of John Benjamin Haygood who was ten years old at the time of his encounter with the law and is an individual on the autism spectrum. Haygood was immediately expelled from school at some point in time, for reasons that are not entirely clear based on mainstream news reports. Five months later when he returned to school, a school resource officer spotted him and told his mother he was going to be placed under arrest. Video from the moment of his arrest went viral on the internet and elicited public outrage over the police's insensitivity about how they handled the situation (CBS News, 2017). Two years later in 2018, the prosecutor still had not dropped the charges after two experts argued that Haygood was incompetent to stand trial (Duffy, 2019).

Let me be clear on where I stand. I feel that we need the police to function as a society. They do good work and help to keep us safe. Without them, we would descend into anarchy. Many police men and women are heroes who risk their lives on a daily basis and we owe them a collective debt of gratitude. Having said that, these aforementioned incidents are far from isolated. Autistic people are sometimes mistreated by the police as a result of the ASD person's condition being mistaken for something nefarious. There are also officers who commit police brutality against autistic people. This is an uncomfortable truth to face collectively as most of us have been brought up to believe that the police are supposed to protect and serve all of us, especially the most vulnerable. I am concerned that the police are often not properly equipped to deal with autistic people and those with cognitive disabilities and sometimes act with cruelty towards them. The question is: what can we do about it? First, I will address the fact that police brutality against disabled people exists.

Police Brutality

One need only look on Google News to see that there is no shortage of mistreatment of disabled individuals and the mentally ill by police. The majority of this chapter will discuss ways to keep autistic individuals out of harm's way when they must interact with the police. But it would do us all good to step back, reflect, and try to understand why this abuse or mistreatment happens and how it got this way. From where does this all stem? Initially, it may seem like the first part of this section has nothing to do with police brutality but please stay with me.

The reader may have a hard time believing that disabled people were once viewed as inherently dangerous. This quotation from 1925 captures the essence of it:

> ...the feeble-minded are a predatory class, never capable of self-support or managing their own affairs...they cause unutterable sorrow at home and are a menace and danger to the community... Every feebleminded person, especially the high-grade imbecile, is a potential criminal, needing only the proper environment and opportunity for the development and expression of his criminal tendencies. (Faunal, 1925, as cited in Nibert, 1995, p.65)

Spitzer and Scull (1977) tell us that modern police forces in the United States emerged as a result of perceived "disorder." In the American South, the genesis of the police force was the slave patrols (Hadden, 2001). The populace that craved social, moral, and economic order turned to police for stabilization so that the right climate for commerce could flourish during reconstruction and into the 20th century. Certain groups of people were thought to be disrupters of both the moral and economic order, especially in the United States. Foreigners, drunks, and particularly those who were thought of as biologically inferior, morally intemperate, or unskilled fell into that category (Potter, 2013). Biological inferiority was seen at one point to be the root cause of all crime. Cognitively disabled men were thought to suffer from exaggerated sexual impulses (Abramov, 2017). A man who served as an expert in autism in the late 20th century said in 1919:

> Feebleminded persons are not merely dull and backward, but are defective in mentality to such a degree that they are incapable, by reason of this mental defect, of receiving proper benefit from the instruction in the ordinary public elementary school... Feebleminded persons are especially prolific and reproduce their kind with greater frequency than do normal persons, and through such reproduction provide a legitimate outlet for the exercise of charitable impulses in each generation, and an endless stream of defective progeny, which are a serious drain on the resources of the nation. (Georgia Commission on Feeblemindedness & Anderson, 1919, p.5)

Early 20th-century America became obsessed with whether the offspring of "feebleminded" people would produce another generation of feebleminded, criminal offspring. Eugenics laws allowed forcible sterilization of people with disabilities or those they labeled defective. It is estimated that around 50,000 people were non-forcibly or forcibly sterilized between 1925 and 1955 (Power, 2016). The 1927 Supreme Court case of Buck v Bell legitimized these forcible sterilization procedures when Oliver Wendell Holmes infamously put pen to paper to say: "Three generations of imbeciles are enough" (Kendregan, 1966, p.133). Ironically, Holmes saw this as compassionate. Instead of "executing" degenerate offspring for their future crimes or letting them starve to death because they couldn't make a living, he figured, why not just save society the trouble by preventing their births in the first place (Lombardo, 2008)? Hitler seized upon what was happening in the United States, which engendered ideas that came into play during the Holocaust of World War II (Kevles, 1999). What would have been considered "feebleminded" in the past would, in many instances, simply be known as "autism" today (Eyal, 2013).

Mid-century sentiment began shifting away from the criminalization of autistic people to institutionalizing them in mental facilities. Notably, Leo Kanner, who was not in favor of eugenics and sterilization, labeled autistic individuals of the day as "feebleminded and idiotic" (Lima et al., 2018).

In the mid 1940s, the United States had the highest number of mental patients anywhere in the world. The same reasons used to justify eugenics were given for the necessity of institutionalization at the time. Children with emotional issues were distinguished from those born with disabilities, since the latter were considered socially incapable and predisposed to committing crime and sexual promiscuity (Malzberg, 1952). Society gave up on them because their conditions were inborn and thus unchangeable or incurable. Autism and other disabilities became medicalized, and forced institutionalization became the norm instead of sterilization and treating people as criminals. Bruno Bettelheim was arguably the individual who was most responsible for autistic people being removed from their homes and placed in institutions. He followed Leo Kanner, who infamously linked autism to cold and emotionally withholding mothers, although Bettelheim took this concept to new heights by comparing children with severe autism to "feral children" raised by animals (Bettelheim, 1959). Though Bettelheim claimed that he strove to treat his patients like human beings, much evidence exists to the contrary. He routinely struck and abused them (Redford, 2010). Animalistic behaviors have been linked to people with disabilities since the 19th century. This has informed policing attitudes towards individuals with disabilities. These attitudes were extremely damaging, despite sometimes giving parents the false hope that a cure was possible. The reasoning was that if the parents, not biology or genetics, were to blame for autism, the child may not have been born with the condition. This was the logic of the times (May, 1958).

It was seen as embarrassing for upper-class individuals to have a child with a disability. Rosemary Kennedy, the daughter of Joseph Kennedy and sister of President John F. Kennedy, was considered "mildly retarded" by the standards of the day. She was given a lobotomy and her cognitive functions were severely worsened by the operation (O'Brien, 2004). The lobotomy of playwright Tennessee Williams's sister, Rose, haunted him for his entire life and caused him to write startling and moving works such as *The Glass Menagerie*, *A Streetcar Named Desire*, and *Suddenly Last Summer*, all of which had lobotomy-laden themes involving the female undergoing, or getting ready to undergo, the procedure (Miliora, 2001). Author Ken Kesey heavily criticized the psychological and psychiatric establishments of the time with his work *One Flew Over the Cuckoo's Nest*, in which his protagonist sees mental institutions as stifling patients' true selves. As a result, the protagonist ends up being lobotomized by the head nurse because of his defiance (Foley, 2001).

Back to Leo Kanner. Even though Kanner felt that some of his child patients started out as feebleminded and idiotic, and with signs of infantile autism (childhood psychosis) that turned into adult schizophrenia (Volkmar

& McPartland, 2014), he saw potential in these children (Kanner, 1943/1973). He tried squaring the intractable nature of an inborn disability with certain potentialities that he believed lay dormant. This is how Kanner attempted to introduce a diagnosis that could differentiate itself from mental retardation and mental illness: one where intervention could make an actual difference. He went on to further differentiate between the degrees of feeblemindedness where the more cognitively abled did not need institutionalization. Instead, intervention and therapy could help youngsters to progress and adjust in society (Kanner, 1949).

Years later came deinstitutionalization, which would take decades to fully implement, not just for autistic people but also for the mentally ill. Improvements in psychopharmacology, family support, and community-based intervention gained traction. And while deinstitutionalization has given autistic people a chance at life outside of the four walls of a hospital—which cannot be emphasized enough as a positive outcome—it has had some unintended negative consequences. The main negative consequence is that we have an unfunded mandate when it comes to our community mental health networks: they have let down people with autism and those struggling with mental illness by making it very difficult to access treatment. And it has made the police become part of the de facto system on the front lines for this population when disabled people need genuine help (Tobin, 2019). In fact, police have been referred to as "streetcorner psychiatrists" (Teplin & Pruett, 1992), which is quite unfortunate, and has become increasingly the case since that article was written in 1992. Without going into too much detail on this subject, I want to focus on just one of the unintended consequences of deinstitutionalization that is germane to this chapter.

Simply put, police have not learned how to interact with autistic people since the wave of deinstitutionalization when these individuals were integrated back into society (Eadens et al., 2016), despite having many decades to learn how to do so. Individuals with disabilities are more likely to be harmed by law enforcement than the general population (Perry & Carter-Long, 2016). This is particularly true for African Americans or Latinos with a disability. A third to half of people killed by police have a disability (Mueller, Forber-Pratt & Sriken, 2019). Other literature confirms that this percentage is indeed around 25–50 percent (DeGue, Fowler & Calkins, 2016). Similarly, The Guardian estimated in late 2015 that individuals with mental illness are 16 times more likely to be killed by the police (Lartey, 2015). Torrey et al. (2013) say that although law enforcement does not keep official track of mental health casualties involving individuals with mental illness, informal studies suggest that around 50 percent of those people killed by police have a disabling condition.

These situations play out daily. Silberman (2017) describes a scenario that is every parent's worst nightmare and one that is all too common. One day, a 14-year-old autistic boy was walking to one of his favorite places in an upscale area of Buckeye, Arizona. His caregiver turned her back for several minutes because he had gained some skills in being more independent and this was a familiar place for him. Suddenly, she turned around and couldn't believe what was happening to the boy. An extremely agitated police officer had pinned him to the ground while he was screaming. It turns out that he was mistaken for a drug user. The officer saw him raise a piece of yarn to his nose to sniff it, in addition to using unfamiliar movements and assuming a rigid body posture.

Unfamiliar body movements may get autistic people killed or badly injured. Take the case of Ricardo Hayes (Associated Press, 2018). Ricardo was an autistic 18-year-old black teenager who wandered out of his home in Chicago around 5 a.m. His caretaker called the police and alerted them to the fact that Ricardo was autistic. A video shows an officer approaching Ricardo as he took a few steps towards the officer. Ricardo was shot by the officer, but fortunately he recovered, in spite of his wounds. The officer thought that he had a gun even though the police department was alerted to his disability in advance. Most neurotypicals probably would have frozen in position and not made sudden moves. They most likely would have been taught to do this. However, this did not come intuitively to Ricardo and it almost cost him his life. The ACLU filed a civil suit on behalf of Ricardo. According to Karen Sheley of the ACLU, black teenagers with disabilities are at a heightened risk for police violence (Associated Press, 2018).

For his dissertation, Abramov (2017) did a Google search and came across 23 cases where the police had used excessive force against those with cognitive disabilities. Thousands and thousands of these cases exist. Abramov did only a random search. Of the 41 percent of African Americans who were sampled, half of those individuals had an ASD diagnosis. Of the Caucasians sampled, all but one person had an ASD diagnosis.

Gardiner, Díaz and Brown (2016) argue that disabled bodies are under attack by the state every day. These three autistic journalists used the disturbing case of Charles Kinsey as an example. Kinsey, an African American behavioral therapist, was shot by police while he had his hands up and in the air. Kinsey's autistic client was a Latino man who was sitting in the street, playing with a toy truck. Police brutally threw him to the ground and then detained him in a squad car for four hours. Similarly, there is the case of another autistic minority man named Reginald "Neil" Latson who was waiting outside a library before it opened. Visiting the library was a routine for Latson. An officer became suspicious and thought that Latson might be carrying a gun.

After realizing that he had no gun, the officer began to question him because of his unusual demeanor. Latson felt panicked and confused, as is common for people with ASD in this circumstance. In an attempt to arrest Latson for not identifying himself, the officer was hurt when Latson tried to move away (Cordell-Whitney, 2017). Latson was imprisoned for a period of time and suffered inhumane conditions. He was also placed into solitary confinement before being pardoned by the Governor of Virginia.

What are we dealing with here? History is repeating itself covertly among the ranks of the police and perhaps society at large. The same attitudes expressed towards disabled people in the 19th and early-to-mid 20th centuries are finding new avenues for expression, even if discrimination is not as overt and out in the open. Dehumanization of those with disabilities is an ongoing theme that has never completely gone away. We have inherited the prejudices of our ancestors. As it turns out, individuals with developmental disabilities experience higher rates, in general, of prejudice, hostility, and dehumanization than their neurotypical peers or what is commonly referred to today as ableism (Parker, Monteith & South, 2018). Over the course of four studies, researchers (*ibid.*) surveyed several hundred neurotypicals using extremely sound and scientifically designed surveys and methodologies. They were looking for unconscious biased attitudes held by neurotypicals towards the developmentally disabled. Survey participants felt that autistic individuals and other developmentally disabled individuals were more likely to cause harm to others than neurotypicals and should be kept separate from others. Furthermore, dependence on others like a caregiver, or needing the services of a group home, *positively correlated* in these studies with what neurotypical participants perceived as an impetus for developmentally disabled people to potentially cause harm in the future. In other words, the participants saw dependence as a predictor of potential future dangerous behavior. This is interesting in light of beliefs in the early part of the 20th century that equated not being a self-supporting person with being a potential menace or danger to the community. Additionally, and perhaps more importantly for our discussion, autistic people were seen as potentially more dangerous to other people than those with Down Syndrome. These prejudicial and ableist attitudes were shown to be positively correlated with decreased support for key social policies that would help to provide individuals with developmental disabilities with greater access to the protection of basic liberties and resources that would help them to lead independent lives. Parker *et al.* (2018) go on to reiterate that these kinds of attitudes are exactly why there are opponents of school inclusion (Thompkins & Deloney, 1995) and why police officers might perceive autistic people to be dangerous, which then justifies their use of force (Parker *et al.*, 2018; Perry & Carter-Long, 2016).

The study regarding unconscious attitudes and perceptions may shock some readers, but consider that police officers, whose job it is to spot differences in human behavior when judging suspicious activity, are far from immune when it comes to these prejudices. In the "see something, say something" culture that we live in, officers are naturally bound to see individuals with differences in human behavior as threats when they don't understand those behaviors. It has always been this way and continues to be so. Autistic people have always been at risk whenever they step outside their front door because of this fact. Collectively, we are afraid of the same things that we were afraid of in the 19th century and probably have been since the beginning of our evolution as a species. It is human nature to associate behavior that doesn't appear "normal" with danger. This is the very nature of what police do. But when it comes to police interaction with autistic individuals, the stakes couldn't be higher in counterbalancing this instinct through better autism education. Many times, it can be a matter of life and death.

Let's return to the quotation that began this discussion from the physician back in 1925:

> ...the feeble-minded are a predatory class, never capable of self-support or managing their own affairs...they cause unutterable sorrow at home and are a menace and danger to the community... Every feebleminded person, especially the high-grade imbecile, is a potential criminal, needing only the proper environment and opportunity for the development and expression of his criminal tendencies. (Faunal, 1925, as cited in Nibert, 1995, p.65)

While today we may not utter such horrible words out loud as some did back in 1925, ableism and stigmatization are alive and well. And since that is true, why should we not be surprised that the police may be susceptible to having at least some implicit biases against autistic people? An uncomfortable and perhaps inconvenient fact that we have to come to terms with is that the police need serious help in learning about autism and so do autistic people themselves. Many officers do not understand autism in the way that they should. As assemblywoman in New Jersey, Patricia Egen-Jones, said:

> There are many things we must train our police officers to do nowadays. I agree with the Attorney General on the need for implicit biased training and cultural awareness and extending that to how we train police officers... Every once in a while we see in the news how someone with autism is treated, or others with disabilities. So there is a need here for this type of training. I have a nephew who is deaf and drives a car. If he were approached by a police officer, his response would be a bit different. Those are the cultural issues I also believe we should be addressing, if we are not already addressing them. (Egen-Jones, 2019)

Indeed, Article 13 of the United Nations Convention on the Rights of Persons with Disabilities mandates effective staff training for everyone working in the field of justice. This is indeed a human rights issue that is taken seriously across the globe (United Nations, 2019).

The rest of this chapter will discuss ways that we can ensure that interactions between police and autistic people go as they should: safely and respectfully.

Do Autistic People Require Accommodations When Being Arrested?

Autistic individuals are subject to arrest every day. In fact, if someone has a disability, their odds of interacting with law enforcement go up dramatically, according to statistics (McCauley, 2017). Even though arrest is inherently a traumatic process for everyone, it is my opinion that individuals with disabilities or mental illness and those on the autism spectrum *should* be entitled to reasonable accommodations during the process. "Should" is the operative word. The Americans with Disabilities Act (ADA) is in theory supposed to offer accommodations to individuals in these situations, but it rarely does. Realistically, this is because police are generally immune from any civil liabilities incurred during an arrest and courts disagree about how to handle individuals who pose immediate and specifically violent threats. Some courts have ruled that threats to human life usurp any protections that Title II of the ADA offers to individuals with mental illness and disabilities for which they would otherwise qualify (Myers, 2017). Titles I and III of the ADA employ language which suggests that reasonable accommodations be made (Rifkin, 2016). Title II says that no individual shall be denied a "service, program, or activity" from a public entity because of their disability. The question is: do the police fall under this category? Do arrests fall under this category? In other words, does being arrested fall under one of the categories of either a service, program, or activity? The answer is yes; in reality, that should be the case. Under the ADA, city governments and local police departments are required to make sure that effective communication takes place with those who have disabilities (Wertlieb, 1991). In practice, Title II of the ADA is supposed to provide a source of liability to litigants/plaintiffs when the police discriminate against disabled people (42 U.S. Code, § 12132). This, however, does not always happen.

A clear-cut case of this involved a deaf man named Charles Lewis, although it wasn't so "clear-cut" to the courts. Police were called to Lewis's home to investigate a custody dispute. Lewis's friends told police in advance, and in unambiguous terms, that Lewis was deaf. His friends also pleaded with police to provide written questions to him. They refused, not believing he was deaf, and instead insisted upon using verbal commands. When he didn't comply (because he was deaf), police proceeded to kick him, hit him, and use abusive and inappropriate language. As a result of the assault, he suffered bruises, contusions, and several internal injuries. He was then arrested for resisting law enforcement. The absurdity of this is that Lewis was not being criminally insubordinate. He could not cooperate because he literally could not hear what was being said. The police knew this. In court, the officers did not dispute that Lewis was deaf, but they argued that he was not a qualified individual within the definition of the ADA. Yet, the court acknowledged that the police were informed about his deafness, took no steps to communicate with him properly, and did not acknowledge anything to the contrary. Ultimately, Lewis's summary judgment was denied. The mental gymnastics used to come to such a judgment are astounding and yet such rulings unfortunately are not unusual (Lewis v. Truitt, 1997).

The Supreme Court "punted the football" on this very question in City & Cnty. of San Francisco v. Sheehan (2015). The facts of the case are as follows: Teresa Sheehan lived in a supportive housing unit that at the time ran cooperatives for adults with mental illness throughout the city of San Francisco (Allen, 2015). Sheehan was 56 years old and diagnosed with schizoaffective disorder, but her condition had significantly worsened over time. She was not eating, not taking her medications, and not attending group meetings.

A social worker named Heath Hodge felt that Sheehan was becoming a danger to either herself or others and needed to be hospitalized. As a social worker, Hodge had the authority to place Sheehan on what's called a 5150, which in California is defined as an involuntary psychiatric hold. Hodge got the pink 5150 form filled out at the police station and an officer immediately arrived at the supportive housing unit, which happened more quickly than Hodge expected. That officer, Katherine Holder, noted to Hodge that she was inexperienced in 5150s in spite of being on the force for over seven years. Holder called a superior named Kimberly Reynolds, who soon joined them. The officers started shouting commands aggressively. Sheehan yelled back at them to "get out," that they had no right to be there without a search warrant, and that she had a knife. She had used that knife earlier in the day to cut fruit because she enjoyed eating alone (Allen, 2015). With no history of violence in her past, she grabbed it. Things escalated quickly. Police backup was called and officers used pepper spray after they finally opened the door. With sirens roaring, police backup, and the pepper spray having no effect on Sheehan, Reynolds decided to fire two rounds of bullets, aiming at Sheehan's torso, although she missed. Sheehan still held on to the knife after these shots.

Reynolds fired again, this time hitting Sheehan's torso, and then finally fired a shot into her head (Allen, 2015).

Sheehan was taken to the emergency room with 14 bullet holes in her body. Doctors said it was a miracle that she survived. With no criminal record, Sheehan was charged with five felonies: making "terrorist threats" and assaults with a deadly weapon on officers of the peace (Allen, 2015).

Many questions were rightly posed after this tragedy. Why did police escalate the situation so quickly? Why didn't they stand down, call for help, get a crisis intervention team involved, and buy precious time before busting down the door? After all, Sheehan was initially not supposed to be arrested nor had she ever been arrested in her life. Sheehan was supposed to go to the hospital because she was in the throes of a psychiatric crisis. So why did police break her door down and then claim self-defense without taking any steps to accommodate her disability?

Sheehan filed a lawsuit against the City of San Francisco, alleging that police did not accommodate her disability during arrest. The Ninth Circuit Court of Appeals held that police officers plausibly violated the ADA when they made no accommodations for her disability during the arrest. But because she was brandishing a knife and causing an "exigent threat," they felt that remanding the case back to the District Court for a jury trial was the best course of action in determining whether Sheehan was denied reasonable accommodation under the ADA.

The City of San Francisco then appealed this decision all the way to the Supreme Court, arguing that the Ninth Circuit erred in saying that law enforcement had to provide a reasonable accommodation to an individual brandishing a knife. The city argued in its petition for writ of certiorari that even if officers were found to have denied Sheehan reasonable accommodations when arresting her, they should be entitled to qualified immunity (Rifkin, 2016). In other words, the city shifted the argument away from their initial position that she was not entitled to accommodations as per the ADA to stating that it was a moot point because she posed a direct threat.

After initially agreeing to hear the case, the Supreme Court declined to take it. In declining, Justice Samuel Alito wrote as the majority set forth a two-pronged test to determine whether future arrests are covered under the ADA:

1. Is the arrest a public activity in which the arrestee "participates" and may "benefit"?

2. Does the treatment an individual receives during an arrest constitute discrimination? In other words, is an "arrest" a "service, program, or activity" from which a disabled person could be excluded or denied the benefits? (Lohmann, 2017)

The court could have answered these questions in Sheehan's case, but they didn't. They basically said, in essence: we don't want to answer these questions as they pertain to the Sheehan case, but these are important questions to consider and the rubrics that we want courts to use when judging such matters in the future. Because they did not answer these questions, individuals with disabilities are not guaranteed the ADA's protections during interactions with law enforcement (Lefkowitz, 2018). Furthermore, the Supreme Court granted qualified immunity to the officers involved. Qualified immunity protects officials from lawsuits by only allowing suits to go forward where a public servant (such as a police officer) clearly violated an established statutory or constitutional right. It asks the person filing the suit to show that a reasonable official (in this case, a police officer) would have clearly known that they were violating the arrestee's rights (Ross, 2015).

There are details to unpack here. When disabled people are killed by police in these situations, the police rarely face consequences. Fewer than 3 percent of these officers are charged with a crime and only 0.2 percent of the charges lead to convictions (Pugliese, 2017). As Pugliese (2017) also points out, the doctrine of qualified immunity often shields officers from liability, thereby nullifying the purpose and intent of Title II litigation. Furthermore, the federal government and the U.S. Department of Justice recognizes that these problems are common and provides guidelines to police officers for when they encounter disabled individuals after the passage of the ADA (U.S. Department of Justice, Civil Rights Division, Disability Rights Section, 2019). The Department of Justice also published a public statement of interest saying that Title II applies to all law enforcement activities including arrests (Bharara & Kennedy, 2015). Therefore, if training was a top priority and officers had standard protocols in place for these situations, qualified immunity would no longer be a viable defense option for officers. It would then be much clearer to officers that their actions would violate the law if they did not take de-escalation steps first whenever it was possible to do so. A reasonable official would then know that they were violating the arrestees' rights under these circumstances. The Supreme Court also left open the question of whether officers are required to undergo training under the ADA or be subject to liabilities, as the circuit courts are split on this question: some have ruled that they are and others have ruled the opposite (Lohmann, 2017). Furthermore, the Supreme Court could have solidified a Tenth Circuit ruling that requires accommodations to be implemented when an agency, like the police, is put on notice that an individual has a disability before the encounter. But the Supreme Court didn't do that (Sperry v. Maes, 2013). This is what happened in the Sheehan case.

Justice Sonia Sotomayor, during oral arguments in Sheehan's case, asked pertinent questions that seem to suggest that she believed that the ADA's intent was to give individuals with mental illness and disabilities a "chance" in these worst-case scenarios. She shared the concern that police shoot and kill 350 mentally ill people each year. She asked whether the ADA's intent was to provide "mitigation strategies" before resorting to violence (Harrington, 2017). These are good questions but unfortunately the highest court in the land failed to answer them. As a counterpoint to Sotomayor, Chief Justice John Roberts seemed to feel that because Sheehan was in a suicidal state, the police probably did what they had to do under the circumstances.

Lefkowitz (2018) feels that when the Supreme Court revisits this issue again in the future (and at some point, they will have to), Title II needs to apply in all but exigent circumstances, meaning whenever there is not a direct threat to people's lives. But this begs the question: would Sheehan have been a threat to Reynolds had Reynolds followed a proper de-escalation protocol with mandatory training? Rifkin (2016) would disagree that exigent circumstances shouldn't count. She argues that the ADA should apply whether or not an exigency exists, saying that doing otherwise strips injured disabled parties of their rights under Title II of the ADA. She feels that courts which focus on exigencies overlook the timing of events, such as whether officers were alerted about a disability in advance (which often occurs) or whether they lacked the necessary training. In essence, Rifkin argues that whether or not a threat exists to the officer's safety, they still should be responsible for their actions if harm to the arrested individual is caused under Title II of the ADA.

If we remember Justice Alito's two unanswered questions of whether arrests are a public activity and lack of protections under Title II constitutes discrimination, Rifkin (2016) answers with a resounding yes. Indeed, when the Department of Justice has acknowledged this to be true, it's hard to argue the contrary.

Understanding our system's shortcomings in addressing systemic police prejudice against disabled individuals and the fact that they don't always receive the accommodations they need during these encounters means mitigating the situation in advance to the best of our ability. We must think of ways to keep encounters and arrests from going tragically wrong before this happens. The following sections will address ways to mitigate potential crises.

What Do They Know?

First, I will discuss trainings that the Department of Justice has stated as being critical under Title II of the ADA. What do police already know about autism spectrum disorders?

In the last few years, police trainings on ASD have increased significantly, although some research surprisingly suggests that increased ASD trainings do not always correlate with more informed practices on the part of law enforcement (Dixon *et al.*, 2012). Still, I believe that they are better than nothing.

Students who are entering the field of criminal justice tend to lack knowledge of ASD, or their knowledge is moderate at best (Mogavero, 2018). In the United Kingdom (where advocacy is more assertive than the United States regarding ASD and the criminal justice system), there are problematic signs. Crane *et al.* (2016) found that 48 percent of officers surveyed believed they were equipped to work with ASD individuals, while 29 percent believed they were poorly equipped to deal with this population. Other studies in the United Kingdom have borne out similar results. Chown (2010) reported that 62 percent of officers received no training whatsoever on ASD, while Modell and Mak (2008) found that 48 percent had no training. Thirty-five percent of officers interviewed in the same study equated autism to "Rain Man," the character that actor Dustin Hoffman played in the 1988 movie (Modell & Mak, 2008). Chown (2010) found 40 percent of surveyed officers did not understand how the terms "developmental disability," "cognitive disability," and "mental disability" were different from one another.

Is it any better in the United States? I don't know, partly because there is considerably less research about it in the United States than in the United Kingdom. However, many signs point to inadequacies. One study from Kentucky indicated that while 78 percent of police officers were somewhat knowledgeable about ASD, the level of confidence in utilizing their knowledge on their beat was much lower (Hoffman, 2018). In several states where police had to complete 400–500-hour trainings, less than 1 percent of the time was devoted to mental illness in general in the trainings, and even less time was spent on ASDs (Laan, Ingram & Glidden, 2013).

Many states don't require police training for interacting with people on the spectrum, and the few that do rarely comply with the law. In New Jersey, for example, police officers complied with the law only 23 percent of the time (Furfaro, 2018), and of those officers who received training, only 50 percent said that it was "somewhat effective or not effective." It's easy to understand why this was the case. Kelly and Hassett-Walker (2016) noted that New Jersey provided officers with both "read and sign" trainings, as well as video trainings. Around 20 percent of officers said that this was their only training and exposure to autism.

In general, female police officers tend to be more receptive to training than male officers. This is problematic, because the majority of police officers are male (Eadens *et al.*, 2016). Modell and Cropp (2007) suggest that officers are often imbued with a "warrior mindset," which fits a masculine temperament. They feel that their job is akin to a war zone and that violence is sometimes necessary.

No doubt, one of the barriers to appropriate training is the understanding of simple definitions. While some readers of this book probably know that autism and mental illness are not the same thing, there are also some police officers who do not (Kelly & Hassett-Walker, 2016). Careful emphasis on autism spectrum conditions as separate from mental illness would help officers to not conflate the two and to respond more appropriately to avoid unnecessary escalation. An overconfidence in an officer's abilities in handling "mental illness" and a generalization of that onto autism may lead officers to think they are more capable than they really are in dealing with this population (Henshaw & Thomas, 2012). Even more problematically and counterintuitively, Modell and Mak (2008) found that officers' ability to recognize autism degraded over time. This means that it got worse. If your only tool is a hammer, every problem looks like a nail.

My initial law enforcement contact has resulted in post-traumatic stress disorder (PTSD), which will probably linger with me for the rest of my life. I'll never know for certain whether the FBI knew of my diagnosis ahead of time, but I do know that their general practice is to conduct a deep investigation into a person's background before conducting a search warrant. Assuming that they did know, it is a safe bet that they either were not trained or simply didn't care that I was on the spectrum, based on how they conducted their raid.

One October morning at around 6:30 a.m., around 12 armed FBI agents busted into my bedroom, awakening me from a sleep. They yelled at me to comply with them while I was still trying to figure out why they were there. My initial thought was that it must be a burglar or the fire department. Instead of fighting or fleeing, I froze. That was very lucky for me because to do otherwise would have probably meant catastrophe. But what if I didn't have the instincts of self-preservation in that situation? What if my autism caused me to panic and mistakenly conclude that I needed to run for my life to escape? What if the sheer sensory overload of the situation, combined with a lack of central coherence to intuit the big picture, resulted in me fighting back? What if my general conclusion was that they were burglars and I needed to defend myself? Could I have ended up like Sheehan?

Training for law enforcement at the federal level (FBI agents and Homeland Security personnel) to recognize and interact with individuals on the autism spectrum should be as much of a priority as it is for local police and sheriff departments. Unfortunately, I have yet to see evidence that such trainings exist.

The Need for Training

I do know that some training is better than no training at all, though I don't have a lot of data on its effectiveness with autistic people. Data among school police/school resource officers shows that those who receive training are likely to offer more rehabilitative solutions rather than automatic suspension or referral to juvenile authorities (Bolger, Kremser & Walker, 2019). This is important because individuals with autism are 2.5 times more likely to be suspended from school than their non-disabled peers (Ambler, Eidels & Gregory, 2015). McGonigle *et al.* (2014) found that emergency medical services personnel reported a significant improvement in both knowledge and comfort levels when working with autistic individuals after being exposed to training. After an "awareness session" in the United Kingdom, colleagues in the criminal justice system felt that they could recognize the role of vulnerable populations in their interactions with them, as well as make more appropriate sentencing recommendations (Hardy *et al.*, 2016). The Crisis Intervention Team (CIT) Program in the United States, which helps officers learn about mental illness, was extremely well received (Compton *et al.*, 2006). Crisis intervention teams with social workers and psychologists tend to handle acute mental health crises more effectively than even trained officers. Ideally, if trained officers were to arrive on the scene of an individual threatening to harm oneself, they should be accompanied by social workers or other mental health professionals with an understanding of ASD and/or mental illness (Pepler & Barber, 2021). Simple desensitization or exposure to autistic people makes it less likely that officers will experience conscious or unconscious negative emotions towards these individuals, which affects the quality of the interactions (Corrigan *et al.*, 2003; Debbaudt, 2002). This is backed up by the research. If an officer has a family member or friend of the family who is on the spectrum, they are likely to handle encounters with autistic people much more effectively (Furfaro, 2018). Standardized training and video instruction is not as effective as in-person training methods (Granpeesheh *et al.*, 2010), and including autistic people as part of the training would contribute the most to officers learning what it is like to be on the spectrum. The bottom line is that there is not a tremendous amount of research citing the efficacy of trainings about autism for police officers at this point. I do know, however, that they are better than nothing.

Simple things that police officers do can make a huge difference; it doesn't take much. To prevent meltdowns, do away with the lights, sirens, and fast-approaching vehicles unless absolutely necessary, while calling in backup in advance (Debbaudt, 2004). Expect that your autistic subject won't look you in the eye, and understand that this is not a sign of a guilty conscience nor is it due to being under the influence of alcohol or drugs (Dalton *et al.*, 2005).

Unfortunately, the need for training is even more urgent when our discussion shifts to autism and minorities. Black Americans are almost three times as likely to be shot and killed by police officers than white Americans (Law, 2017). For Holly Robinson Peete, the struggle is personal. Her advocacy was born out of a tragedy in North Miami, Florida that involved the shooting of Charles Kinsey whom I spoke of earlier. After hearing about Kinsey, Peete instinctively knew that her son wouldn't handle such a situation and became scared for him, as most black parents are for their children in relation to encountering law enforcement. Peete invited Kinsey to be part of a panel discussion, and from that, Spectrum Shield was born. Spectrum Shield pairs police officers with older African-American autistic children as part of a training so that both populations can learn from each other. The weekend training is designed to teach officers that "If you have met one person on the spectrum, you have met one person on the spectrum." In other words, there's no one monolithic way that autistic people present, even though there may be general commonalities. Participants, on the other hand, are taught what not to do when law enforcement initiates an encounter with them. Among the skills taught are the following:

- Minimize one's nonverbal communications. Laughing or spontaneously reaching for something in one's pocket will be interpreted as aggression and will usually be met with a harsh and sometimes lethal response.

- Follow instructions explicitly. If they tell you to get down on the ground, do it. Don't ask questions.

- Ask permission to do anything, whether it is reaching for one's driver's license in the glove compartment or one's iPhone. (Law, 2017)

Autism Registries

You read me right. Not sex offender registries but autism registries. Some communities have adopted autism registries that let officers identify autistic individuals who are willing to put their names (or the names of their children if they are under 18) into a police database so they can respond accordingly (Furfaro, 2018) when confronting that individual. Ideally, one would hope that police officers armed with proper training would allow these registries to augment the resources they have at their disposal to respond appropriately when confronting autistic individuals. You can go online right now and do a simple Google search, and you'll see how popular this idea has become with many police departments.

An example is the "Samuel Allen Law" that was passed recently in Texas (Cabrera & Rice, 2019). Samuel's mother, Jennifer, pushed for the law, as she became afraid of what might happen if her autistic son was ever pulled over by the police once he started to drive. This new law allows anyone with a "communication impairment" (including deafness and autism) to bring to a police station a diagnosis notice from a doctor and be placed on an internal police registry with the code "A Communication Impediment with a Peace Officer" besides their name. Any officer in Texas approaching a vehicle and doing a check on the license plate would see the code before getting out of the car to interact with the person.

There are several reasons, though, why a parent may not opt for this as their chosen method of protection. First, it does invite bias on the part of officers. People with disabilities are often subjected to negative stereotypes and prejudices (Bagenstos, 2000). Families of young people understandably worry about misleading reports and statistics that suggest autistic people are violent by nature, using examples like Nikolas Cruz (Ortiz, 2018), Adam Lanza (Harmon, 2014), and Elliot Rodger (Gnaulati, 2014), even though the scientific community knows that violence is not largely associated with autism (Allely *et al.*, 2017). The word "registry" also has such an emotionally charged meaning, being associated for so long with sex offender registries, that parents may be reluctant to place their child's name on it even though the purpose here is to protect the autistic child. And finally, an autism registry truly works only when an officer pulls over a driver or has time to do a check in a non-emergency. But what about when an identification can't be made immediately? Officers can't always rely on these registries when they have to make split-second decisions before going to their database to check whether the person has autism or not. If they are posed with an immediate threat, they have to act within seconds, not minutes.

The other obvious limitation with this method is proximity. Suppose the autism registry was limited to the town in which the ASD person lives. What would happen when they leave and go to a neighboring town? Would officers in that jurisdiction have information about the individual? The same question could be asked if this was implemented on a state-by-state basis. If the answer is that the registries are limited to jurisdictions, counties, or states, it brings into question the efficacy of such a proposal since it is quite easy to come into contact with police from other cities, towns, and states. And if the answer is that there are no limitations, it invites serious privacy concerns, no matter how well intentioned the idea is. For such a registry to be perfect, officers everywhere should have access to this information, since autistic people can theoretically travel anywhere. But most people probably don't want the FBI or Homeland Security knowing the personal details of their autistic children.

Writer David Perry (2017), of the magazine *The Nation*, is not a fan of this approach. He says:

> The second suggestion, registries of disabled people, is even more concerning. There have long been advocates for making lists of disabled people to give police more information, but people should not have to hand their names to the police to be guaranteed basic civil rights.

Identification Cards or Bracelets

The idea of an "autism alert card" is a little older and less complex. It's been embraced by police departments in the United Kingdom and America. It allows an autistic person to carry a card in their wallet that alerts authorities to their diagnosis, as well as any differences in perception and communication that help the officer to understand the person's behaviors (Maras & Bowler, 2014). Other forms of identification have become more sophisticated as technology has developed. Recently, a grant application was written for one such program called Immediate Recognition Increases Safety (IRIS) (Lewis, 2019). Parents who give their permission can register their children and IRIS notifies first responders in their communities. They receive an ID card and a bracelet with an autism recognition symbol and a PDF copy to be used on other articles such as backpacks and jackets. The bracelet they receive has a USB port that can connect to a computer and provide first responders with more specific information on the person. Additionally, police officers are given a free app that is accessible from their iPhone or Android stores and provides de-escalation strategies to use in a crisis. Some alert cards today have barcodes that can be scanned for additional information. Some cards allow the autistic person or their parents to check off boxes regarding behaviors that may apply to them when triggered. Other cards display the prominent information of the autism diagnosis on the front of the card and instruct the officer or first responder to turn over the card for more specific information on the back.

There are other variations of these kinds of identification markers being proposed. In my home state of Michigan, for example, one autistic man asked his state legislator to have an optional autism identification license plate so that police would immediately know of someone's diagnosis when they pull them over (Putnam, 2019). This license plate would visibly show all drivers that this person has an autism diagnosis.

Identification cards or plates might be helpful in those instances where autistic individuals are suspected of being under the influence of alcohol or a drug after being pulled over. ASD suspects may fail the field sobriety test because of the complex motor skills required and/or not understanding all of the verbal directions involved (Bolton & KUSA, 2014). In some cases, ASD defendants have also had dilated pupils even though they were not intoxicated.

Since there is limited research on the efficacy of these programs, I must rely on what I know about autism. These cards and bracelets can only be effective to the extent that a situation has not yet begun to escalate out of control. De-escalation tools themselves can be highly effective if the officer, for example, recognizes the bracelet symbol of the rainbow jigsaw puzzle and immediately associates it with autism through their training. They can be successful if the autistic person has the presence of mind to calmly ask the officer if they can reach for the card or bracelet. But if they reach for an item suddenly and without asking permission, an officer can also react with aggression.

In one online video (Dietz, 2015), there are several dramatizations showing the effectiveness of the autism alert cards. But in all of the fictionalized depictions presented, the autistic individuals are somewhat calm and the situation has not reached the point of no return where force needs to be used. If an officer feels immediately threatened at the beginning of the encounter, it's very unlikely that the situation will proceed to a point where an autistic individual can reach for their wallet card without getting seriously hurt. It would be too late.

Virtual Reality Training

Another method of police training is through virtual reality (VR). As part of a federal consent decree in Chicago (Rhee, 2019), mandating training has taken this route (Gorner, 2019). The Chicago superintendent of police estimated that 55 percent of the people he encountered on the street had either autism, bipolar disorder, or schizophrenia (Francescani & Margolin, 2019). Officers are presented with videos where they have to make choices in simulations with autistic and schizophrenic individuals. Officers use headsets similar to those used for VR video games and pick a different scenario, each one lasting about five minutes (*ibid.*). The video simulations put one in the shoes of the individual needing intervention, so the officer gets to understand the autistic individual's perspective firsthand. Preliminary research suggests that this could be an effective model of training officers because it is so interactive (Garcia, Ware & Baker, 2019).

Self-Incrimination

So far, I have limited the discussion to keeping autistic people safe when they have to interact with law enforcement. The tone has been focused on complying with what police demand in order to keep the autistic person out of harm's way. But it's important to also keep in mind the distinction between complying with commands to stay alive and knowing one's rights in an encounter. There are genuine concerns that arise when we think about the specific set of traits that autistic people possess and the greater possibility of unintentionally giving up one's rights and possible false confessions. Worse yet, there are instances of defense lawyers' representation of autistic people being subpar at best and completely abominable at worst.

Let's take a case that most people are familiar with: Brendan Dassey from the hit Netflix documentary series *Making a Murderer.* Brendan was a developmentally disabled juvenile who, along with another individual, Steven Avery, was accused of murdering a woman named Teresa Halbach. While I can't substantiate that Brendan is autistic, court records showed he had a severe language-based learning disability that placed his communication and processing skills in the lowest percentiles of all juveniles his age (State v. Dassey, 2007). In spite of this, he was questioned about his possible role in Ms. Halbach's murder without a parent or guardian present. The interrogation, some of which was viewable on the Netflix documentary, left many viewers with a horrible taste in their mouths. People could tell that something wasn't quite right. Brendan seemed to answer questions he didn't understand, and he most likely wasn't aware of the significance of the interrogation. This was evidenced by him asking if he could "go back to class" after they were through. The answers Brendan gave were full of contradictions and physical impossibilities. His answers appeared to be aimed at pleasing the officers so he could leave the room rather than comprehending what he was being asked (LaVigne & Miles, 2018). Brendan was extremely compliant. He nodded a total of 236 times and said yes 247 times, even when he couldn't possibly have understood the questions. Police officers' verbiage was above and beyond what his test scores indicated for his comprehension level (*ibid.*). One may argue that nodding was a sign of acquiescence on Brendan's part, but he also nodded when officers were speaking gibberish. One may also argue that false confessors do not provide details, they simply confess to a crime. But, in fact, 95 percent of false confessions provide specific details of how a crime occurred (Schatz, 2018). Brendan is currently serving a life sentence in federal prison for murder and rape where, in my opinion, a good case could be made that he is actually innocent (Keatley, Marono & Clarke, 2018).

One of the issues that the court took into consideration when ruling against Brendan was that detectives read him his Miranda Rights twice; therefore, he must have understood what it meant. He "voluntarily, knowingly and intelligently" waived them, to be exact. However, with a quick glance of the literature, one can see that this means very little with regards to his actual understanding of the warning at the time. The fact is: autistic individuals are highly vulnerable in the interrogation room (North, Russell & Gudjonsson, 2008) whether they have been read their Miranda Rights or not. With regards to Brendan, individuals with intellectual disabilities will generally have difficulties with Miranda Rights comprehension (Fulero & Everington, 1995) due to individuals' suggestibility to leading questions and response to detectives' perceived friendliness. North *et al.* (2008) found in a study of 26 "high functioning" autistics to 27 matched controls that those in the ASD group were significantly more compliant in the interrogative setting than their counterparts. Goldstein *et al.* (2003) studied 55 adolescents whose cases had already been adjudicated to see if they comprehended or understood what Miranda warnings meant using the Miranda Rights Comprehension Instruments II (MRCI-II). Participants were asked to use their written expression skills to demonstrate their knowledge of Miranda Rights. They were also asked to answer a series of multiple-choice questions. The results of the study found that those individuals who were cognitively impaired had a difficult time in comprehending Miranda Rights. But what was perhaps most surprising about this study was that students who had received any kind of special education were less likely than their general-education counterparts to comprehend Miranda Rights. Once Miranda Rights are waived, any confession sticks, whether it is true or false. The conviction is almost always upheld on appeal as a result of the confession. Perske (2008) showed how common false confessions are for people with intellectual disabilities when he compiled a list of 53 cases. Individuals displaying characteristics of an intellectual disability represent 25.7 percent of those who have falsely confessed (Schatz, 2018).

As we can see, Brendan's case is far from being an outlier. Detectives receive little training when it comes to autism spectrum disorders (Trainum, 2016). Therefore, they don't learn that anxiety and eagerness to please can contribute to both being suggestible and a willingness to comply in the interrogative setting (Gudjonsson *et al.*, 2002). North *et al.* (2008) believe that being suggestible in this setting is due to a combination of fear of negative evaluation by others, high anxiety, and a dash of paranoia. Debbaudt (2004) says that the "concrete thinking" part of those with ASD can lead to false confessions. Mogavero (2016) says that standard interrogative pressure, which utilizes deception, could be extremely confusing to an ASD individual who tends to be literal minded.

By now, we have reached a concern that is even more pressing than not understanding Miranda Rights, and I believe that it is overlooked by almost everyone: detectives often conduct a "pre-interrogation interview" during the investigative phase before an arrest takes place. These interviews happen when detectives have a "hunch" that a suspect might be guilty of a crime but don't necessarily have probable cause to make a formal arrest or even get a search warrant. So they'll frequently ask a suspect at this point in the process if they will come down to the station for an interview, while emphasizing that they are not under arrest and are free to go whenever they want to. This is a trap, since it gives a naive suspect the impression that all one has to do is cooperate and one may not be in trouble. I believe that this incentivizes incrimination since, when agreeing to an interview, it doesn't appear to the suspect that the "gloves are off." This is all intentional, as one is more likely to talk freely if one feels less threatened. If a confession happens during the pre-interrogation interview, it is game, set, and match for the government, most of the time. In some states, defendants in the United States District Court can bring in confession experts to dispute the validity of the confession, but not all jurisdictions allow this (Cutler, Findley & Loney, 2014). Worst of all, there's no formal requirement to Mirandize someone under these circumstances if the police claim the defendant was never "in custody" to begin with (Kamisar, 2017). Any appellate case looking for a dismissal along these lines would be denied if the defendant had not yet been arrested and claimed he wasn't Mirandized. But who would know that? Certainly not most laypeople and especially not autistic people and individuals with cognitive impairments who haven't had prior involvement with the legal system.

The pre-interrogation interview is largely based on hunches, nonverbal behavior, gestures, and detectives' suspicions that arise based on a suspect's behavior (Inbau *et al.*, 2013). Interestingly, research has emerged to suggest that detectives are not very good judges of truthfulness using the Reid technique (the "go-to" protocol for United States detectives) (Bond & DePaulo, 2006; DePaulo *et al.*, 2003; Vrij, 2008; Vrij, Granhag & Porter, 2010). In other words, detectives make personal judgments on a suspect's guilt based on what they have been trained to do according to the Reid model of interrogation and they are often not accurate. Consider this: how much worse would detectives be when judging truth or falsehood with the developmentally disabled individual whose nonverbal behavior often differs significantly from the rest of the population? This is potentially catastrophic as far as autistic people are concerned. But I have jumped the gun. We will return to the Reid technique in a moment. I need to finish our discussion of the pre-interrogation interview as it applies to ASD individuals.

The pre-interrogation interview is a litmus test of sorts for detectives. If a suspect appears to be guilty based on their behaviors, law enforcement moves in for a full confession, typically using the Reid technique later on. The pre-interrogation interview has the detective ask "behavior provoking" questions (Kassin, 2014) and observe the suspect's verbal and nonverbal reactions, attending to such cues as eye contact, pauses, qualified denials, posture, and fidgeting. It's no secret that ASD individuals have trouble sustaining eye contact in stressful situations (Kliemann *et al.*, 2010), so it is a bit frightening that an uninformed detective would use this yardstick to determine whether an autistic person is being truthful. Furthermore, it is very apparent that prosody and pragmatic ability in speech are highly altered in ASD individuals, which may account for long pauses (Peppé *et al.*, 2006; Kim *et al.*, 2014). Additionally, a large body of research suggests that postural control is diminished or even "immature" in ASD individuals, for numerous reasons (Radonovich, Fournier & Hass, 2013). Setting aside the substantive words spoken by the ASD individual in this setting, most of their nonverbal communication might cause a detective to believe that they are a guilty suspect even if they are completely innocent. Which brings us to the Reid technique.

First, the detective isolates the individual in a small, enclosed room with bright lights and sensory deprivations, such as a lack of natural light, for hours upon hours and sometimes days upon days if necessary. Second, the detective conveys, on an absolute, factual basis, to the suspect that they are guilty and may say that they have proof that the person committed the crime, even if no such proof actually exists. They may show fake evidence to the suspect. There is nothing that a suspect can say that will sway the detective or change their mind; the suspect might as well be whispering into the wind. The idea is to get the suspect to believe that their denials are completely futile and that they may as well just give up. Third, the detective will act sympathetic to the fact that there may have been a reason for the crime. They might say: "You know, I've struggled with addiction myself. People do crazy things when they are addicted. It's okay to talk about it and admit what you did. This is your only chance to get the help you need." Police are encouraged to develop themes that justify or excuse the crime, such as a detective saying: "Everyone looks at porn every now and then. Heck, I've even looked at porn myself. But you let your porn viewing get out of control, didn't you? Let's talk about this thing and be honest about it here. This is your chance." This can lead a suspect to believe that they may get treated more leniently if they confess. In fact, police are allowed to lie about future lenient treatment while knowing full well that no such leniency promises will be kept. Detectives will also present false choices to suspects where an "alternative question" will imply guilt but is considered to have a more socially acceptable answer than a full admission of guilt. An example could be: "Do you want us to think that you have abused lots of little kids or that you had a problem or an addiction with child pornography? If you had a problem looking at pictures...fine...

just tell us. We know what is on your computer, so you might as well tell us. Staying quiet and not saying anything only makes you look more guilty in our eyes." This "false choice" of admitting to using the computer to download child pornography still gets the detectives what they want in the end, which is a confession. Once a confession is made, the detectives will then do the investigatory work necessary to see whether actual sexual abuse took place with other children.

This kind of psychological warfare leaves an autistic person or someone with an intellectual disability unprotected and vulnerable, with potential life-and-death consequences for the person if they confess, falsely or not. There are several reasons for this. Schatz (2018) identifies the following:

- Autistic people and those with intellectual disabilities are easily overwhelmed by stress and will be less capable of handling both the sensory deprivations and bombardments of being in an isolated room for prolonged periods of time. Without truly realizing that they can leave if they have yet to be arrested, it may seem imperative to them to say anything they can just to leave that environment.

- Problems with reading nonverbal cues, theory of mind, and understanding the intentions of the officers will make autistic individuals more easily manipulated by fake evidence (fake evidence is not illegal for detectives to use) and any trickery officers decide to employ. Autistic individuals might use such logic as: "A police officer can't lie to me." Or: "Even though what he is telling me doesn't make sense, he is showing me proof that I committed this crime. Does that mean I did it?" Autistic individuals tend to be more trusting than their typically developing peers (Yi *et al.*, 2013).

- Autistic individuals and those with intellectual disabilities have difficulties parsing out the differences between blameworthiness and unforeseen circumstances. This can cause some of these individuals to accept blame for events in which they were not culpable. People like this can be known as "guilt grabbers" because they not only elicit signs of guilt at doing something wrong, they also elicit signs of guilt *at the mere thought* of doing something wrong (Lilienfeld, Lynn & Lohr, 2002). ASD individuals are often very sensitive to normative rules (if they know what they are) as they are a way to cope and overcompensate for their social limitations. Any deviations from those rules can bring about a panicked response. So being told "It is unfortunate this crime took place" could bring about a guilty response since the crime itself is so grotesque to the ASD individual.

> It is very much like a child who feels guilty his parents are getting a divorce and thinks it is his fault. The unforeseen circumstances of the divorce morph into blameworthiness that the child feels.

Furthermore, Schatz (2018) gives a final reason for false confessions that I believe is extremely significant and compelling. Individuals with mild cognitive impairments or those on the "higher functioning" end of the autism spectrum may deny that they have a disability in the first place, may be undiagnosed, or may overrepresent to the interrogator/detective what they are capable of understanding out of human pride or the desire to reduce stigma. Doing this puts the suspect at a huge disadvantage because, if by small chance the detective had training and understanding in ASD, they could modify their approach. We often call autism an "invisible disability" (Neely & Hunter, 2014). It becomes even more invisible when it is not even acknowledged in the first place.

These life-and-death consequences can lead to lengthy prison sentences and sometimes the death penalty. Consider this: according to The National Registry of Exonerations, individuals with an intellectual or learning disability who were accused of committing murder made up 69 percent of those exonerated. For sexual assault, the number was 12 percent. For child sexual abuse, the number was 11 percent (Johnson, Blume & Hritz, 2018).

England and Wales implemented a program where "Appropriate Adults" (AAs) safeguard the welfare of children and adults with special needs who have difficulty in the interrogation setting (Crane *et al.*, 2016) in an act passed in 1984. AAs are there to safeguard against false confessions (Bath *et al.*, 2015). They are meant to act as a check against the abuse of police powers (*ibid.*). An AA can be someone that the accused disabled defendant knows well, such as a friend, family member, caregiver, social worker, or someone else who can protect their rights.

While this is a vast improvement on anything done in the United States, it has not been a perfectly implemented program. Some adults do not receive an AA for parts of their custodial process, which risks miscarriages of justice happening to those defendants (*ibid.*). There is a lack of both adequate funding and the quantity of AAs needed for all defendants when friends and family are not available to act in that role. Furthermore, no agency has a statutory duty to provide AAs for disabled people, which poses a problem for those with no family ties and few or no friends (*ibid.*). The success of such a program depends on officers being able to identify suspects with disabilities and direct appropriate resources towards this population. Some people believe that AAs should be trained individuals who can assess the situation professionally without becoming overinvolved or antagonistic to the defendant. Bath *et al.* (2015) said that senior stakeholders interviewed for their project recommended that AAs need to be both trained professionals and on call.

Either way, how different this is from the United States criminal justice system, which provides absolutely no safeguards whatsoever against self-incrimination in individuals with developmental disabilities. While the program in England and Wales is not perfect and is not utilized as much as it should be, in theory it is a good model and one I would endorse.

Apparently, so would a man who helps the police to learn about autism for a living, Dennis Debbaudt, whose own idea of an Autism Response Team (ART) is very similar (Debbaudt & Brown, 2006). Debbaudt envisions the team being involved in every phase of the process—from arrest, to the charging and investigation phase, to the probation and sentencing phase. Implicit in this is that a responsible person or team should be in place to help the autistic person exercise their constitutional rights, especially for someone who lacks the capacity to understand them.

Autistic People as Witnesses

Autistic people also have contact with the police when they serve as witnesses to a crime. The previous section stressed the importance of autistic people preserving their rights when they encounter police so that they are not taken advantage of. But does this suggestion generalize about how reliable autistic people are as witnesses to crime? That's a complicated question and the answer deserves explanation.

Autistic people are reliable witnesses, with some caveats. Autistic people simply need more supports than neurotypicals do in these situations. McCrory, Henry and Happé (2007) reported in their study that autistic children were just as accurate in recalling events from a live classroom demonstration as their typically developing peers even though they recalled less information (about a third of the amount). The fact that episodic memory is impaired in autism isn't surprising given that much of our knowledge comes from both social and emotional contexts, and that this information is encoded in different ways in autistic and neurotypical brains. The amygdala, which is the limbic area of the brain that processes emotions, plays a crucial role in encoding affective or emotionally charged stimuli. The amygdala is altered in ASD individuals. As a result, people's faces and social situations are not processed in the same way in autistic individuals as they are in neurotypicals (Norbury *et al.*, 2009; Spezio *et al.*, 2007). The cognitive demands of processing complex auditory linguistic instructions and then integrating them with the emotionally charged event in question may prove difficult (Maras & Bowler, 2014). Certainly, memory recall will be more difficult for these individuals in a sensory-rich environment (Dawson & Watling, 2000). Therefore, it wouldn't make much sense to take written statements from autistic individuals in sensory-rich environments like police stations, courthouses, and the like. For visual learners, it would be prudent to reduce the verbal-to-visual pathway and augment questions with greater visual supports. Studies have shown that this can be successful (Maras & Bowler, 2014). When allowing for recontextualization of an event by placing the autistic individual back where the event occurred, for example, ASD individuals showed just as much recall as their matched neurotypical controls. Of course, going back to the scene of a crime could be traumatic for certain individuals, which would render this suggestion impractical in some situations. Yet the point remains that inclusion of the visual sensory modality is key. Some newer research also suggests that eyewitness identification in autistic children and neurotypical children is about the same. As a result, there is no research-based consensus on this question yet (Wilcock *et al.*, 2019). Where there does seem to be consensus is that autistic individuals can recall information as accurately as their neurotypical peers, even if they cannot give the same quantity of information (Henry *et al.*, 2017). Ideally, if an autistic witness had to testify verbally or with other accommodations at trial, these visual strategies conducted by investigators could at least help prepare them for trial testimony.

What else can we do to help autistic people be reliable witnesses? Officers need to make adaptations to their usual communication style, using specific, concrete, and literal language (Maras *et al.*, 2018). Allowing some individuals to draw sketches as opposed to having them give long, drawn-out verbal answers might help to elicit information not otherwise obtainable (*ibid.*). One study showed that sketching reinstatements were more beneficial to a group of autistic children than their neurotypical peers (Mattison, Dando & Ormerod, 2016). Having an autistic person draw a sketch—as opposed to directing a series of rapid-fire questions at them, which can be harder to process—minimizes complex verbal instructions (Goldstein, Minshew & Siegel, 1994). This makes sense given the fact that recontextualization is more difficult for autistic people when environmental cues are missing. The drawings themselves help the person decontextualize and thus trigger memories for the autistic person (Gaigg, Gardiner & Bowler, 2008).

In the United Kingdom, registered intermediaries provided by the Witness Intermediary Scheme are present during police interviews and are there to provide best practice and recommendations on how to best obtain information. While not necessarily shown to increase accuracy, they have been able to decrease autistic witnesses' anxiety (Maras *et al.*, 2018).

Autistic People as Victims of Crime

There are times when autistic people will have to interact with police when they have been the victims of crime. A report compiling data from 2009 to 2013 estimated that the risk of violent victimization towards individuals with disabilities was 36 per 1000, versus 14 per 1000 for neurotypical individuals (Fitzsimons, 2016). People with disabilities in general are at an increased risk for interpersonal violence. One reason for this is the communication barrier that hampers the reporting of the violence, which the perpetrator would likely know to be the case in advance (Hughes *et al.*, 2012; Quarmby, 2011). Mate crime (where the perpetrator is known to the victim) seems to be high among autistic people. One study found that 80 percent of autistic individuals have been victims of behaviors that may be linked to mate crime (Wirral Autistic Society, 2015). Common types of behavior associated with mate crime that autistic people experience are coercive and threatening behavior directed towards them and verbal abuse (Clayton, Donovan & MacDonald, 2016). This abuse is seen across the lifespan because disabled and autistic people may be dependent on their perpetrator for daily-life activities (Lund & Thomas, 2017). Edelson (2010) argues that some autistic individuals may not recognize dangerous situations that they are faced with due to a lack of understanding of the social cues that they are forced to encode by the situation. Hughes *et al.* (2011) reviewed 6000 PsycINFO and PubMed abstracts that were published between 2000 and 2010, along with 177 full-text articles. The prevalence of interpersonal violence for women with disabilities was 26.0–90.0 percent for lifetime, 4.9–29.1 percent for the past five years, and 2.0–70.0 percent for the past year, while the prevalence of interpersonal violence for men with disabilities was 28.7–86.7 percent for lifetime, 24.9 percent for the past five years, and 36.7 percent for the past year (*ibid.*). And finally, Brown-Lavoie *et al.* (2014) say that both male and female individuals with ASD are much more likely to be sexually victimized.

Some reasons that researchers believe developmentally disabled individuals are more likely to be sexually abused include the following.

- Lack of sex ed training

- Relationships where dependence on the other person is a key factor and gives that individual an element of power and control

- Little privacy if the disabled person requires an extra amount of personal care

- Lack of assertiveness in situations requiring it, or an eagerness to please

- Not inherently knowing their own rights when it comes to their bodies

- Undeveloped communication skills. (Contreras, Silva & Manzanero, 2015)

When a person with a communication disability (including autism) reports a crime, sometimes the problem is that the police officer believes that autistic individuals cannot possibly explain their experiences in clear and simple language, which discredits the story in the officer's mind (Bryen & Wickman, 2011). The Victorian Equal Opportunity and Human Rights Commission (2014) gives some striking and frankly infuriating examples of this. I encourage you to visit the website listed in the references section of this book to read this report for yourself. On page 42 of the report, one officer refers to a person with a cognitive disability who had his bag snatched as a "spaz bag" case. Some people felt that they would end up being hospitalized if they went to the police and reported a crime (p.35). Indeed, this correlates with other research that suggests that these attitudes can negatively influence the way that police officers see disabled crime victims when they report a crime (Bailey & Sines, 1998). Violence committed by staff against disabled residents of group homes was sometimes dismissed by police as necessary restraints (p.38). Like some cases of rape where police won't test rape kits and blame the victims (Maier, 2008), some police blame the victims of crime with disabilities (p.41). One informant in an undercover study told researchers that victims are told not to go to certain places again to avoid crimes being committed against them. A separate study showed that women with intellectual disabilities were not believed after making sexual assault allegations to the police (Keilty & Connelly, 2010).

In fact, the most disturbing element that emerges from the literature again and again is that individuals with disabilities are sometimes seen by police as not being credible (Modell & Mak, 2008). Some officers will ask themselves if the testimony of the autistic or disabled victim will hold up in court when they are deciding whether or not to move a case forward (Doak & Doak, 2017). Some police officers will not take the time to hear a victim out if they feel that a conviction in court is not possible (O'Mahony, 2009).

It is clear that the police need to be trained to deal with autistic individuals as crime victims. A survey asked 133 law enforcement agencies about the protocols they used to serve victims of crime with disabilities, such as providing basic accommodations. Most were found to lack such protocols (Oschwald et al., 2011). This correlates with findings from one study that found that 69 percent of autistic adults were unhappy with the police after their dealings with them (Crane et al., 2016). Simply put, crime victims with disabilities feel less than satisfied with the police after encounters with them (Brucker, 2015).

Ultimately, this is a human rights issue (Viljoen, 2019). The human rights model of disability acknowledges the inherent human dignity of persons with disabilities and that impairments associated with the disability may hinder certain rights. Those rights include the right to file a police report. As we have seen, having a disability increases the likelihood that one will be a victim of crime. And it also creates barriers to reporting that crime, which creates further barriers towards accessing justice. People with autism and disabilities have historically faced barriers in this regard. Ortoleva (2010) cautions that disability rights activist groups need to work hard to incorporate human rights, education, media, engagement, grassroots empowerment, mobilization, and budgetary analysis into their advocacy. Many groups do this already, such as the Autistic Self Advocacy Network (2011) and others.

The United Nations has, for about one-and-a-half decades, recognized that protecting the rights of disabled individuals is essential for the democratic societies to remain that way. And while regional treaties existed throughout the United States and Europe prior to 2006, the United Nations made it a human rights issue by addressing it at world level. With the United Nations Convention on the Rights of Persons with Disabilities (CRPD) moving away from the medical model and adopting the social model for disabilities in 2006, the United Nations made it known that disabled people's full participation in every aspect of society was of paramount importance (Stein & Lord, 2009). This historical framework states that human societies must eliminate the stereotypes of people with disabilities, promote accessibility, and protect disabled people's equal recognition before the law. This would include a disabled person as a complainant or victim of a crime. The International Criminal Court's Rule 102 also says that victims of crime with disabilities are entitled to accommodations throughout the process when needed (Ortoleva, 2010).

Article 13 of the CRPD says that parties should ensure equal access to justice for persons with disabilities, and they should be provided procedural and age-appropriate accommodations, in order for them to effectively take part in legal proceedings (United Nations, 2019). As I see it, there is one troubling provision of Article 13 of the CRPD (United Nations, 2019) as it relates to accessing justice for autistic people. It is not a small point. Article 13 says that "age-appropriate" accommodations must be made in these justice-related settings. The reason for this language (i.e., "age appropriate") is that disabled people (and many autistic people) want to see themselves as fully functional adults who can succeed in life with age-appropriate accommodations and not as "eternal children" who will never grow up.

Being viewed as having "Peter Pan" qualities is seen as extremely demeaning and ableist (Stevenson, Harp & Gernsbacher, 2011). The "eternal child" description offends some autistic people, including myself at times, if I am completely honest. Autistic characters such as Rain Man or even Lennie from *Of Mice and Men* are often characterized as childlike (Freeman-Loftis, 2016). A guest blogger on an autism advocacy website indicates very clearly that autistic people are not eternal children: "An autistic 20 year old is not a toddler in a 20 year old's body—they are an autistic 20 year old" (Think Inclusive, 2017). Leslie Scobie of the Henry Ford Health System in Detroit says that the myth of the eternal child is often a barrier to sex education (Henry Ford Health System, 2017). And advocates are very quick to point out that it was Mental Age Theory that historically divided people into extremely prejudiced classes, such as a moron versus an imbecile, or a low-grade imbecile all the way down to an idiot (Smith, 2017). Autistic people who are conscious about their need for self-determination (making their own decisions in life) do not like to be infantilized. Again, this is understandable given that much of disability history is not pretty: stripping away the rights of people; forcibly institutionalizing them; sterilization; and all the subjects I talked about at the beginning of this chapter.

It is worth reemphasizing that there are extremely successful autistic people in the world like Greta Thunberg, Temple Grandin, and Tim Page. It is not unusual for an autistic person to be a fully functional, successful, and independent adult living in the world. But as the old saying goes: "If you have met one person on the autism spectrum, you've met one person on the autism spectrum" (Stavropolous, 2019). The problem with not providing "maturity-related" accommodations to people when they may need simpler explanations, a softer touch, or the "kid gloves" treatment is that some autistic people truly feel emotionally and developmentally younger than their age. Some autistic people have a lower mental age than their typically developing peers, which is an uncomfortable fact. According to Anderson *et al.* (2016), many autistic people do not attain adult roles as they are typically defined. Adulthood is traditionally defined as the completion of an education, entering the labor force, establishing an independent household, and then marrying and having children (Shanahan, 2000). Much literature suggests that these milestones are less likely to be attained by autistic individuals after completing high school (Anderson *et al.*, 2014; Chiang *et al.*, 2012; Orsmond *et al.*, 2013; Taylor & Seltzer, 2010). Certainly, many people would argue that the goalposts for what defines adulthood have shifted and that they are now more evolved than they were some generations ago. Many people today see adulthood as being about attaining qualities of character rather than achieving developmental milestones (Arnett, 1998), and many autistic people are wonderful individuals who act morally and ethically. In that sense, they are very "adult." The point is, though, that it's not fair or "inclusive" on society's part to expect that someone to possess the same knowledge as those of the same age who have had different life experiences. One could argue that not providing accommodations related to one's maturity is in fact the very definition of discrimination if the person truly needs them. Therefore, we *do* need to make accommodations that we might make for younger individuals for an adult when the situation warrants it. It is unfortunate that Article 13 of the CRPD misses this point. If an autistic person walks into a police station to file a report, is intimidated, and has never done so before, a trained officer should immediately contact a third party with whom the autistic person is comfortable. This could be seen as infantilization by some but it is also necessary in certain circumstances. In addition to making sensory accommodations (which are not "age appropriate"), perhaps the officer could conduct the interview in a "safe space" such as the individual's bedroom if that is what the person wants. Again, this is an accommodation that acknowledges a person's younger state of being and also one that might put the autistic person at ease and elicit more accurate information. We should not confuse these accommodations for thinking that the ASD individual lacks credibility or certainty regarding what happened to them because their emotional age is delayed or younger than their chronological age. That would be the single greatest mistake that police could make. We should not "infantilize" autistic people by discrediting what they have to say when they've been the victims of crime; we should instead give them what they need (regardless of what it is) to break down the barriers to accessing justice. This was the United Nations' intended goal.

I will return to this theme of the tension between self-determination and accommodations throughout this book, particularly as it pertains to adjudication.

Conclusion

Here are some suggestions as I close out this chapter.

We need to end qualified immunity when officers are alerted to the presence of a disability in advance. With training being mandatory under Title II of the ADA, and the Department of Justice acknowledging that Title II applies to arrests, there is simply no reason to use force when de-escalation has not been attempted. This should no longer be a defense that officers, police departments, and cities can rely upon in these situations. Some legal scholars even believe that qualified immunity should be abolished in its totality (Baude, 2018; Schwartz, 2017).

We need to use budgetary discretion wisely to make disability and autism training mandatory at the federal level and withhold funding for states, cities, counties, and municipalities that don't meet these requirements. Furthermore, we must involve autistic people at every level of the training.

We need to provide layers of protection so that anyone with a cognitive and developmental disability has the right to an "Appropriate Adult" when the police attempt to question a person for a suspected crime. Miranda Rights warnings are not enough.

We need to ensure that a human rights perspective and the intent of the United Nations CRPD is upheld when autistic people come forward to report crimes.

We need to do away with internal investigations and let oversight of officer misconduct be investigated by an independent office.

We need to bring crisis intervention teams with trained social workers and mental health professionals to intervene on behalf of ASD individuals in situations that need de-escalation, and not just trained officers.

CHAPTER 3

Autism and the Adjudication Process

Once an individual on the autism spectrum has landed in the criminal justice system, a tragedy has begun to unfold, one that in all likelihood is irreparable. Once the genie has been taken out of the bottle, it cannot be placed back in. As an advocate, I have been involved in helping parents, autistic individuals, and those with cognitive disabilities. None of these stories have happy endings. Unless there is an acquittal or the prosecutor drops the charges, the best that can be done is to try to make a terrible situation slightly less terrible. In this chapter, I will first look at the practicalities of what families face in this situation and what they may be able to do to achieve a slightly better outcome (I say "slightly better" because no outcome in the criminal justice system is good). In the end, I will advocate for an alternative to how we currently handle the adjudication of autistic people in the criminal justice system. This alternative takes into account public safety but also catches up with the 21st century.

I am writing this chapter from the perspective of having received countless emails from parents after they have learnt that a justice-involved situation with their child is inevitable. They tell horrendous, unimaginable tales. Many describe their autistic loved one languishing in jail because the caregivers cannot afford bail. Some ask feverishly what lawyer they should use. Many are below the poverty line and rightly worry that they may not get preferential treatment if they cannot put down a $5000 retainer. Most simply do not know what to do or where to start. Many of these families know nothing about the criminal justice system. The arrest and subsequent charging of their son or daughter is the first taste that they get of what the system is like—outside of courtroom shows that they may have watched on television.

The Selection of an Attorney

In every case, ideally an ASD individual would have the means to hire a lawyer with complete expertise in the subject. In a perfect world, public defenders would get the training necessary to understand not only mental illness in its entirety but also autism spectrum disorders. But since we are living in a world that is far from perfect, I am going to offer some suggestions that I believe are extremely important regarding the selection of an attorney when an ASD defendant has been criminally charged.

It would be very unfortunate if a person on the autism spectrum did not have supportive family members who could, along with the defendant, communicate facts of importance to their trial counsel at the very beginning. Any attorney familiar with autism who is representing a client needs to know this. Deficits in the reading of nonverbal cues (Bird, Press & Richardson, 2011), difficulties with both expressive and receptive language (Kwok *et al.*, 2015), emotional regulation difficulties, or potential outbursts (Mazefsky *et al.*, 2013) put the ASD defendant at an inherent disadvantage as far as communicating effectively with their attorney, especially if the lawyer is not familiar with autism or does not know that the client is on the autism spectrum. Perhaps the lawyer will just ascribe the behavior of the client to being "difficult," which would, again, be most unfortunate.

Imagine the following scenario: an undiagnosed ASD defendant meets his trial counsel for the first time. The lawyer walks into the room, introduces himself, and sits down at the table across from his client. The handshake is strange or awkward (ASD individuals can present with abnormal handshakes) (Golubchik *et al.*, 2012), and the defendant looks down at the table, makes no eye contact, and has a flat affect in saying "Hi" or "Hello." The lawyer is startled by the awkward handshake but decides to brush it off and proceed. He then explains to his client: who he is, why he is there, and the charges that the state or government is bringing against him. While he is talking, however, the defendant continues to look down.

"Hello, excuse me. I am talking to you. This involves you, you know? The case is about you, not me. I am not here for my own benefit, I am here to help you, so please look at me," the lawyer implores of his client. But the client still looks unengaged and keeps staring down.

"Don't you know how much time you are looking at here? Hey, I am trying to help you," the lawyer continues. The autistic person replies: "How much time are we looking at? When will this meeting be over?" The client doesn't say this sarcastically. He misunderstands the word "time" in its proper context and inappropriately misapplies it when asking this question to his attorney.

How would a lawyer who is completely unfamiliar with autism handle this scenario? Many would undoubtedly be frustrated and promptly order a forensic psychological examination. My hope would be that this exchange might also "flip a switch" in the mind of the lawyer and make him question whether such a diagnosis might be present in his client. In the interim, I would also hope that this lawyer would realize that communication deficits such as these require the marshaling of family members to help to fill in the blanks on an as-needed basis.

According to Steve Gordo (Gordo & Kelley, 2019), picking a defense attorney for his autistic son was the most important decision of his life. His son, Paul, who was considered "high functioning autistic," was involved in an incident at a library that changed the course of both of their lives. One day, Steve and Paul went to the library; Steve remained present while his son received tutoring instruction. After about 50 minutes, Paul became restless and agitated. As Steve and the instructor were debating whether to continue with the lesson, Paul went to the restroom. Upon returning to the library, Paul was even more agitated than before and made a dash to exit the building. As he ran past the counter, he pushed himself into two men. Luckily, they were not hurt. But as he was going through the exit doors, he accidently pushed an older woman with Huntington's disease. She fell and was immediately knocked unconscious; she later suffered a mild concussion. Paul stopped, turned around, and apologized, but of course, it was too late. Her husband lunged at Paul in anger, called him an "animal," and said he should go to jail. When the police came and questioned Paul, they asked him if he knew what he did was wrong. He said, "Yes." (Is it clear that he actually knew it was "wrong" in the heat of the moment?) He was committed temporarily under a 5150 and released the next day. However, several months later, the family got a notice through the postal service, which Steve Gordo had been dreading. It was a "notice to appear," which stated that charges were being filed against Paul for assault and battery and that he needed to turn himself in to go through the booking process. At this point, Steve knew that he "needed a hero," as he put it. But he didn't know how he would get one. How does one go about choosing a lawyer? He didn't know. He never thought he was going to be placed in this situation. Most parents of children on the autism spectrum don't.

The first lawyer Steve hired was an out-of-town attorney, which he recognizes now is usually a mistake. "The locals have the inside track," Steve said. The out-of-town attorney had very little influence on plea negotiations with the county district attorney, even though strong mitigating factors were presented. So, with little hope in the ability of his out-of-town attorney to ensure that reason prevailed, Steve stormed onto social media and began an aggressive campaign. He canvassed Facebook, Twitter, and change.org, messaged well-known local politicians and media outlets, and "friended" every big-name person possible. None of these efforts made any difference. (It has been my personal experience of observing cases over the years that prosecutors are used to these kinds of campaigns and are not intimidated, influenced, or moved by them.) Prior to the preliminary examination, the assistant district attorney offered to reduce the felony to a non-strike felony (some states have a "three strikes and you're out" policy, meaning that after three felonies a person is indefinitely detained). This is known in other states as "habitual offender laws." Paul, Steve, and his attorney refused the offer and the prosecutor then added a misdemeanor assault charge relating to the man who Paul accidently pushed at the library, who was not hurt. This is when Steve began to fully understand the importance of having a defense attorney who could guide him through this Kafkaesque maze where nothing made sense to him or his family. So, that evening, he hired a local defense attorney who was an insider on the local workings of the prosecutor's office and judiciary in his county. After protracted negotiations between the parties, they were able to get the charges dropped down to a misdemeanor.

Paul was lucky. Cubby Robison was lucky. I was lucky. We all had families who could collaborate with our attorneys during our respective perilous times. In this case, Steve was there for Paul. If it wasn't for Steve's efforts in finally selecting the right attorney and the collaboration between them all, Paul's adjudication most likely would have ended in a much worse situation. In fact, we know many autistic individuals who are not as fortunate as Paul. It was reported in Minnesota that 170,000 cases were allocated to 400 public defenders. One public defender there said he was only able to spend about 12 minutes on each client's case (Mador, 2010). Another public defender in Louisiana, as reported in *The New York Times* (Oppel Jr. & Patel, 2019), had a total of 194 felony cases at the same time. Many high-level felonies carry a penalty of over ten years in jail. It is recommended that each of those cases gets 70 hours of attention. This kind of superhuman effort is simply impossible for any lawyer who has to oversee almost 200 cases. The public defender from Louisiana also noted that what is truly required of him would amount to two years of work. In sum, this lawyer needed to do the work of five full-time attorneys to properly serve all his clients. Schoneman (2018) writes that only 21 percent of state-based public defenders have enough staff to manage their caseloads. In Florida, the average annual felony caseload per year for public defenders is 500. In Missouri, they can handle up to 150 felony cases at once. Kentucky is no better: in 2016, the average public defender worked on 460 cases (*ibid.*).

I am not putting down public defenders. They are the heroes who help to fulfill the Sixth Amendment's promise that all defendants shall be able to enjoy the right to assistance of counsel. I know many public defenders personally and they are champions for their clients, when they can be. They are not to blame. The system is to blame. Many public defenders are simply overworked and frustrated by this limitation because it hinders them doing their job. It is, therefore, possible to get a public defender who does an extraordinary job and spends a lot of time on one's case. And privately retained lawyers can be lousy too, if their heart and soul is not truly in it. There is no guarantee whatsoever that privately retained counsel will perform better than a public defender.

I offer the following advice based on nine years of experience of watching people go through the same process as me and observing what works and what doesn't. It is easy to do a Google search for "autism," "sex crimes," "defense lawyer," "burglary," "arson," etc. and be directed to a bunch of websites of lawyers who advertise under those specific keywords. These websites will entice you into thinking that these lawyers are experts in these areas and that they have achieved wonderful results for their clients. While some may have had variable amounts of experience, many are far from being true experts in autism spectrum disorders. Despite their self-pronouncement, the advertisements are deceptive. Furthermore, no serious lawyer will ever make promises to a client about specific outcomes because there are always too many unknown variables in a criminal case. Avoid finding attorneys this way.

If searching for a reputable lawyer on the internet doesn't work, where should you look? Start by contacting organizations such as The Arc, the Autism Society of America, or a reputable autism agency near you. If you do not know of any attorneys in your geographic radius, you can always ask key people, who most likely will know. If an autism-focused organization endorses a specific lawyer, it means they have a proven track record in representing ASD individuals beyond what they say about themselves on their sponsored websites.

Second, take Steve Gordo's advice: hire a local attorney who knows the ins and outs of your county, state, or federal court and the prosecutors in that particular office. This is important when it comes to plea negotiations and achieving a better outcome than one would get with a person without these local connections.

Third, meet the attorney and see if you are comfortable with their communication style and presence. Ask how many assistants they have working for them. Do they return phone calls in a reasonably timely manner? If someone is interviewing the defense lawyer because of an alleged sex crime, for example, ask if the attorney has handled a reasonable number of sex crime cases in the past. Can they highlight to you any successful case results in their experience defending ASD clients or more broadly, clients with mental illness? Have they ever been able to get charges dismissed, reduced or obtain diversion agreements for their ASD clients? Are they receptive to a different communication style when interacting with the autistic client? Do they promise to work extremely closely with family members as a condition of employment (assuming that the autistic client gives consent for this)? And are they willing to admit that they probably need to learn more about autism, regardless of how many cases they have handled in the past? These are good questions to ask before approaching the topic of a retaining or fee agreement.

This is one of the most important decisions that parents, guardians, spouses, or family members will ever help to make with the ASD individual. The stakes are extremely high. Making the correct choice is crucial.

Competency

If a client is unable to help or assist their attorney in their own defense, the lawyer can try to show that the client is not competent to stand trial (Kois *et al.*, 2017). Lack of competency is an extremely difficult standard to meet. The defendant must be able to understand the nature of the charges against them and the potential consequences they face (U.S. Department of Justice, 2015a) and assist their attorney. This brings up some interesting questions. What if an autistic defendant works against their own best interests and insists they are not autistic? Such was the case with Theodore Kaczynski, also known as the Unabomber. To our knowledge, he was not autistic. Although he was diagnosed as paranoid schizophrenic by a psychiatrist, he did not want this used during his trial and also during death penalty mitigation (Litwack, 2003). Dylann Roof also refused to identify as autistic and did not want this information introduced by his attorney during the death penalty phase of his trial (Allely & Faccini, 2019).

This issue gets enormously complicated because a defendant can potentially be competent in one legal setting but not in another over the long term. For example, if the defendant has to be present for a short procedural hearing and is not required to give much or any input to or collaboration with his lawyer in this setting, perhaps he would be competent—but only in that setting and context. He may not be competent, however, over the course of a long trial, particularly if he has not been bonded out of jail (Reisner, Piel & Makey, 2013). Much more is required of him to defend himself as time progresses. As we saw in the previous chapter, autistic adults struggle with episodic memory under the best of circumstances (Millward *et al.*, 2000). Episodic memory is related to a conscious recollection of experience and events (Shalom, 2003). Furthermore, problems with executive functioning (which encapsulates episodic memory) and the skills of planning, flexibility, and organization are exacerbated with stress and anxiety for ASD individuals (Wallace *et al.*, 2016). Further research corroborates that anxiety and depression weaken executive functioning (Han *et al.*, 2016), which is already an inherent difficulty for most ASD individuals. Anxiety and depression will affect ASD defendants who are in jail awaiting trial or even those who are bonded out and waiting to learn their fate over an extended period of time. Even if an ASD individual has episodic memory recall under the best of circumstances, it usually takes much longer for them to remember certain facts (Crane & Maras, 2018). This can be problematic when time is of the essence and lawyers need information expeditiously. Outside of the discovery evidence that prosecutors are required to turn over to the defense attorney, the best source of information a lawyer has at their disposal to defend their client is the information their client gives them. We have to ask ourselves if an autistic defendant is in the best position to factually relay information to their attorney based on the circumstances of their own case. The obvious response is that most of the time the answer is: probably not. But this extreme impairment does not matter in the eyes of the law. To establish competency or a lack of it, in the eyes of the law, either the individual can fully collaborate with their attorney or they can't at all. There is no middle ground. It is an obvious shortcoming of the current criminal justice system, which coerces people into either standing trial or pleading guilty. As Reisner *et al.* (2013) note, competency is usually considered for those whose thought disorders are so severe that they cannot, to any degree, assist their attorneys in a rational defense. But Reisner *et al.* also argue that lack of competency should extend to those defendants who lack insight into their mental illness or, in this case, developmental disability. Additionally, they argue that this requirement be expanded to any defendant beyond those who simply fail to consider an insanity defense to those who will not allow their attorneys to introduce a mental illness or developmental disability into the record.

I agree with Reisner *et al.* and will give a hypothetical scenario to show why. Suppose a man downloads child pornography and is subsequently arrested. He sits down with his attorney to strategize the best way to present a viable defense or mitigating factors in his case. During the course of the conversation, the attorney suspects that his client might be on the autism spectrum based on facial mannerisms and bodily gestures. Additionally, in subsequent interviews, his parents tell the attorney that they always thought their son had autism but never got him tested. The attorney then suggests a forensic evaluation to his client and the client vehemently objects. The client does not want to be identified as autistic and sees that as an insult. The lawyer tries to explain rationally that a forensic exam would be in his best interests and that he is only requesting this in order to minimize jail time or get a probationary sentence. It all falls on deaf ears. The client insists that he does not want a forensic exam and does not want autism used as an excuse, and that if his lawyer tries to do any of that, he will fire him. What should happen here? What is the client's goal? Does he have any goal at all? Is it just a matter of pride or is his ASD itself, and lack of central coherence (of not seeing the big picture), preventing him from giving his lawyer what might be needed to attain the best possible result at sentencing? Should we just allow clients, who may not be in a complete psychotic state or classified as insane, to take the wheel when their strategy (if there even is a strategy to begin with) goes against their own best interests? These are questions that courts have considered time and again. Usually, in the end, they leave it to the defendants to fend for themselves.

To illustrate this further, let us examine a study on the subject and how overconfidence can play a role. One study examined the question of fitness to plead or stand trial in the United Kingdom with individuals on the autism spectrum. The study (Brewer, Davies & Blackwood, 2016) found that ASD individuals have a poorer understanding of the courtroom process than their neurotypical counterparts. The researchers excluded from the study individuals with an intellectual impairment or a mental illness. The ASD individuals were defendants awaiting trial, while the control group was found by advertising in an East London newspaper. The ASD group and the control group did not differ as far as their overall profiles on the WAIS-IV (Wechsler Adult Intelligence Scale, Fourth Edition) and the WMS-III (Wechsler Memory Scale, Third Edition) but did differ on measures related to processing speed. This meant that the neurotypical group had superior recall. Participants in this study were asked to watch a "fitness to plead" video based on realistic trial material that was scripted by actors and filmed in an actual courtroom. The video showed a victim being given direct and cross-examination by the two sets of attorneys. The vignette was stopped throughout the video at several different points and the viewer participants were asked a series of standardized questions related to comprehension of pleading guilty versus not guilty, the roles in a courtroom, and the overall judicial process. The questions were subdivided across several categories:

- FTP (fitness to plead) knowledge—understanding knowledge regarding entering a plea

- FTP evidence—understanding the evidence and case (meaning whether the defendant can understand the evidence being used against them)

- FTP instruct, which is whether the defendant can properly instruct their lawyer as part of their defense

- FTP roles, which measures a defendant's knowledge of the roles that courtroom personnel play throughout the process.

Questions to rule out malingering were also incorporated. Results indicated that the control group scored significantly higher on three of the four subscales: FTP evidence; FTP knowledge; FTP roles. The authors of this study say these results suggest that adults with ASD had more difficulty in understanding aspects of the trial process and proceedings in spite of having past involvement in the criminal justice system. They attribute some of the scores to slower information processing skills by the ASD group, though the authors remain inconclusive about whether these cognitive differences played a role in the score discrepancies between the two groups. They correlated lower theory of mind as found by the Reading the Mind in the Eyes Test (which was also administered to both the ASD and control groups) with the FTP evidence and FTP roles subscales. The authors believe this might suggest that lower theory of mind plays a role in one's fitness to plead but that more research is needed. Even though the ASD individuals considered themselves familiar with courtroom procedure (more familiar, in fact, than the control group), the opposite was actually true. The authors see this overconfidence as potentially masking deficits in understanding that fact can slip past legal professionals. In other words, the ASD group's confidence may not be a reflection of their actual skills to assist in a defense.

There are some important implications in this study that I will be returning to later in this chapter, but I want to plant a seed where the ground is fertile: the criminal justice system judges people in a black-and-white way. Is a person intelligent, or isn't he? Can he drive a car, or can't he? Is he competent, or isn't he? Is he criminally responsible, or isn't he? I am going to suggest that the issues are not always this clear-cut for the ASD population, which was clearly shown to be true in this study. Both groups of individuals had the same intelligence and yet the ASD individuals struggled more with comprehending what was happening in the courtroom, even though they projected more confidence than the neurotypical group. In mounting a defense or mitigating factors, this unevenness in one's developmental profile or level of understanding is a consideration I will investigate later in the chapter.

Sometimes, lack of competence can lead to a dropping of the charges. A federal prosecutor agreed to drop charges against an ASD man from Miami, Florida, who had an IQ of 73 and had been charged with downloading and disseminating child pornography, after he was found not competent to stand trial by a court-appointed examiner (Weaver, 2016). The facts of the case remain somewhat unclear to the lay public. According to Weaver's article, the man's own defense attorney felt frustration that no federal pretrial diversion program was put into place and suggested that his client get recharged at the state level so one could be established for him. Absent a formal requirement for mental health treatment, all parties expressed dismay that this man was not going to get the psychological and mental health support he so badly needed.

Defense attorney Mark Mahoney (2019) says that findings of competence or lack thereof have been a factor for him in a number of "successful" cases he has overseen and that the subject needs considerably more attention with regards to autistic people. Mahoney takes a checklist proposed by Murrie and Zelle (2015) to access competence in a legal setting and argues that this is relevant to the ASD individual. The areas are:

1. understanding relevant information

2. appreciating the situation and its consequences

3. reasoning

4. assisting the defense

5. decision making.

So, let us begin with understanding relevant information. Mahoney (2019) argues that while many ASD individuals attain a rote sort of ability to correctly answer questions about the proceedings, what can still be missing is a holistic view of what is happening to them. For example, I know from the literature that individuals on the spectrum often present with deficits in perceptual integration processes, which weaken the ability to perceive the gestalt (Plaisted, 2001). Plaisted (2001) attributes perceptual abnormalities (or what would normally be called "lack of central coherence") to reduced generalization. It's been found that autistic people tend to process the unique elements of stimuli fairly well (e.g., strong visual acuity) but have difficulty when it comes to tasks involving discrimination. One example that has been used to illustrate this is Roger Penrose's impossible triangle (Penrose & Penrose, 1958), which is the optical illusion of a triangle that couldn't exist as a solid object. Numerous studies have shown that autistic people have difficulty with distinguishing the possible triangles from the impossible triangles (Booth & Happé, 2018). In other words, for autistic people, they were all triangles. The idea of the triangle did not generalize well, and there was no perceptual discrimination among them. Though I note that many visual learners, such as Temple Grandin, excel at tasks involving visual acuity, which could be due to the right hemisphere of the brain's unique ability to overcompensate for the weaker areas of the brain that are necessary to perform executive functioning (McGowan, 2013). And, in fact, visual discrimination is a strength for most individuals on the autism spectrum (Baron-Cohen *et al.*, 2009). However, the lack of an ability to generalize in novel situations is still a weakness for most individuals on the spectrum (Church *et al.*, 2015) in spite of splinter skills, which may strengthen visual discrimination. Church *et al.* (2015) attribute deficits in generalization at large to reduced levels of brain plasticity in autistic people. Individuals with ASD sometimes see issues in "black and white" terms with zero shades of gray, and this can be understood as a corollary to difficulties with generalization they experience.

A more simplistic example of lacking an ability to generalize would be the following. Suppose an ASD child learns that he is supposed to shake hands with everyone he meets and applies this new command to every situation in his life. He tries to shake hands with the child in the next bathroom stall, or the teller at a bank, or a Transportation Security Administration (TSA) agent. This child has not generalized the lesson of shaking hands well. This is one of the reasons why autism is generally considered to involve social communication. It's because, contextually, autistic people miss out on the "gist" of what is happening. The reasons for this are too numerous to contemplate. One reason I mentioned is the differences in the neuroplasticity of the brain of some individuals on the spectrum (Church *et al.*, 2015). Some of it might be due to high cortisol levels in autistic individuals (Corbett *et al.*, 2010), which tends to keep a person in a fight-or-flight mode, and their anxiety can cause them to not take in the gestalt. Part of this can be attributed to biological psychiatry and brain functioning, where there is a reduced pattern of information processing concerning long-distance communication between different regions and areas of the brain, leading to less "holistic control" of one's global information processing ability (van Elst, Riedel & Maier, 2016).

Each phase of the legal process is a piece of a larger whole. If an ASD individual gets fixated on one aspect of the legal proceedings without considering the totality of the circumstances, the whole gestalt, and the end game, it can affect that person's judgment in making crucial decisions. The literature shows that global processing is an issue for individuals with ASD. Mahoney's (2019) contention, based on experience in hundreds of cases, is that his ASD clients lack an adequate comprehensive understanding in processing all of the information in a case in a pragmatic way.

I now come to number two on this list, which is appreciating the situation and its consequences. Mahoney argues that it should not be enough that the autistic person knows they are in trouble with the law and needs help. Rather, they need to appreciate the dynamic understanding of the proceedings and how information applied at one stage of the legal process applies to the next. As I've said, in Mahoney's experience in representing autistic individuals, most of them lacked a full appreciation of their predicament and consequently could not be considered as being in the best position to make crucial decisions. This is fully consistent with what has been seen in an ASD individual's potential lack of understanding.

Mahoney believes that concern number three, reasoning, is the area of greatest importance. Here, Mahoney says that problems with fluid and abstract thinking, combined with a reliance on caregivers, make this a concern. In other words, if an individual with ASD lacks the fluid reasoning necessary to live on their own and make daily decisions about their lives, how can they be expected to make crucial decisions about defending themselves in a criminal case? Let us now flesh out whether fluid reasoning is indeed problematic for ASD individuals.

Mahoney is partially correct. A certain kind of fluid reasoning does exist for ASD individuals who may actually be above average on certain tasks, but it has to be parsed out to make sense to a court. What is lacking here is *social reasoning*, which is even more detrimental. As for fluid reasoning, studies actually show that for some ASD individuals strong visual acuity and enhanced reliance on visuospatial processes in parietal regions of the brain when engaging in fluid tasks (Mottron *et al.*, 2013) is above average. Visual processes involve the occipital and temporal regions of the brain in conjunction with the superior frontal gyrus, superior parietal lobe, inferior temporal gyrus, and middle and inferior occipital gyrus (Simard *et al.*, 2015) and are superior in some autistic people. This is why an autistic individual like Stephen Wiltshire can fly over the city of Singapore in a helicopter and draw it perfectly from memory (Serena, 2019). However—and this is what is important—although tasks involving visual cues create increased occipito-temporal activity in these individuals, there is a decrease in activity in the prefrontal cortex region of the brain for the same tasks (Pua *et al.*, 2017; Watanabe *et al.*, 2012).

Social reasoning, upon which client decisions in court cases are based, involves the prefrontal cortex region of the brain. The prefrontal cortex involves tasks dealing with higher-order social, communication, and emotional processing (along with the amygdala) and cognitive development (Courchesne *et al.*, 2011). Deficits in the medial prefrontal cortex, which helps to identify what emotions we are feeling at a given time, are disrupted in ASD individuals (alexithymia) (Shalom, 2009). Additionally, the adversarial process that the legal system presents to a client requires each defendant to have reasonable ideas about other people's mental states. More specifically, a defendant would need to know about someone's beliefs, desires, intentions, and so on. The autistic defendant may need to have a sense of the victim's mindset regarding whether to proceed to trial or not. The defendant may also need to be aware of the beliefs and desires about the parents of the victim and have a knowledge of the impact of their crime, and not just use superficial parroting back to their attorney. They need a "mind-reading network," as Khalil *et al.* (2018) call it. This mind-reading network model (*ibid.*) involves social decision making, social cognition, reasoning, and cognitive perspective taking. Khalil *et al.* say that the mind-reading network, which most of us take for granted, is disrupted by abnormalities in the prefrontal cortex, anterior cingulate cortex, and temporoparietal junction.

This has practical consequences. For example, one study examined choice behavior during the Iowa Gambling Task (IGT) in autistic adults who were compared with healthy controls to see if participants could make sound decisions based upon feedback in the form of monetary gains and losses. The autistic group was more focused on the losses and negative reinforcement than the wins (Johnson *et al.*, 2006). Furthermore, other studies have shown that the autistic individuals switched their choices regardless of whether the feedback was positive or negative (Chevallier *et al.*, 2012; Shafritz *et al.*, 2015).

So, Mahoney is correct to the extent that it is reasoning that is disrupted, but it is social reasoning and not necessarily "fluid reasoning," as it is usually defined.

Which brings us to the fourth concern of Mahoney's, which is assisting defense attorneys. Here, Mahoney's concern rests with the fact that a client may not be able to testify as a witness on their own behalf in a case where it might be otherwise advantageous to do so. Mahoney puts forward the problems that autistic people have with working memory, the inability to understand the intention of the questioner, an inability to sense how the jury might respond to their answers and demeanor, and an inability to avoid deliberate traps set by a prosecutor on the witness stand.

Last, I address the fifth item pointed out by Mahoney, and that is decision making, which I have touched on already. During the course of a case, many decisions have to be made by a client. These include: whether to accept a plea agreement or proceed to trial; which plea to enter (there may be multiple charges that carry different mandatory minimums or lack thereof); and which witnesses to call at trial.

Difficulties with decision making for autistic people are pretty easy to spot in a quick glance of the literature. Temple Grandin (2000, p.17) says that her mind can become "locked up and overloaded with pictures coming all at once," and that making decisions on the spot is very difficult for individuals with autism. Other self-reported data from ASD individuals suggests that autistic individuals tend to freeze, experience tremendous anxiety, exhaustion, slowness in reaching a decision, and a tendency to collect too much information, and have impaired flexibility and difficulty making decisions based on previous choices (Luke, 2011; Luke *et al.*, 2012). Robic *et al.* (2015) add to this by saying that decision making in autism is accompanied by marked reliance on formal rules of behavior and social conventions, but a fair question that needs to be asked is: what if they don't understand the rules of the judicial process in the first place?

Robic *et al.* (2015) conducted a study with a group of autistics without an intellectual disability and a control group of neurotypicals, where changing variables and inducing an "unstable environment" were tested to evaluate effective choices under these conditions. The autistic group was greatly affected by the unstable environment and performed much more poorly than the neurotypical group. This suggests two things. First, anxiety can truly make it hard for ASD individuals to make sound decisions under pressure. Second, the legal system is dynamic, pressure filled, and always changing, where one set of rules in one situation do not always apply to other situations. One is also facing an uphill climb from the very beginning in that the legal system is adversarial and the goal of the prosecutor is to convict a defendant and get a substantial amount of prison time.

Mahoney's reframing of competence (2019) is revolutionary because it expands the definition from rote understanding to a more holistic framework. Many ASD individuals may show rote understanding of the process and can parrot certain phrases back but still do not intrinsically grasp what is really happening. Mahoney is therefore stating the following: autistic people have a difficult time navigating life. Individuals on the spectrum struggle tremendously with remaining employed (Ballaban-Gil *et al.*, 1996; Cimera, Burgess & Bedesem, 2014; Howlin *et al.*, 2004; Roux, Rast & Shattuck, 2018; Taylor & Seltzer, 2011), even in light of advanced degree obtainment (Baldwin, Costley & Warren, 2014). Some cite an unemployment number of around 85 percent for autistic people (Lyn Pesce, 2019). It is not uncommon for parents to set up special-needs trusts for their ASD children (McCoy, 2014). So, in essence, Mahoney's question is as follows: if autistic adults have issues making daily and long-term decisions that affect their lives, how can we possibly expect them to make decisions in a criminal matter where the stakes are much higher? Life-and-death decisions are potentially at play in a criminal courtroom.

In the cases where Mahoney (2019) has apparently been successful in the court and found his clients incompetent to stand trial, the charges were eventually dropped or a pretrial diversion program was put into place. But this is not usually how incompetency works. Restoration to competence is much more common than outright dismissal or diversion. Most of the time, being incompetent to stand trial is not a get-out-of-jail-free card. Usually, there is a long period of administering psychotropic medication to the defendant within a hospital setting to eliminate or decrease any delusions that may be present, while simultaneously giving a series of psychiatric exams to ascertain whether the defendant understands the charges against them and can also assist in their defense (Heilbrun & King, 2017). Restoration to competence is not indefinite. Eventually, either the defendant is civilly committed to an institution forever, or the charges are dropped if restoration is not possible, as was true for some of Mahoney's cases. Restoration to competence is the eventual goal, however, by and large.

Skepticism

Many parents of ASD children are shocked at the notion that those involved in making decisions regarding adjudication are generally skeptical of any mitigating circumstances. Many of these parents simply expect to have their lawyer sit down with the prosecutor and have a long and frank discussion, and everything will eventually work itself out for the best. Unfortunately, it doesn't usually work out that way. Parents of ASD children are truly bewildered to learn that they are entering a system where foundations run deep and are influenced by the Code of Hammurabi and the Mosaic Law of seeking an eye for an eye. The notion that this system would view their fairly immature, sheltered, and law-abiding autistic child in the same way that biblical justice viewed lawbreakers in the days of the Old Testament makes them feel like they are tumbling down a rabbit hole where nothing seems real anymore. It was never that way for these same parents when they sat down to make an Individualized Education Plan (IEP) with their educational team. It wasn't that way when they were helping their children to navigate the ins and outs of college or getting a professor to make an accommodation consistent with the ADA. The criminal justice system is different from anything else with which these parents have had contact. Throughout our history, retribution runs deep, and nuance is usually left out of the equation. An illustrative historical example of this in action is that of the executioner Franz Schmidt of the 1500s, who lived in what is now Germany and conducted executions in Nuremberg. He felt no sympathy for those with mental disabilities whom he was about to execute and whom he felt were trying to "game the system" (Harrington, 2013).

Part of the reason such skepticism exists today is that mental illness is quite prevalent in those who pass through the criminal justice system. It is very difficult to make one's case stand out as unique to prosecutors and judges when so many other cases look similar to yours. Those defendants who had mental illness were not treated particularly leniently. Jails and prisons have become the de facto place where individuals with mental illnesses go (Cuddeback, 2019). Numbers vary depending on the sources, but it is a problem of epidemic proportions. One study in Iowa showed that 48 percent of all inmates in the state had a mental illness, while 29 percent had a serious mental illness (Al-Rousan *et al.*, 2017). The Department of Justice's own statistics showed that those with a mental illness or an "emotional condition" were 3–12 times more likely than community prison samples to be in prison, reaching as high as 64 percent (Prins, 2014). In 2017, the Bureau of Justice released statistics which found that 14 percent of prisoners and 25 percent of those in jail had a mental health episode within 30 days, compared with 5 percent of the general population. Meanwhile, 37 percent of prisoners and 44 percent of jailed individuals had a history of mental health struggles (Bronson & Berzofsky, 2017). Furthermore, 50 percent of defendants with mental illness were rearrested after serving their sentences, making prosecutors that much more reluctant to take a chance on someone (Judd & Parker, 2018).

Some "progressive prosecutors" have recently shown an openness to new, innovative, and more compassionate approaches towards adjudicating the mentally ill, like the former public defender Larry Krasner, now the District Attorney in Philadelphia (UCLA Law, 2018). The current St. Louis District Attorney, Wesley Bell, is another example of an individual pushing for such reforms (Medina, 2019). Unfortunately, these people are few and far between. Even more unfortunate is that few "progressive prosecutors" are not particularly progressive when it comes to how they negotiate plea deals for sex crimes (Hoechstetter, 2020), which has been this book's focus because of its impact on autistic individuals. I believe it is important that society deals with the issue of better mental health care in the community. This will help everyone to avoid slipping through the cracks and falling into a system that does not address their underlying needs. In fact, the current system can make mental health much worse for individuals. However, this book is about autism, not mental health. While autism often presents with mental health comorbidities (Lai *et al.*, 2019), autism is my primary focus. With so many individuals in the criminal justice system who are presenting legal experts with complicated situations and potentially mitigating factors because of their mental health, the challenge becomes how to appeal to a prosecutor's use of discretion by explaining why autism is different from a case involving a neurotypical individual or someone with a mental illness. I will return to this theme shortly.

Prosecutors have a very difficult role and this accounts in large part for their overall skepticism. They play a paradoxical role in the criminal justice system. To explain this, let us begin with a quote from an early 20th-century Supreme Court case.

In the case of Berger v. United States (1935), Justice Sutherland remarks:

The [prosecutor] is the representative not of an ordinary party to a controversy, but of a sovereignty whose obligation to govern impartially is as compelling as its obligation to govern at all; and whose interest, therefore, in a criminal prosecution is not that it shall win a case, but that justice shall be done.

In other words, prosecutors are tasked with seeking justice in any given case and not necessarily getting convictions (Kugler, 2016). Theoretically, they are under no obligation to even charge someone with a crime unless they feel moved to do so. We as a society trust that they will perform this function honorably because of the almost limitless power it gives them. And many prosecutors do perform in an honorable fashion. But the issue is not quite as simple as it seems. The obligations that prosecutors have towards defendants are actually quite minimal, and sanctions that would keep them in check should misconduct arise hardly exist. Prosecutors are not allowed to charge a defendant with unsupported evidence. They *are* expected to make timely disclosures of exculpatory evidence (and all discovery material in general) and they are expected to allow the accused to exercise their procedural rights. They are supposed to be known as "ministers of justice" (Gershman, 2011) but are also expected to be fierce advocates at the same time. Yet, these ethical codes are often confusing and conflicting. On the one hand, prosecutors are supposed to be ministers of justice, but on the other hand, they are, in fact, zealous advocates for their client—the people and society at large (as are defense attorneys for their own clients). The political nature of a prosecutor's office means that success will be measured by rates of conviction, with the goal of currying public favor towards reelection. Or perhaps certain prosecutors have higher aspirations, such as running for political office if they can demonstrate that they care enough about public safety. Even low-level prosecutors who want to move up the ranks within their own office need to show that they can amass convictions at a high rate. Dennis (2007) calls this schism between their roles of "ministers of justice" and "zealous advocates for the people" a "schizophrenic muck and must bend them into psychological pretzels to fulfill the duties of their office" (pp.138–139). As Dennis notes, many commentators believe that it is simply impossible to reconcile these conflicting ethical roles. Are there any checks in place to prevent these dichotomous roles from creating unethical behavior? Not realistically. Prosecutors have absolute civil immunity. In a nutshell, this means that no matter how egregious their misconduct happens to be, they cannot be sued or held liable (Niles, 2017). It is the state and the taxpayer who pay for a wrongful conviction if an innocent man sits in prison for 30 years because the prosecutor acted unethically, not the prosecutor. If a prosecutor fails to turn over evidence that might help a defendant (exculpatory evidence), they are, in theory, supposed to be punished for this, but this rarely occurs. Brady Violations (not turning over said evidence) happen all the time (Leonetti, 2012). As former Attorney General Robert Jackson stated almost eight decades ago: "The prosecutor has more control over life, liberty and reputation than any other person in America" (Bellin, 2019, p.171). This is still true today.

What can happen when these abuses are taken to the extreme? One former prosecutor (Godsey, 2017) says that when he was an assistant United States attorney, it was part of his job to dehumanize defendants. Defendants were "otherized." His fellow prosecutors used the phrase "bad guy" amongst themselves to describe defendants. "Bad guy" was code for, in essence, "don't give that guy such a sweetheart plea deal" when a supervisor didn't approve of a lenient agreement between their office and a defendant. In one of the more gross examples of how the adversarial system can be corrupted, prosecutors in Chicago participated in a contest amongst themselves known as the "Two-Ton Contest." The goal of this contest was to convict "4,000 pounds of flesh" by handling the most overweight defendants more harshly in order to win (Pollock, 2014).

This preamble was created intentionally to foster an understanding in the reader of why prosecutors are so skeptical by nature. They have to be. Trials are a form of civilized warfare. It is an adversarial system and prosecutors want to win and amass strings of convictions. In order to do that, they have to discredit or even exclude as evidence claims of mitigation if it is not related to insanity, should a case go to trial. (The federal government does not recognize a diminished-capacity defense, though this can vary from state to state.) Non-insanity evidence is not permitted at trial if the defense does not involve insanity. This includes mitigating circumstances (18 U.S. Code, § 17). An insanity defense is exculpatory for the defendant, while diminished capacity is merely mitigating and might provide for a downward departure for sentencing at the federal level (Levy, 2019). This requires the legal suppression of expert testimony that is possibly favorable to a defendant regarding mitigating circumstances at trial. Each time that parents of autistic children are told that evidence of their child's diminished capacity can't be used at trial, or the prosecutor does not take seriously the mitigating circumstances, they can't believe that these people would ignore what is right in front of them. It feels cruel to them. But it's actually part of how our very imperfect system works.

In addition to being zealous advocates, prosecutors are also, in fact, "skeptical advocates" (Nora, 2007). Nora (2007) says that our adversarial system casts prosecutors in the role of the skeptic by its very nature. First, prosecutors are almost always skeptical about the claims of innocence that defendants might make (Gershowitz & Killinger, 2011). Second, they are skeptical regarding "excuses" that defendants might make through their attorneys as to why they committed a crime. They think that they have heard every excuse in the book. So, when they have to, they try to undermine proof of mental illness or its effects on a given crime (substitute developmental disability for mental illness, for our purposes) (Nora, 2007). Sometimes, the undermining isn't even necessary to win. In fact, most of the time it isn't. Assuming that the prosecutor has the evidence they need to convict and plans to bring information or indictment, and the defendant chooses not to go to trial, the prosecutor can simply waive off the mitigating circumstances, knowing full well that the defendant will plead out and leave it all up to a judge (97–99 percent of cases end in guilty pleas, not trials [Dezember & Redlich, 2019]). In other words, most of the time, prosecutors don't even need their own forensic psychologist's expert witnesses to rebut what a defendant's witness says. Defendants are literally at the mercy of whether the prosecutor has an open mind.

In the rare instances where a plea doesn't happen and trial preparation leads the defense and prosecution to disagree on the extent to which mental illness affected someone's criminal responsibility (and, inevitably, they usually do disagree), expert witnesses become necessary on both sides. This seems fair, and to some extent it is. Forensic psychologists are guided by a code of ethics and their job is not to act in a therapeutic sense. Their job is to be information gatherers, guided by truth in the pursuit of justice on behalf of the system. They are hired by either prosecutors or defense lawyers or appointed by the court (the judge). Rule 702 of the Federal Rules of Evidence allows expert witnesses to testify if they have scientific, technical, or other specialized knowledge that would help the trier of fact (a judge or a jury) to understand a piece of evidence where a fact is being contested (this varies by state but exists at the federal level) (Graham, 1999). But as has been widely noted by legal scholars, providing "factual assistance" is actually a highly subjective determination that both sides try to use to their advantage (Oh, 1997). Let me explain.

One study had forensic health professionals do a "file review" of a case using the exact same information for both parties (Murrie *et al.*, 2013). A file review is where a forensic psychologist looks at the data pertaining to a defendant without meeting that person face to face, a practice that is used in real life and one that I question the ethics of using. Data for a file review can include a defendant's academic, intelligence, and neuropsychological test scores, background and history, discovery materials, and evidence, etc. The researchers in the study deceived the psychologists, who thought they were writing a report for an actual case to be submitted to the judge when, in actuality, it was for the research study. The only experimental manipulation in this study was whether the referral source came from the defense or prosecuting attorney. The results strongly suggested "adversarial allegiance." This meant that experts who were assigned to the prosecution assigned higher risk scores to offenders and experts assigned to the defense were given lower risk scores, even though the data they were looking at was exactly the same. Other studies indicate that the prosecutor's experts report higher scores for psychopathy among defendants than experts obtained by the defense (Lloyd, Clark & Forth, 2010; Murrie *et al.*, 2008, 2009). This is no secret. It's been known for more than a century that medical expert witnesses are influenced by the party that pays their fees (Foster, 1897; Hand, 1901; Wigmore, 1923). Judges frequently say that their primary frustration lies in the bias that expert witnesses possess (Shuman, Whitaker & Champagne, 1994). Judges acknowledge that expert witnesses often abandon their objectivity, skewing it more to the side that retained them (Krafka *et al.*, 2002).

Skepticism does not end with prosecutors for individuals on the autism spectrum entering the criminal justice system. In fact, it extends to the judiciary. The vast majority of judges are former prosecutors who retain a prosecutor's bias. According to an article by the Cato Institute, the ratio of former prosecutors to former defense attorneys sitting on the federal bench is four to one (Neily, 2019). Most studies conclude that judges who are former prosecutors are more likely to vote against a defendant (Nagel, 1962; Robinson, 2011). Similarly, federal judges with aspirations of being promoted to higher courts are less likely to rule in the defendant's favor than judges who don't have such aspirations (Epstein, 2016). State court judges with similar ambitions also show such tendencies (Brace, Hall & Langer, 1999). According to the Brennan Center for Justice (Berry, 2015), adding to this conflict is that 87 percent of state judges are elected or reelected and their constituents tend to vote for candidates who they feel will protect the community and be tough on crime. Mounting evidence suggests that elections threaten a judge's ability to be impartial arbitrators in criminal cases (*ibid.*). The vast majority of criminal cases in the United States take place in state courts where this dynamic comes into play.

So how is this judicial skepticism actually demonstrable? Take, for example, something that the late Supreme Court Justice, Antonin Scalia, said in a dissent from Atkins v. Virginia (2002). Scalia said that nothing has changed in 300 years since Lord Matthew Hale discussed the easiness of counterfeiting mental disability. (If Scalia had got his way, "mentally retarded" individuals could have been subjected to execution by the government.) A "fear of faking," that a defendant would fake an illness in order to avoid responsibility for a crime, has been an issue in the legal system for centuries. Perlin (1996) calls it perhaps the most compelling and dominating myth in all of criminal procedure.

There are several reasons why Scalia's statement about counterfeit mental disability is a huge exaggeration. First, as Perlin (2016) has said, individuals with mental disabilities will often feign wellness out of pride, even when they are facing prosecution and when it is not in their best interests to do so. Second, as I have already established in this book, skepticism is baked into the system to act as an inherent check against Scalia's concern. Any expert witness/forensic psychologist worth their license will use a symptom validity test to measure for malingering, such as the Test of Memory Malingering, the Miller Forensic Assessment of Symptoms Test, and the Minnesota Multiphasic Personality Inventory-2 (MMPI-2) (van Impelen et al., 2017). Even cognitive tests such as Digit Span from the Wechsler Adult Intelligence Scale (WAIS) have malingering indices built in (Reese, Suhr & Riddle, 2012). The International Society for Autism Research posted preliminary research that suggests that the Morel Emotional Numbing Test (a PTSD screening instrument) has the potential to detect malingering in individuals who appear autistic. ASD individuals with an IQ over 80 and neurotypically matched controls who were instructed to malinger both completed the instrument, and the control group performed worse. This strongly suggests that the test might detect validity with regards to malingering, though more research is needed (Dubbelin et al., 2016).

Since autism as a diagnosis of one's developmental history is determined mostly by past records, interviews with family members, and standardized testing, feigning the disorder would be almost impossible in a criminal case. There are too many safeguards in place.

Scalia was not a complete judicial aberration when it came to this skepticism. He represented the way that *some* judges think. Not all judges, but some. In United States v. Dolehide (2011), an autistic defendant was seeking a downward departure for a five-level increase that was applied to his base-level offense, which was possession of child pornography. In her ruling, District Judge Linda R. Reade said:

> The sentencing argument du jour for possession of child pornography in federal court is the allegation that a defendant suffers from Asperger's Syndrome and thus is entitled to probation. Individuals who were previously diagnosed with ADHD and other personality disorders are now re-labeled as afflicted with an "Autistic Spectrum Disorder," one of which is Asperger's Syndrome.

She also states:

> Defendant is at least of average intelligence and according to Scaramella, of "superior intellect." He is polite, can carry on a conversation by listening and

responding to questions. His answers during the July 2009 interview with law enforcement were not overly verbose as suggested by Holmes but rather were straightforward... Defendant has lived independent of his family, gone to school and had sexual relationships with females in his own age group. He has friends.

In order to clarify the previous statement about the defendant having friends, she goes on to state in item 3 of the appendix:

His interest in playing video games seems to be consistent with other "neuro-typical" [sic] young adults who use technology to interact rather than engaging face-to-face, thus preventing development of fluent social skills in generations of Americans.

As previously noted, most defendants do not go to trial. An informal but quantifiable penalty exists if a defendant goes to trial and loses. This penalty is a much longer prison sentence than they would receive by simply pleading guilty, and it is commonly referred to as "the trial penalty" (Abrams, 2013). This leaves most autistic defendants with a truly awful choice to make. On one hand, if they firmly believe in their innocence or plan to use an insanity defense, they can take the risk of going to trial, hoping to be either acquitted or committed to a mental institution. But long stretches of prison time are not tenable for most autistic people. Yet, even with the avoidance of the trial penalty and trying to plead out for a shorter sentence, depending on the severity of the crime and one's criminal history, plea bargaining does not guarantee a shorter stay in prison. Furthermore, even very short stays in custody can turn into completely traumatic ordeals for autistic individuals. So why doesn't everyone go to trial to avoid long prison sentences? Because if everyone took their cases to trial, the system would grind to a halt. The system is designed to encourage plea bargaining by threatening a "trial penalty" if one does not plead out to keep the proverbial blood of the system flowing so that it doesn't clot. This means that defendants are forced to rely upon a prosecutor's use of their discretionary power, which is vast. I noted throughout this section that prosecutors are skeptical by nature and their skepticism presents a huge obstacle in the process. While this is not completely insurmountable, it's far from easy.

Charge Bargaining

Before I talk about the ways some autistic defendants and their lawyers have successfully appealed to a prosecutor's role as a minister of justice, I need to discuss one of the inherent, structural limitations involved in this process for the uninitiated, which is "charge bargaining." Prosecutors make the initial decision of whether to prosecute and determine the preliminary charges, charge reductions, and plea negotiations (Piehl & Bushway, 2007) before a sentencing judge becomes involved. As Reiss (1974; quoted in Forst, 2002, p.518) says, prosecutors arguably exercise "the greatest discretion in the formally organized criminal justice network." This is to say that they arguably have more power than anyone, including judges. Let me explain what this all means.

One way to get a defendant to plead guilty is by overcharging them (Davis, 2007). Here's a fairly common scenario: in the federal court system, a prosecutor will often charge a defendant with distribution, receipt, and possession of child pornography, three separate charges that carry different sentencing recommendations and mandatory minimums. Mandatory minimums force the judge to hand down a minimum prison sentence to a defendant based on what they plead guilty to (Criminal Justice Policy Foundation, 2014). Regarding receipt and possession, from our example, the reader may wonder what the difference is. Usually it is not possible to be in possession of something unless you have received it from somewhere. Indeed, this conundrum has stumped legal scholars. Judge Posner in United States v. Richardson (2001) put it this way: "The puzzle is why receiving…should be punished more severely than possessing, since possessors, unless they fabricate their own pornography, are also receivers." A receiver of child pornography is subject to a mandatory minimum of five years in prison whereas there is no mandatory minimum for a possessor. Bacon (2010) correctly says that no meaningful distinction exists between these two offenses other than to "punish" receiving child pornography more harshly than possessing it, and sums it up nicely:

> When a prosecutor elects to charge a defendant with "receipt" instead of, or in conjunction with, "possession," he or she strips the judicial branch of its authority to fashion an appropriate sentence in light of the defendant's conduct. Federal prosecutors…can always hedge the risk that a judge will depart downward by charging defendants with just "receipt." This effectively ties the judge's hands and ensures that the defendant will serve five years in prison if convicted, regardless of what he would have been sentenced to had he been convicted of "possession" alone. … Not surprisingly, defendants affected by § 2252's paradox have looked to avoid the five-year mandatory minimum sentence that accompanies "receipt" convictions. (pp.1030–1031)

In this example alone, one can understand how a prosecutor has enormous power over the outcome. By deciding which charge ends up on the indictment or information when a defendant pleads guilty, the prosecutor (and not the judge) can determine whether that defendant serves a five-year prison sentence or gets probation.

The same is true with distribution, which also carries a mandatory minimum, unlike the charge of possession. I have personally met many individuals on the autism spectrum who did not know they were disseminating this illegal material to others at the time of their arrest. If you find this hard to believe, consider it is possible (not likely, but possible) to be in possession of child pornography and not know it. As an example, United States v. Kuchkinski (2006) (Marin, 2008) was a case in which the defendant's computer contained some 15,000 illegal images. But the defendant successfully argued that he was unaware that a computer mechanism downloaded any and all images viewed. In other words, he was not aware that he had those 15,000 images on his hard drive. Ultimately, he was able to get the number of images knocked down to 110 (*ibid.*).

Similarly, as I mentioned, some individuals are charged with "distributing" child pornography when they are not aware that they have actually distributed anything. If an individual is using a file sharing network, it can be impossible to know which if any files are unknowingly being shared with others (Fisk, 2009). Peer-to-peer internet sites permit the general public to download items from one's computer without one's knowledge and without one committing an affirmative act (Douard & Schultz, 2017). Furthermore, in a PowerPoint presentation given to help explain child pornography viewing in autistic individuals, Schutte and Schutte (2018) note that many individuals who use peer-to-peer software are not aware that downloaded files are, by default, automatically uploaded. If we assume that Schutte and Schutte's statement can be true under some circumstances, then certain individuals are not aware that they are distributing files to anyone.

Neither the federal government nor many of the states require proof that the defendant acted with mens rea (intent or knowledge of wrongdoing) in order to convict them on the charge of distribution, receipt, or possession. An exception to this, in regard to distribution, comes from a Florida appellate court. In Biller v. State (2013) the appellate court in Florida voided for vagueness when a defendant was charged with transmission of child pornography because, according to him, he did not affirmatively dispatch or send the images to others as a function of his computer. They were sent for him by his computer, without his knowledge. But this ruling is, again, an exception, not typical of cases involving child pornography. Douard and Schultz (2017) point out that, elsewhere (in most states and at the federal level), possession and distribution is a strict liability crime and only prosecutorial discretion can save someone from being charged with these crimes. Strict liability is when the legal system deems it insufficient on the part of the defendant to excuse someone on the grounds that they did not act intentionally, recklessly, or negligently in the commission of a crime. In other words, the defendant is not even offered an opportunity to present an explanation or an excuse for their behavior (Carpenter, 2006). It would not matter whether a defendant knew that they were distributing child pornography, nor would it matter whether a person did not know that possession of child pornography was illegal. All that is necessary to establish a conviction, under strict liability, is the knowledge that the defendant had the images in question. Another example of a strict liability crime is statutory rape. It does not matter whether the defendant knew that the person they had sex with was underage. The only thing that matters is whether they were, in fact, underage. Even if they deceived the defendant by showing a fake driver's license, they looked 18 or older, and the defendant tried to verify their age in every other way possible, it still would not matter. The defendant would still be committing a crime if they had sex with the person who was younger than 18, under strict liability.

So, charge bargaining plays an enormous role in the plea-bargaining process. As a result of having the final say as to the charges that stick, charge bargaining allows prosecutors to enjoy tremendous influence over the sentencing severity of a defendant (Nagel & Schulhofer, 1992). Charge bargaining curtails judicial discretion in order to increase prosecutorial discretion (Tonry, 1996). Richard Frase (2000) stated it rather eloquently when he said: "Prosecutors in American jurisdictions wield enormous 'sentencing' power because they have virtually unreviewable discretion to select the initial charges and decide which charges to drop as part of plea bargaining" (p.440). In our previous example using possession, receipt, and distribution of child pornography, a prosecutor can ensure that a defendant serves a mandatory minimum of a specific length of time in prison, depending on which charges they decide to hold on to. Their decision of which charge to reduce (or not reduce) while negotiating a plea deal could very well make the difference between a sentence of probation and as much as 10–15 years in prison, with the judge having no role whatsoever in that process.

Given that the role of prosecutors (and to some extent judges) is to be skeptical to protect society, *and* given that so many individuals present in the criminal justice system with mental health issues, how can we appeal to a prosecutor's discretion regarding autism? Moreover, how does charge bargaining factor into the equation? Armed with this information, I will now tackle these important questions.

A Different Approach to Obtaining Prosecutorial Discretion

Generally speaking, seeking prosecutorial discretion for serious crimes is a bit like a spider asking a Venus Fly Trap for mercy. Yet defense attorney Mark

Mahoney feels differently about his autism cases. His experience tells him that when prosecutors are thoroughly informed about how autistic individuals may unwittingly engage in criminally sanctioned conduct, they are capable of responding humanely (Mahoney, 2017). Although he cites that, as of 2017, there were no reported cases of pretrial diversion for a sex crime at the federal level, Mahoney was able to obtain reduced charges where the final disposition resulted in a non-SORA (Sex Offender Registration Act)-based offense in several cases. In other words, the reduced charges allowed an individual to not have to register for the sex offender registry. This happened in United States v. Rubino (2008), for example, where an autistic defendant was originally charged with crimes related to child pornography but eventually got the charges reduced to an obscenity charge, which is not a registrable offense in most states. Furthermore, the defendant did not go to prison. I will repeatedly return to Mark Mahoney throughout this section since he is the most experienced and arguably the most successful trial attorney in the country who defends autistic individuals charged with sexual offenses.

Mahoney (2017) admits that his approach to lawyering in these situations is a little different from the norm, but he believes that it is the only hope for a good outcome. He does not act as though prosecutors are Venus Fly Traps. Usually, lawyers pay deference to the state or government when a client is guilty. They also try to show mitigating factors to the prosecutor, hoping that they will be merciful. (This is true with mentally ill clients, as well.) Mahoney, however, believes that a defense lawyer has to show that it is "morally wrong" (p.2) for the state or the federal government to punish a person because of their autism if the autistic defendant does not have the mental or moral culpability of a typically developed person. Mahoney is arguing here for pretrial diversion, which I will also argue for later in this chapter. However, this is a bold strategy that, while it has clearly been successful for Mahoney in getting non-registry convictions and sentences without incarceration attached to them, can easily backfire if a prosecutor feels attacked or put on the defensive. Telling a prosecutor that they are "morally wrong" could easily be seen as an affront unless there is a clear way to back up that statement. I believe there is. Therefore, one of the primary burdens for me in this section is to explain how to distinguish autism from a mental illness because, as I have talked about, prosecutors are extremely used to hearing excuses. This is going to require us to delve deeply into how an autistic person in the criminal justice system is fundamentally unique from others.

Mahoney (2017) believes that when a fee agreement is drafted between the client and the lawyer, a parent or guardian should have a role as a guarantor and adviser. This is because, as I discussed earlier in the book, he believes that some people with autistic disorders give an appearance of understanding a situation when, in fact, they do not understand due to their autism. In other words, it seems as though Mahoney believes that it would be malpractice not to include this clause in a fee agreement. The fee agreement clearly states that the attorney's sole duty is to serve the client but that consulting with parents on every aspect of the case, making disclosures, and even making some routine decisions on behalf of the client will be performed, while all major decisions will always be made by the client. In essence, Mahoney is expanding the scope of the attorney-client privilege to parents, assuming a client agrees to it.

Many factors come into play when a defense attorney handles the case of an individual with autism and, of course, each case is different. The most important factor is whether the person is guilty. A defense attorney is concerned with whether an individual has committed crimes in the past, easy access to travel and money, an arrest record, or even a juvenile record. Of course, this goes beyond the purposes of getting a reasonable bail. This is important since it demonstrates one's tendency to be law abiding, which later on will affect plea bargaining, as well as calculations made in the presentence report, which helps to determine one's sentence.

Next, the gathering of past records on the part of historians (parents or guardians) is crucial. This includes all previous psychological testing and reports, IEPs, and medical reports that might be relevant to the mitigating factors. These records serve all vested parties. They help defense lawyers to learn more about their clients; they supplement the forensic psychologist's report with a life history and more data to flesh out the person's life; they can ultimately be helpful in persuading a prosecutor or a judge later on. Even if an individual was not formally diagnosed with autism before the arrest, if medical/psychological or historical records from the past indicate that there were differences in development, this strengthens the validity of a new diagnosis. Differences in development could include a speech delay, dyspraxia, lack of friendships, extreme sensory issues, and any special education services that one received. As we have learned, prosecutors are skeptical. My experience has been that when an individual is diagnosed after an arrest, it arouses more suspicion in prosecutors. That bolsters the need to make historical records available to the defense team so that they can give credence to a diagnosis. This is of paramount importance.

Fleshing out the narrative arc of the individual that led to the charges also includes a thorough developmental history that goes beyond one's treatment records (Mahoney, 2017). Mahoney encourages parents to write a narrative of their child's history and development. Parents or guardians should include in this narrative all perspectives, including those of siblings, uncles, aunts, and anyone who has had intimate contact with the defendant. Mahoney sees this narrative as being a mosaic of the individual's autism via detailed reporting.

This includes descriptions of the person's developmental history, such as not fitting in at school, missing social cues, having security objects (such as blankets or stuffed animals) beyond the appropriate age, children's television shows they still watch, or anything that may not match their chronological age. If the person has always been extremely "rule bound" in their thinking, this should be highlighted as well. Documentation for being rule bound could come from: an employer; a former high-school principal or college dean (such as a notarized letter indicating that there were no disciplinary issues or notations on the person's record; obtaining school records is also recommended for a well-behaved person); and/or a psychotherapist with whom the person has worked, who can attest to the person's cooperativeness and motivation in treatment. Mahoney also recommends showing the lawyer home movies of the client as a child if they capture rule-bound or autistic qualities. This makes family and defendant testimony to the lawyer literally "come alive" and allows for better advocacy in the end.

A defendant's narrative is also concerned with their psychosexual development history. Mahoney (2017) notes that parents may not be the best historian on these issues simply because their child may not have talked much about their sexuality (Ballan, 2012). Therefore, a parent may have assumed that their child was simply not interested in sex. It is definitely possible to provide simple empirical statements. Did the person ever have a girlfriend or boyfriend? Did they have many friends growing up? If such friendships or relationships existed, what were the nature of them? Were they one-sided or did they include reciprocity? If, for example, a 33-year-old is arrested for a child pornography offense or in a sting operation and he had no sexual experience to draw from in his life, this fact is important. Each case is different, but one can infer that a social disability might make sexual intimacy and relationships more difficult in general. Hénault and Attwood (2002) cited a study in which there were nine virgins among a group of 25 autistic participants. Their lack of sexual experience was accompanied by psychological and physiological symptoms, such as nervousness, loneliness, and anxiety. Recent research by Dewinter et al. (2016) has contested this by saying that parents underreport the sexual experiences of their autistic children, whereas autistic people overreport it. While acknowledging that this reporting will vary from person to person, we must keep in mind that teens in general, and even adult males, often overreport and exaggerate their sexual activity to prove their prowess (Limmer, 2014). "Don Juanism," or the appearance of it to others, traditionally helps to confer status among males in our society, particularly for adolescents. So, a lawyer needs to be aware of whether the client's self-reporting while recounting their sexual experiences is coming from a place of insecurity or is the actual truth. In my experience, some or even many autistic people know that individuals who don't have sex are very often considered "uncool" by their peers. I certainly considered people in this way, and I know many other autistic people who think this way too. So, if an autistic person has not, in fact, had any or much sexual experience, it would certainly be in their best interest to tell their lawyer the truth. But sometimes clients cling to normality as much as possible—if only to hold on to their pride in a situation where their pride is all but gone, or if they don't know that to do otherwise would be for their own good. Yes—even when it goes against their interests to do so, clients can sabotage themselves. Good lawyers don't let them do so.

Alongside a thorough debriefing with family members and the creation of a narrative arc, Mahoney (2017) suggests a thorough interview with the client (everything about this interview assumes that the client did commit the crime). Mahoney uses child pornography as his example, since that is the crime for which he most frequently sees autistic people prosecuted. It is important for the lawyer to conduct this interview in the presence of someone with whom the autistic defendant feels comfortable. That could be a therapist. For accuracy and convenience, it is best to tape record and then transcribe the interview. This interview is an attempt to understand the client's state of mind. At the beginning of Mahoney's interview, the questions relate to the difference between an act being wrong and being illegal. Mahoney wants to get a sense of whether his clients know this distinction.

The next set of questions has to do with pornography in general. Mahoney wants to know how the person began viewing pornography. Was it at the behest of someone online? How did it start? Assuming that the defendant viewed adult pornography too, did they think that viewing these legal images was wrong or even illegal? What was their methodology for searching for these images?

The next set of questions is perhaps the most difficult: getting to the heart of why the person viewed the illegal images. Mahoney wants to get a sense of whether the person was aware that taboos about this behavior exist. So, he asks a similar set of questions relating to how the person began their viewing, how they obtained the images, how they imagined the images came into being, why the images were on the internet, their awareness of wrongness or illegality, etc. Mahoney stresses that by the time this interview is conducted, the lawyer will have already emphasized to the defendant why the acts in their totality were illegal, morally wrong, and societally taboo. Therefore, it is necessary for the lawyer or interviewer to stress that the client repositions their mindset to what was occurring in their mind *before* the arrest and not post-arrest. Finally, Mahoney wants to know if a person was aware that the files on their computer were being sent to others, perhaps without their knowledge. He asks these questions in an open-ended way so as to encourage honest responses.

What's the point of all of this? First, it's to get at the truth. But of almost equal importance is that if the answers show naivete, lack of awareness of what was illegal or the taboos involved, or lack of understanding of the fact that real victims were in those pictures, this demonstrates an entirely different mindset on the part of the autistic individual than for a neurotypical. One could argue that it shows significant diminished capacity or, in some cases, lack of criminal responsibility. These kinds of questions can apply to other criminal situations where autism is a factor and they must be asked. The example of John (pseudonym), discussed earlier in the book, is a perfect example of this. John was not aware that touching a woman to feel her silky clothing would constitute any kind of sexual offense. In his mind, it was a sensory issue. He was not even attracted to the woman. His trial attorneys ignored this issue and encouraged him to plead guilty prematurely, and this landed him on a sex offender registry. The important question is: is it morally right to prosecute and punish John, an autistic individual, in the same way as a person who intended to violate someone sexually? Mahoney argues that it is extremely "morally wrong" to prosecute an autistic individual in the same way as a neurotypical individual who intended sexual violation, and that the defense attorney needs to convey this to the prosecutor with exactness and urgency.

Consider another striking example. Most people would argue that a futures trader who triggered a "flash crash" by wiping billions of dollars from publicly traded companies and earning 70 million dollars in commissions had to have had criminal intent when he committed the crime. What else could motivate such a crime other than greed? It's hard for us to conceptualize any other reason. But, in the case of autistic trader Navinder Singh Sarao (Tarm, 2020a, 2020b), there was another reason. He saw it as a videogame. Both prosecutors and defense attorneys noted that he was able to spot numerical patterns in split seconds and saw his acquisition in points rather than money. Additionally, after getting the 70 million dollars, he ate at McDonald's using coupons. He continued living on his modest government benefits. His most expensive purchase in ten years was a used Volkswagen that was not worth much. He lost millions of dollars to people who took advantage of him. His defense attorney described him as "innocent, guileless, trusting and childlike" (Reid, 2020), and he was even able to make the FBI agents investigating his case and his prosecutors fall in love with him. He could not do simple, everyday, ordinary tasks such as the laundry. Yet, in exchange for a cooperation agreement, he helped prosecutors to learn the techniques he had used, for future investigative purposes. His crime was committed in

2010. He was indicted in 2015, and in 2020, he was finally sentenced to home confinement. I find it fascinating that, in spite of his cooperating with the government, ten years going by, and the extraordinary circumstances of his case, he was not given a diversion agreement. Particularly because he spent four months in a British prison, which was "unbearable," as he described it, and "amounted to torture of sensory stimulation, sleep deprivation, and forced socialization" (Tarm, 2020a, 2020b) that made him suicidal. Did he really need home confinement as a punishment when, according to the article (Verity, 2020), he barely leaves his home anyway? A year of home confinement is better than imprisonment, but after ten years, what is the point?

This case illustrates the importance of Mahoney's thorough debriefing with the client. To state the obvious, we need to look through a different lens to understand whether a crime was committed and whether the defendant had a lack of understanding about the nature of the crime. For example, it would be harder to argue in court that a man made excessive amounts of money and got rich because he was in a manic phase of a bipolar depression. Being in the manic phase certainly inhibits a person's control over their behavior (Swann *et al.*, 2011), but even in a manic phase, a person conceivably knows right from wrong. This differs markedly from certain autism cases where the autistic individual was clearly not aware of their wrong behavior.

There are several reasons for this. I will get into this in detail so that advocates or defense lawyers reading the book can help to educate prosecutors. It will begin to make sense as I explain it. First, to reiterate a point made earlier, daily living skills and adaptive functioning as measured by instruments like the Vineland Adaptive Behavior Scales can actually *diminish* for autistic people as they age, as counterintuitive as that might sound (Smith, Greenberg & Mailick, 2012). What is adaptive functioning, anyway? Adaptive functioning describes how well one is able to function independently in one's environment (Pugliese *et al.*, 2016; Turygin & Matson, 2014). Behaviors that measure adaptive functioning include communication, socialization, and a daily living skills domain that includes items related to self-care, home living, community use, health and safety, leisure, and occupational skills (Ditterline *et al.*, 2008). It is no surprise that autistic individuals struggle in the domains of communication and socialization (Volkmar *et al.*, 1987). However, autistic individuals, even without an intellectual impairment, score low in daily living skills domains such as hygiene, grooming, housekeeping, and meal preparation, which encompass the domain of daily living skills (Matson, Dempsey & Fodstad, 2009).

Let me explain this in greater detail. Vineland Adaptive Behavior Scales is a test that measures adaptive functioning in everyday life. The Vineland test can be taken by any person up to the age of 90. After survey participants (or their caretakers) answer a variety of questions based on the participant's life, the test then takes the raw data from across the domains and subdomains and converts them into an adaptive-levels determination, as well as age equivalents in years and months (Raggio, Massingale & Bass, 1994). Within the communication domains are the subdomains of:

- written communication
- expressive communication
- receptive communication.

Within the socialization domains are:

- interpersonal relations
- leisure time
- coping skills.

And within the daily living skills domain are the subdomains of:

- personal
- domestic
- community.

The personal subdomain under the domain of daily living skills refers to how a person eats, dresses, and practices hygiene. The domestic subdomain under the daily living skills domain refers to what household tasks the individual can perform or is able to perform. And the community subdomain under the daily living skills domain refers to how a person uses money, the telephone, a computer, and job skills. For example, in the domain of daily living skills, if a person scored 4:6 (four years and six months) in the subdomain of personal, 6:5 in the domestic subdomain, and 6:6 in the community subdomain, their score for the daily living skills domain averaged together would be 5:9.

In the Smith *et al.* (2012) study, the authors found that the age of daily living skills for ASD adults begins to decline somewhere in people's early 30s. A slight improvement in daily living skills can be seen through late adolescence but then it typically slows down. According to Taylor and Seltzer (2010), daily living skills for ASD individuals oftentimes slow down or even sometimes stop once an individual exits secondary school and enters their early 20s. As Smith *et al.* (2012) go out of their way to point out, the gains made during adolescence are not due to a ceiling effect or a mastery of skills. On the contrary, by the end of the study period, the ASD adults could not complete over a third of the measured daily skills of adult independent living. In fact, Down Syndrome adults show a higher level of daily living skills across the board in adulthood than ASD individuals (Esbensen *et al.*, 2010). In a study between 70 ASD individuals and 70 age-matched controls with Down Syndrome, it was shown that the ASD group had less residential independence, less social contact with friends, and more limited functional abilities (daily living skills) and exhibited more "problem" behaviors than the Down Syndrome group (*ibid.*).

Now, here's the part that really pertains to our discussion for prosecutors. For the general population (or neurotypicals), adaptive functioning and IQ are related. Studies measuring the correlation between scores on the Adaptive Behavior Assessment System Second Edition (ABAS II) and the WAIS-IV in the general population show that they remain constant (Nyrenius & Billstedt, 2019). This means that one's IQ can reasonably be assumed to match one's adaptive functioning. If someone has an above-average IQ, it can usually be said that they know how to take care of themselves, establish relationships, and have functional independence relative to their intelligence. Recent research shows significant gaps between IQ and adaptive functioning across all age groups for individuals with ASD (Chatham *et al.*, 2018; Pugliese *et al.*, 2015; Tillmann *et al.*, 2019). Researchers tend to emphasize different aspects of autism to account for this discrepancy. Some put the emphasis on the core social communication deficits related to autism (*ibid.*) to account for this discrepancy, while others attribute it to executive functioning deficits (Kraper *et al.*, 2017). The bottom line is that despite an ASD individual possessing an average or even above-average IQ, there are likely to be deficits in adaptive functioning (Duncan & Bishop, 2015). I want to repeat this because it is that important: a higher IQ for ASD individuals does not predict higher adaptive functioning—it often predicts the inverse, particularly with respect to daily living skills (Klin *et al.*, 2007; Lee & Park, 2007; Liss *et al.*, 2001). And even when IQ should be a strong predictor of adaptive functioning, this is less relevant because it often decreases with age in ASD individuals with higher intellect (Kanne *et al.*, 2011). Moreover, a 20-year longitudinal study of ASD adults with IQs in the normal or higher range showed very little evidence to support the belief that cognitive factors are associated with adaptive functioning, as measured by the *Vineland Adaptive Behavior Scales, Survey Edition* (Farley *et al.*, 2009). In the Farley *et al.* study, there were individuals with high IQ scores but limited adaptive skills. However, there were also people with borderline IQs (in the 70–85 range) who were fairly independent and obtained "good" or "very good" outcome ratings. ASD is considered a heterogenous disorder because of its spectrum nature

(Georgiades, Szatmari & Boyle, 2013). Yet in spite of this, there is greater uniformity in adaptive functioning across the spectrum such that even when intellectual ability is intact, adaptive functioning is still impaired, particularly in the areas of socialization and daily living skills (Charman *et al.*, 2011; Duncan & Bishop, 2015; Klin *et al.*, 2007).

Earlier in this chapter, I noted how prosecutors can be skeptical of clients with mental illness. I noted that part of my burden in this section was to show how a developmental disability like autism presents differently from a mental illness and why prosecutors should adhere to Mahoney's creed that, under some circumstances, it is immoral to prosecute an autistic person. The above discussion of the Vineland test, daily living skill age equivalents, and uneven profiles between intellectual functioning and adaptive functioning illustrates a unique marker in autism that does not exist in mental illness. The fact that individuals with autism test as low as they do on these measures is not for lack of effort. It does appear that lack of daily living skills is directly tied to issues with executive functioning, which concerns one's planning ability, generativity, flexibility, working memory, motivation, concept of time, and ability to shift attention (Gillberg, 2007). Two studies have shown clear correlations between trouble with executive functioning for autistic people and low daily living skills, as measured by the Vineland test (Gilotty *et al.*, 2002; Kenworthy *et al.*, 2005). In fact, several more recent studies of individuals with ASD and without intellectual disability demonstrate real-world links between deficits in executive functioning and adaptive functioning (Wallace *et al.*, 2016). This makes intuitive and practical sense when we think about what daily living skills entail, such as cooking, dressing, and hygiene. Performing in the kitchen requires executive functioning skills to formulate goals, plan strategies, and self-evaluate during these activities (Lezak, 1982). It is well recognized that occupational therapists have to help autistic people with practical issues, like cooking, across the lifespan (Katz & Hartman-Maeir, 2005). Autistic individuals have a variety of daily living challenges with skills such as dressing, cooking, bed making, shopping, and ordering food at a restaurant (Mechling & Gustafson, 2008). We can attribute some of these deficits to poor motor skills, too. Atypical motor performance can affect tasks such as grooming, dressing, and household chores (Fournier *et al.*, 2010). Research suggests that manual motor skills, like grip strength, significantly correlate with daily living skills in autistic individuals, even after accounting for age and IQ (Travers *et al.*, 2017). Another study found that motor impairment affects quality of life for autistic individuals (Günal, Bumin & Huri, 2019).

The adaptive functioning skills mentioned above are extremely difficult for prosecutors to fully understand because they are counterintuitive to how prosecutors, and frankly people in general, think. Prosecutors cannot imagine a scenario in which a person with above-average intelligence has difficulties managing the simple skills of daily living. It seems like an impossibility and yet it is merely a facet of autism. How else could one explain a savant who can play a Rachmaninoff concerto blindfolded but can't carry a conversation or tie their own shoes? Uneven development is a hallmark of autism, to varying degrees. And Mark Mahoney (2019) believes that it is morally wrong to prosecute someone with age-equivalent scores of a child for the three domains. According to Mahoney, who has assisted in hundreds of these cases, autistic adults who take these tests often come back with scores that measure in the range of preadolescence. The research backs this up.

If we assume that the above impairments are valid (communication, socialization, and daily living skills), we can begin to understand how autism is unique and how it creates age discrepancies between chronological age and functional age, as well as extremely uneven developmental profiles. Mahoney (2020) believes although the vast majority of ASD individuals are not pedophiles, they may emotionally identify socially (not sexually) to the age range of the photos they are looking at. As Mahoney (2019) puts it:

> The importance of the chronological age equivalent of social adaptation ability cannot be overstated. The power of this lies in the ability to objectively describe to the prosecutor and the judge the degree of impairment in critical "interpersonal" social skills. The prosecutor would not contemplate prosecuting and imprisoning a severely intellectually disabled person, or a small child. Why would it be any different for one whose ability to understand the wrongfulness involved in looking at sexually explicit images of minors is no better than a ten-year-old? Few of those with ASD charged in these offenses will test out at a higher level than that. (p.14)

As I have noted, intellectual ability or IQ was not a predictor of functional, day-to-day success in these studies. So, even though in some cases it may look like an individual has accomplished certain goals in life, this needs to be offset by the understanding that this means very little if an individual still lives at home, can't make daily decisions that affect their life, depends on their parents for advice that most grown-ups would have a handle on in their own lives, needs help tying their own tie, can't drive or cook their own food, doesn't know how to initiate an encounter with the opposite sex, etc. Functional independence is a marker of the ability to navigate the world and make judgments on a daily basis. If a person has issues with this, one can presume that they either can't make those judgments or have not been trusted to make them by their family or loved ones. Therefore, when Mark Mahoney says that, in some domains of life, prosecuting an autistic individual is like prosecuting a ten-year-old, he is right. Their body may have grown up to match their chronological age, along with all of the hormones that accompany that, but the complete understanding or holistic thinking needed to understand why something may have been wrong could very well have been absent from the picture.

This idea is beginning to pick up traction across the country. Recently, in Virginia, for example, a bill was sponsored by a former prosecutor and Republican State Senator, Richard Stuart, that would give a judge the authority to defer findings of guilt and dismiss a criminal case where an individual has been diagnosed with autism or an intellectual disability (Green, 2020). The bill passed 40-0 in the senate and, as of this date, still has to go to the state house (Virginia's Legislative Information System, 2020a).

A short summary of the proposed bill can be found on the internet (Virginia's Legislative Information System, 2020b). It is public record and reads as follows:

> § 19.2-303.6. Deferred disposition in a criminal case; persons with autism or intellectual disabilities.
>
> A. In any criminal case, except an act of violence as defined in § 19.2-297.1 or any crime for which a deferred disposition is provided for by statute, upon a plea of guilty, or after a plea of not guilty, and the facts found by the court would justify a finding of guilt, the court may, if the defendant has been diagnosed by a psychiatrist or clinical psychologist with (i) an autism spectrum disorder as defined in the most recent edition of the Diagnostic and Statistical Manual of Mental Disorders published by the American Psychiatric Association or (ii) an intellectual disability as defined in § 37.2-100, without entering a judgment of guilt and with the consent of the accused, after giving due consideration to the position of the attorney for the Commonwealth and the views of the victim, defer further proceedings and place the accused on probation subject to terms and conditions set by the court. Upon violation of a term or condition, the court may enter an adjudication of guilt; or upon fulfillment of the terms and conditions, the court may discharge the person and dismiss the proceedings against him without an adjudication of guilt. This section shall not limit the authority of any juvenile and domestic relations court granted to it in Title 16.1.
>
> B. Deferred disposition shall be available to the defendant even though he has previously been convicted of a criminal offense, been adjudicated delinquent as a juvenile, or had proceedings deferred and dismissed under this section or under any other provision of law, unless, after having considered the position of the attorney for the Commonwealth, the views of the victims, and any

evidence offered by the defendant, the court finds that deferred disposition is inconsistent with the interests of justice.

Please keep in mind that the sponsor of this bill is a former prosecutor who comes from the conservative commonwealth of Virginia and is a Republican acknowledging that discretion should be shown for this population for reasons contained throughout this book. I will return to the important concept of diversion as a capstone for this chapter, because that is ultimately what I am arguing for.

However, I have one more burden to address before advocating for diversion. As I have mentioned, the question that prosecutors typically ask is: "How is autism, or a developmental disability, different from a mental illness?" I have already established within the context of developmental disabilities that while one's IQ can be intact or above average, the disability nevertheless can impact all aspects of growing up from birth to adulthood. Thus, a person can be considered extremely disadvantaged if they only have the life experiences of a child, which can be quantitively measured with standardized tests. Furthermore, paradoxically, some people still test out as average or above average on IQ tests and may have some life accomplishments.

Though these lower scores would be unusual in the case of someone with a mental illness, they are not impossible when it comes to regression due to life circumstances. For example, individuals who have experienced extreme trauma and PTSD might have much lower than average Vineland scores (Becker-Weidman, 2009). In the nature-and-nurture context, the environmental factors (or nurture) that occur when a child or adult is exposed to complex trauma can disrupt the basic sense of feeling safe in the world. These experiences can create a loss of emotional regulation and can affect one's neurochemistry, cognition, self-concept, and a host of other characteristics that can cause regression. Children who were reared in orphanages, experienced sexual abuse, or received abuse from their primary caregiver are all susceptible to this type of complex trauma, which might predict a lower chronological age score on the Vineland test (Becker-Weidman, 2009). On the other hand, lower Vineland scores were not seen in a study conducted by Matson *et al.* (2006) for bipolar individuals. On yet another study, researchers found that depressed and impaired preschoolers did not score lower than average on the Vineland test and did not show developmental delays, suggesting a window of opportunity for early intervention (Luby *et al.*, 2009). In one study examining schizophrenia, it was found that older age was a predictor for a higher score on the Vineland test (Ania *et al.*, 2018), whereas with autism, it was just the opposite. Scores on the Vineland test actually dropped for autistic people as they aged. Additionally, executive functioning skills played a key role in whether someone in the schizophrenia group had a lower Vineland score. Notably, a psychotic illness or episode was not a predictor of a lower score.

The above paragraph is not intended to trivialize mental illness or its seriousness. I do not suggest that mental illness shouldn't sometimes have a significant mitigating effect on the dispositions of certain criminal court cases. As a matter of fact, I think it is becoming clear that there is a growing epidemic in the United States of jails and prisons becoming the de facto place where these individuals are warehoused, which is extremely regrettable and unfortunate. But my burden of persuading prosecutors that autism is unique requires me to show how developmental disabilities and autism differ from mental illness, including PTSD. And the differences are as follows. First, the signs and symptoms of autism manifest between the ages of six months and two years (Ozonoff *et al.*, 2010), whereas age of onset for most mental illness is not so early in life. Second, autism is a neurological disorder (Mesibov & Sreckovic, 2017) that is present from birth. Just because the symptoms are not normally visible to the untrained eye until the second year of life does not mean a person is not affected by autism from birth. In the first six months of life, motor skills (Estes *et al.*, 2015), visual reception (*ibid.*) language (Swanson *et al.*, 2017), and eye gaze patterns of social scenes and situations (Chawarska, Macari & Shic, 2013; Jones & Klin, 2013; Shic, Macari & Chawarska, 2014) are observable in autistic infants. And while larger head circumference was confirmed in autistic toddlers of two to three years of age quite some time ago (Courchesne *et al.*, 2001; Hazlett *et al.*, 2005; Nordahl *et al.*, 2011), other studies show that autistic infants have an excessive amount of cerebrospinal fluid in the subarachnoid space surrounding the cortical surface of the brain (Shen *et al.*, 2017) before some of the more obvious symptoms of autism begin to appear. Infants at the six-month marker also have abnormalities in white matter from multiple fiber tracts across the brain (Wolff *et al.*, 2012). Additionally, functional connectivity MRI scans, which detect abnormal brain connectivity, were measured on 59 six-month-old infants and successfully predicted: abnormal brain connectivity in 9 of 11 infants who received an ASD diagnosis at age two; all 48 infants who did not receive a diagnosis by age two (Emerson *et al.*, 2017). Overall, it had a positive predictive value of 100 percent.

There is even some evidence that autism can (but doesn't necessarily) occur as a result of what happens in utero (Atladóttir *et al.*, 2010; Chess, 1976; Fox, Amaral & Van de Water, 2012; Xiang *et al.*, 2015; Zerbo *et al.*, 2013) and is also the result of genetics (Hallmayer *et al.*, 2011). While addiction, mental illness, and PTSD may all share a genetic component (Broekman, Olff & Boer, 2007; Kreek *et al.*, 2005; Uher, 2009), the age of onset for all of these conditions is usually later in life than 6–18 months. However, unlike Fragile X, Rett Syndrome, Williams Syndrome, Cohen Syndrome, Gillespie Syndrome, and 9q34 Deletion Syndrome, which are all present at birth, autism spectrum disorders have a tremendous amount of genetic heterogeneity. In other words, there is no complete knowledge of the genetic origin for autism spectrum disorders. While the etiology for most people with ASD is unknown, ASD can in some cases be explained by a specific genetic alteration (Rogers, Wehner & Hagerman, 2001). Future research needs to investigate how other disorders, such as the ones described above, affect a person at birth and how they might correlate with criminal justice involvement. If a link is found, what can be done to ensure fair and compassionate justice for both victims and perpetrators? Anecdotally, I have seen many cases where individuals with Fetal Alcohol Syndrome have ended up in the criminal justice system, so it is clear that this area of research needs more attention.

To bring it all back home, Mark Mahoney has argued that, in some cases, it is immoral to prosecute an autistic person. I have tried to flesh out the reasons for his position. Is he right? Let's briefly review what I have written to see if this position makes sense. Autism is unique and differs from mental illness. Though there is often a high comorbidity in autism with mental illnesses in general and anxiety in particular (Cage, Monaco & Newell, 2018), autism itself is a distinct condition. It occurs at birth through no fault of the autistic person. Every phase of development from birth onward is processed through the lens of autism, whereas an individual who develops schizophrenia or some trauma-based illness in their early 20s has not been impacted since infancy. Being born with autism shows. Autistic children aged 9–18 were observed to have the emotional maturity of someone two-thirds of their age (Weissman & Hendrick, 2014). Achievements in certain areas and extreme deficits in other areas exist side by side. Every defense lawyer representing an autistic client should know this. Uneven development is a hallmark of autism (Russo et al., 2007). Theory of mind, which means extreme difficulty in accessing the beliefs, desires, intentions, and subjectivity of another person (Haskins & Silva, 2006; Volkmar et al., 2005), is often apparent. As to Mahoney's position, I recognize that the autistic population is an extremely heterogenous group of people and that each case needs to proceed on an individualized basis, based on the facts and merits of each case. But when the situation allows for it, I strongly agree with Mahoney that, based on what we know about autism, some circumstances would make it immoral to prosecute an autistic person, assuming that they are a low risk to the community (no one is "no risk" entirely) and are amenable to treatment. In the best-case scenario of low risk, why would we want to imprison and almost certainly endanger a human being with the social or emotional age of a child, who does not present a danger to the community and is capable of learning from a situation? That cannot be defined as justice in any rational sense.

There is one last thing that needs to be mentioned. It is often noted in the literature that, supposedly, ASD individuals lack empathy. If prosecutors read this out of context, they may believe that this makes autistic people more dangerous and unfit for a probationary sentence, let alone a diversionary program. This myth of dangerousness is the opposite of the truth. To be crystal clear, autism is not associated with an antisocial personality disorder, sadism, or psychopathy. Simon Baron-Cohen in his ambitious and revolutionary book *The Science of Evil* (2012) puts empathy on a curve from zero to six. An individual who scores six may be extremely empathetic and attuned towards others, while an individual who scores zero has extreme trouble with this skill. Baron-Cohen says that having lack of empathy can be either useful or harmful. He calls these two dichotomous states of being zero positive and zero negative. A zero-negative person is someone who not only lacks empathy but also has no conscience. If a person has no conscience, it will lead them to do horrible things to others because they lack a moral code. As Baron-Cohen points out, empathy in a traditional sense is not the sole route to developing a moral code and a conscience that naturally lead to ethical behavior. In fact, Baron-Cohen points out, paradoxically, that zero-positive people (including some autistic individuals) can be "supermoral" (his word) rather than immoral.

He explains it this way: the main thing that autistic people want in the world is predictability. He thinks of autistic individuals as systematic thinkers and puts systems thinking on a curve from zero to six. In contrast to what we would think of as a typical autistic person, a zero-level systematic thinker can deal with lots of change and is not particularly interested in patterns. They can multitask, deal with interruptions, and handle surprises. A level-zero systems person, says Baron-Cohen, might notice that some church bells chimed but wouldn't be able to tell if they chimed in groups or how many different chimes there were. This could also be the case if two neurotypicals are sitting under an umbrella outside Starbucks and drinking coffee; they might hear the church bells but ignore them because they are focusing on each other. The two individuals engaging in conversation are, thus, participating in an emotional flow and exchange where conversation is unpredictable, changes from subject to subject occur, and success is determined by their emotional attunement to each other. On the other end of the systematic-thinking spectrum, by the time you get to level six, says Baron-Cohen, change is *toxic* to the individual. Level-six systematic thinkers have extreme anxiety when even small changes in their environment take place. He gives the example of an autistic child who watches the washing machine go round and round and screams if anyone tries to pull him away. Baron-Cohen says that this is why an autistic savant like Daniel Tammet (who could recite pi to 22,514 decimal places) is comforted by sameness and constancy. Pi never changes. Systemizers want the timeless, the predictability, the changelessness. In essence, they want to live in a completely controlled universe (Baron-Cohen, 2012), which is not possible in our world. Baron-Cohen notes that while huge talents can be conferred upon hyper-systematizing people as a result of being aware of the many details that neurotypicals would not pick up on, this often comes at a great price. This price is the tremendous difficulty in coping with change. Baron-Cohen argues that zero-positive empathy individuals might score zero or one on an empathy quotient but six on a systematizing quotient. This kind of empathy, argues Baron-Cohen, is not harmful and can actually lead to a highly ethical human being.

Baron-Cohen seems to say that difficulty coping with change leads to lack of empathy. This, however, can be compensated for when strict rules and guidelines that make logical sense to an autistic person are put into place to bring a sense of constancy back to their lives. We can use Baron-Cohen's model to understand why some individuals mentioned throughout this book fell afoul of the law. Darius McCollum wanted nothing more than the safety, predictability, and perceived security of conducting the subway, something he knew how to do and was good at. He felt that the outside world was unpredictable, changeable, and hostile to him, so he retreated to the underground world of subways where life remained the same. Neil Latson's routine of waiting outside the library was disrupted by the police who ordered him (a suspicious-looking person) to move away. Cubby Robison's fascination with explosions was his attempt to learn about a special interest in a controlled environment and in a way that would not hurt someone.

So, how can we account for this paradox of low empathy but high morality and ethical behavior? Baron-Cohen says that individuals with autism develop very strong moral codes through trial and error, though not in traditional ways. Unlike sociopaths or psychopaths who lack affective empathy and just don't care, autistic people live by codes of rules and the expectation of fairness. Of course, since these moral codes sometimes develop outside the boundaries of shared experience, it can result in misfires and errors and possibly land someone in trouble with the criminal justice system. But autistic people's inherent desire to act morally and do the right thing has enormous implications for the purposes of rehabilitation and whether someone is fit for a diversion program. I will speak to this shortly in more detail.

Even saying that autistic people "lack empathy" is not entirely true.

Empathy is no longer a unitary concept, but instead comprises two parts (Baron-Cohen, 2012; Decety & Meyer, 2008; Dziobek *et al.*, 2008, 2011; Jones *et al.*, 2010; Schwenck *et al.*, 2012; Singer, 2006; Zaki & Ochsner, 2012). Those two components are cognitive and affective empathy. Autistic individuals have a difficult time inferring the mental states (Zaki & Ochsner, 2012) of other people. This is related to the cognitive processing of emotions, which is different in ASD individuals (Fletcher-Watson *et al.*, 2014) than it is for neurotypicals. I would call this type of empathy "cognitive empathy" since it is based upon cognition, which leads to appropriate perspective taking, or lack thereof. However, affective empathy relies upon empathetic concern, which tends to be present in individuals with ASD (Davis, 1980; Dziobek *et al.*, 2008; Jones *et al.*, 2010; Rogers *et al.*, 2007; Schwenck *et al.*, 2012). Put another way, affective empathy is the recognition and response to other people's emotions (Blair, 2005), which we would not see in other diagnoses such as conduct disorder and other antisocial personality disorders (Jones *et al.*, 2010) or psychopathy (Blair, 2008). Where there is affective empathy, there is an emotion contagion. An example would be one baby crying triggering a second baby to cry (Holt *et al.*, 2018). Someone without cognitive empathy but with affective empathy might see an individual in distress and be personally distressed by this—but they may not know why that person is in distress. A person with cognitive empathy, however, uses inferential processes to attribute mental states to others by understanding the thoughts and feelings of the other person to comprehend why they are distressed. Additionally, as Blair (2008) points out, a psychopath has to have their cognitive empathy intact because otherwise they wouldn't know how to find other people's weaknesses and then exploit them. The key difference between autistics and psychopaths is that psychopaths are seemingly able to turn on and off their cognitive empathy and use it only when it is a means to an end (Drayton, Santos & Baskin-Sommers, 2018) and it helps their cause. A sociopath or a psychopath can turn their affective empathy on and off at will. They also lack remorse but have good mentalizing abilities, which is to say their cognitive empathy is intact (Blair, 2008). They can know exactly what their prey is feeling but not be swayed emotionally by that if they choose (Vrij, Granhag & Mann, 2010). This is in stark contrast to autistic individuals, who, on the whole, respond when other individuals are distressed but may not know what is causing the distress because they can't mentally process the thought or feeling states of others.

To restate: autism is not related to psychopathy (Loureiro *et al.*, 2018). It should be pointed out that the biggest risk factor in sex offender reoffending, particularly in the cases of touch offenses, is antisocial personality disorder (Hanson & Bussière, 1998; Hanson & Morton-Bourgon, 2005; Lehmann *et al.*, 2014; Mulder *et al.*, 2010; Seto & Eke, 2015), which is usually not seen in autistic people. In contrast, autistic people seem to be at a greater risk of offending when there is social naivete, social rejection, sexual rejection, and family conflict, and when they have been bullied (Allen *et al.*, 2008). Howlin (2004, p.302) lists the following scenarios as to why an individual might break the law.

- Individuals with ASD who have increased social naivete may be vulnerable to manipulation by others.

- An ASD individual's disruption of routines, or over-rigid adherence to rules, might lead to them becoming aggressive.

- A lack of understanding of social situations might lead to people with an ASD becoming aggressive.

- An ASD individual's obsessional interest might lead them to commit an offense in the pursuit of that interest, perhaps exacerbated by a failure to recognize the implications of their behavior for them and others.

So a psychopathic person may not care if they are breaking the law. Conversely, autistic people generally are more law abiding *as long as they know what the law is* (Mouridsen *et al.*, 2008; Woodbury-Smith *et al.*, 2005, 2006) and can receive treatment for the underlying issue. Evidence for this comes from the fact that autistic individuals reoffend at a low rate (Allen *et al.*, 2008) and are also more likely to complete their probation without a violation (Cheely *et al.*, 2012). Cheely *et al.* (2012) speculate that this is due to a combination of rule following, closer supervision by the adults in their lives, and less severe legal conditions/sanctions as a part of an autistic person's probation due to leniency.

Now that we have reviewed a different approach to seeking prosecutorial discretion in order to ask for a diversion agreement, let's look at how one might get to that goal.

Finding the Right Experts

The above information might be valid for autistic people on the whole, but unless these general facts fit into the specific facts of any particular case, they are useless. Whether a person is autistic or not, they have to demonstrate that they are a low safety risk to the community, on an individual basis.

How does a defense attorney find a competent expert to write an individualized risk assessment and translate autism into relatable terms for a prosecutor or judge? It's a valid and important question because it is not an easy task. From my anecdotal experience, most clinicians in the field of autism are child-centered, meaning that they do not do much work with autistic adults. In addition to that, many experts lack experience in forensic settings, leading to tepidness for becoming involved in matters where they may be asked to testify in court. In the vast majority of these cases that do not go to trial, not every expert who writes a report is asked to testify. But some are, for example at the sentencing hearing. Therefore, finding someone who is not only qualified but also wants to take on this role can be hugely challenging.

There is no shortage of forensic psychologists in the world. And there is no shortage of forensic psychologists saying that they know a lot about autism when, in fact, that is not their area of specialization. This is a big trap to avoid.

The Trap of Comorbidity

There is no question that comorbidities are common amongst the ASD population (American Psychiatric Association, 2013; World Health Organization, 2004), in general. Research shows that comorbidities, such as a mental illness, are very often but not always present in autistic offenders (Hofvander et al., 2009; Howlin & Moss, 2012; Tantam, 2000). The psychological comorbid diagnoses most often seen alongside autism are anxiety, depression, attention deficit hyperactivity disorder (ADHD), and intellectual disability (Masi et al., 2017) but can also include conduct disorder, oppositional defiant disorder, and PTSD.

Readers of this book should keep several things in mind. First, those in clinical settings observe that ASD diagnoses are often precipitated by the observation of other mental disorders, leading to difficult diagnostic procedures for even the most trained psychologist (Kamio et al., 2013). Takara and Kondo (2014) reported that 16 percent of all recently reported depressed patients actually were diagnosed with ASD after being diagnosed with depression. Therefore, autism is a diagnosis not usually suspected at first by clinicians treating adults. It is extremely important that any forensic psychologist be attuned to the possibility of an autism diagnosis. They also must know that the *Diagnostic and Statistical Manual of Mental Disorders, 5th Edition* specifies that for an ASD diagnosis to be valid, it has to have occurred apart from other child-onset diagnoses such as ADHD, social anxiety disorder, etc. (Ousley & Cermak, 2014). Thus, the diagnosis of autism should be considered primary.

Second, although there are instruments available to assess comorbidities in the ASD population, there is no gold standard (Belardinelli, Raza & Taneli, 2016). Would we really trust a forensic psychologist with limited training in autism to know what tests might be normed to screen for comorbidities in an ASD population? Would they even take the time to look up those tests and use them appropriately? These are questions that need to be considered.

Third, a secondary diagnosis can be misinterpreted as the primary diagnosis. For example, an individual who has been diagnosed with "conduct disorder" may in fact be having chronic meltdowns (Tick *et al.*, 2016) due to environmental triggers such as sensory overload or unexpected changes to their routine. This was the case for Neil Latson, mentioned earlier, who acted violently when his routine was disturbed. The literature often reports ASD individuals who have acted violently, and, indeed, there is literature to suggest that autistic individuals can behave in more aggressive ways than the general population (Hofvander *et al.*, 2019). To an unknowledgeable forensic psychologist, such people may easily be diagnosed as "oppositional defiant" rather than autistic. The question that a forensic psychologist would have to ask is: why does this violence happen within the context of autism? Some clues can be found in studies. One study found that, on blood draws, autistic children were aggressive 23 percent of the time, whereas the neurotypical control group scored at 0 percent aggression (Bronsard, Botbol & Tordjman, 2010). This was attributed to poorer coping skills and higher anxiety on the part of ASD children when faced with the stress of dealing with a needle. Bronsard *et al.* (2010) found that the antecedents to most of these aggressive behaviors were anxiety-related behaviors such as anxious agitation, paleness, screaming, sweating, or a facial expression of fear. A physiologically overactive sympathetic nervous system that is always on guard for danger (which is the case for autistic people) (Panju *et al.*, 2015) is naturally going to produce excitations and overreactions that can result in unintended violence or perceived self-defense. Taken in the wrong context, these behaviors might appear to be purely anxiety related or attributable to conduct disorder, but they are, in fact, rooted in autism. Anger contributes to some of these outbursts, but alexithymia (seen in about 55 percent of ASD individuals) (Milosavljevic *et al.*, 2016) can account for a reduced recognition of anger, which can be mitigated through interventions that are appropriate for this population. (Violence in ASD tends to be most associated with younger populations, specifically under the age of six, and between the ages of nine and eleven [Kanne & Mazurek, 2011].) Even depression can sometimes be a manifestation of autism when it is viewed as hopelessness related to the consistent failure to adapt to life and new situations, and the individual's recognition of their own limitations (Cashin & Yorke, 2016). Symptoms of autism, such as social withdrawal and abnormal speech patterns, can be confused with fatigue or psychomotor retardation normally associated with depression (Stewart *et al.*, 2006). With regards to PTSD, Haruvi-Lamdan, Horesh and Golan (2018) suggest that autism serves as a vulnerability marker by increasing the risk of exposure to traumatic events. Events like being bullied and/or experiencing sexual abuse as a child (Cappadocia, Weiss & Pepler, 2012; Edelson, 2010)—which unfortunately are highly common experiences for ASD individuals—can give rise to PTSD. More severe PTSD symptomology includes deficits in emotional regulation, negative self-perception, and interpersonal issues, which are the same symptoms that are exacerbated by ASD (King, 2010). Additional ASD traits that might exacerbate PTSD include maladaptive coping strategies, reduced help seeking, and cognitive rigidity (Haruvi-Lamdan *et al.*, 2018). As we can see, heterogeneity and comorbidity are so common in ASD that some researchers have even suggested subtyping other diagnoses under the umbrella of autism, with autism remaining the primary diagnosis (Lynn & Lynn, 2007; Ousley & Cermak, 2014).

An Autism Expert is Best

To avoid the trap of comorbidity, Mahoney (2019) strongly advises seeking an expert with a primary expertise in ASD. According to Mahoney, most non-ASD-oriented psychologists will use personality inventories and will arrive at a confusing array of diagnoses. The behaviors listed in the inventory or exhibited by the individual will be described in terms of personality disorders or mental illness when, instead, the behavior may simply be a common manifestation of ASD. Mahoney recommends that the lawyer look for a psychologist who is well versed in ASD to do an evaluation and then build from there. The ASD expert is in a better position to consider differential diagnoses than any original general forensic psychologist. As has been emphasized throughout this chapter, the ASD expert should tailor their exam to the individual. This includes receiving the detailed narrative that the family writes about their loved one, a detailed history including IEPs and other important school records, and diagnostic testing and lengthy interviews tailored to meet the needs of the individual on the spectrum. This may take multiple days or even several lengthy sessions to complete. After that, Mahoney recommends building a collaborative team by uniting additional professionals once the first report is established. The goal with the first report is to build a record of solid information backed up by data that the person in a forensic capacity can build upon later. Keep in mind that forensic psychologists and psychiatrists have different areas of specialization. Forensic psychologists will typically be more skilled at using neuropsychological testing, while psychiatrists are considered medical doctors with broad expertise (though they can specialize in various areas too). Also, the expert being hired should have no "blackmarks" on their record, such as disciplinary measures of lawsuits against them, and it is up to the lawyer to vet this. The expert should be board certified under a main accreditor, while also having professional certification and continuing education in the areas of specialization he or she works in. If the expert has testified in the past for the prosecution in the past, this can be a plus as it shows impartiality on the part of the evaluator in the eyes of the court or prosecutor. Finally, no reputable expert will make any kind or promise or guarantee to a lawyer that is necessarily favorable to their client. This is normal.

Using the Vineland test to augment life history data, as discussed earlier in this chapter, is highly recommended, along with a personality assessment like the MMPI-2. Most importantly, if an ASD diagnosis has not been made in the past for the individual, a battery of neuropsychological diagnostic tests should be given to firmly establish the diagnosis.

The Second Forensic Evaluation

From my own anecdotal experience, based on seven years of talking to people in the field, in order for even a lighter sentence to be considered for an autistic person, let alone diversion, several things have to be demonstrated.

- No matter what the charge, the evidence has to fit the client's story.

- The prosecutor has to be absolutely convinced that the person isn't a danger to society.

- When there is a direct victim, what do they want? (Sometimes prosecutors check this out and sometimes they don't.)

- Is there precedent to do so? In other words, have other prosecutors offered diversion under similar circumstances?

Let's take a look at the first and second points, because they have a direct bearing on the second forensic psychologist's examination; I will address the others in a later section.

First, metadata is everything. Consider a child pornography case, for example. The FBI investigators ask people under investigation which search terms they used to find the material, but they will eventually find this information anyway when the computer is sent to the lab for analysis. If the person tried deleting files or even the peer-to-peer software itself from the computer, this will eventually be recovered and used as part of the discovery evidence to establish consciousness of guilt. But I have drawn the conclusion, from every defense lawyer I have talked to, that deleting the software out of a compulsive habit and then downloading it again does not necessarily mean that a person undertook this act to cover up their actions because they knew they were committing a federal crime. One would have to measure their level of sophistication in carrying out these actions. Did they do it sloppily? Did they take extra precautions that the average person wouldn't have known about? Did they encrypt their files? Were there saved chats with others that showed consciousness of guilt? These are all important questions. As I have already stated, many sexual crimes that ASD individuals fall into involve masturbation (Haracopos & Pedersen, 1992; Ray, Marks & Bray-Garretson, 2004), which not only is inherently shameful for most people but can also be a compulsive behavior. Merely deleting the software is not an overly sophisticated thing to do, nor is it a "policeman at the elbow" test that carries any significance of consciousness of guilt. There are many behaviors that all individuals display that they may be ashamed of and want to cover up. Those behaviors, however, may not necessarily be illegal. All lawyers should be prepared to ascertain whether their client deleted the software and to argue that this doesn't necessarily display consciousness of guilt, especially when looking at the bigger picture. Additionally, lawyers must be prepared for the possibility of false confessions, as discussed earlier in the book. A second forensic psychologist who does not specialize in autism spectrum disorders should ideally follow the lead of the autism expert on this delicate and complicated issue.

Second, the prosecutor has to be convinced that the defendant isn't a danger to society. There are both good and bad ways to do this for an autistic defendant. First, earlier research in this chapter outlines what makes the autistic personality unique in a criminal setting and distinctly differentiates those qualities from someone with low or no empathy. Those individuals with low or no empathy include a psychopath or a malignant narcissist, or someone with low impulse control. The defendant's attorney/advocate must work to tie the alleged criminal activity to the behavioral characteristics of the defendant and to their life before the crime took place. If it can be shown that the autistic defendant has always been law abiding and has no criminal record, this can strengthen that position. But oftentimes, this will not be enough for prosecutors. They will want what is referred to as a psychosexual examination and sometimes a polygraph test. Unfortunately, there is scant research on how both of these procedures apply to individuals with developmental disabilities or autism spectrum disorders. However, I want to examine why they may be areas of concern. In doing so, I hope to teach advocates ways to help convince prosecutors that they should question the legitimacy of these instruments when they are being used on autistic individuals.

Forensic psychologists have several risk assessment tools at their disposal. Some of the tools have more validity than others. For example, the Child Pornography Offender Risk Tool (CPORT) developed by Seto and Eke (2015) is considered by Lawrence A. Dubin, Esq. (the author's father) and Allely (2018) to be an appropriate assessment tool to use for autistic people because it does not count volume (or number of images) as a measure of dangerousness. Anthony *et al.* (2013) found that collecting items related to special interests is common among autistic people and not necessarily indicative of a sexual interest. The CPORT comprises seven static areas related to the age, life history, and content found on the defendant's computer. Other assessment tools such as the Children, Internet, and Sex Cognitions Scale are used to determine the likelihood that someone has engaged in a contact touch offense beyond looking at child pornography (Kettleborough & Merdian, 2013). There are many other evaluations that forensic psychologists use, and their efficacy among autistic populations has yet to be determined. However, my experience in helping families over the years has proven to me that the two evaluations that prosecutors are most interested in are the Abel Assessment and the polygraph.

The Abel Assessment is based upon the principle of "visual reaction time" when a person views the image of another person from any specific age demographic, such as a boy, girl, man, or woman (Gray *et al.*, 2015). It purports to measure how long it takes a person to react to the age of a person and then make a judgment about what age group is most attractive to the test taker. Gene Abel, an American psychiatrist and the designer of a sex offender assessment instrument that screens for sexual deviancy in test takers, emphasizes that visual reaction time is not the only factor used in degerming whom one is attracted to. It is combined with 15 other factors that are used as a secret propriety algorithm that only Abel and his company know about (Gray *et al.*, 2015). Needless to say, Abel has received criticism for this secrecy but says it is designed this way as a safeguard against someone beating the test. Test takers are presented with images of both scantily clad and fully dressed individuals in different age groups: adults (21 or older), teenagers (14–17), grade-school children (6–13), and preschool children (5 and younger). Among the pictures are slides depicting exhibitionism, voyeurism, children in swimsuits, a male and female hugging, a male and female "suffering" (no clear meaning as to how), two males hugging, and two females hugging (Wilson & Miner, 2016). The test takers see these sets of images twice. The first time they see them, they are asked to familiarize themselves with the images. On the second go around, participants are asked to rate each image on a scale of one to seven, where one is very arousing and seven is highly disgusting. Their visual reaction time, or how much time they spend looking at each of the photos, is also measured to see if written responses are consistent with reaction time. This occurs on the second viewing of the pictures.

Visual-reaction time testing is based on a few assumptions. First, it is assumed that the longer a viewer looks at a picture, the more attracted they are to that age group (Laws & Gress, 2004). In the 1950s, it was found that heterosexual men took longer to look at pictures of women than men, while homosexual men took longer to look at pictures of nude men than nude women (Zamanski, 1956). Researchers explain this through a cognitive mechanism known as sexual content induced delay (SCID) (Greer & Bellard, 1996; Greer & Melton, 1997). SCID simply means that when sexual content is introduced to an individual at random, an involuntary longer lag time will follow, out of sheer curiosity, since it is such a novel stimulus. This presumes that viewers will take a longer time to move on to the next slide when sexual content is present. Finally, researchers believe that the longer the latency period is (meaning how long one waits to press the button to move on to the next image), the more one is attracted to the picture and thus the age group. Researchers believe that denying sexual attraction is easier than affirming sexual attraction, which likely requires a longer look at the stimulus (Imhoff et al., 2012). In other words, we typically do not stare at people we are not attracted to.

There are several problems with this approach being utilized on autistic people. To begin with, I could not find a single study corroborating its efficacy for the autistic population or a version of it normed for those on the spectrum. The test seems to rely on visual reaction time to determine one's level of sexual attraction to an age group, plus other factors we are not privy to, since Abel's methods are propriety. To our knowledge, the test does not seem to take into consideration other factors such as variabilities in visual spatial processing, sustained attention in someone with a neurological difference, and sensory integration and motor differences in disabled populations. For example, when taking the Integrated Visual and Auditory (IVA) Continuous Performance Test (CPT) designed to measure visual reaction time, autistic individuals showed significant impairment in their ability to control their response to visual cues (Chien et al., 2014). Another study showed that visual reaction time tends to be prolonged in autistic children and adolescents (Bhakare & Vinchurkar, 2015). (Keep in mind that prolonged response time would indicate an attraction to a particular age group, using Abel's methodology.) Other studies using electrophysiological and behavioral indicators (audiovisual reaction time tests) of processing visual and audio stimuli have revealed deficits in general audiovisual temporal processing in

ASD individuals (Martínez-Sanchis, 2014). Moreover, autistic individuals have consistently shown problems with over-focused attention (Todd *et al.*, 2009) and with shifting visual attention from one stimulus to another (Tager-Flusberg, Joseph & Folstein, 2001; Townsend, Harris & Courchesne, 1996; Wainwright-Sharp & Bryson, 1993). Psychomotor retardation (or slower motoring functioning) can be seen in autistic individuals (Ghaziuddin & Al-Owain, 2013), which may indicate how slow or fast their visual reaction time to an image is. Research is definitive that ASD individuals have difficulties with sensory integration, and McKeen (2013) believes that, in light of this fact, more research should be conducted on visual reaction time testing with autistic individuals.

An adapted assessment of the Abel is purported by its creators Gene Abel and Gerry D. Blasingame, (Blasingame *et al.*, 2011) to be normed for individuals with intellectual impairments and developmental disabilities. Called the Abel-Blasingame Assessment System for individuals with intellectual disabilities (ABID), the ABID differs from the Abel in a few ways. Most of the differences appear to be the ways in which the testers gather information from the test takers in the pre-test phase. First, the clinician reviews the test taker's file for an IQ score and if one does not exist or is not documented in the records, he or she determines this before beginning the ABID. Second, the pre-test interview between the tester and test taker is semi-structured, as opposed to being completely self-generated by the test taker. This allows the evaluator to adapt language or wording of a particular question to the unique characteristics of each case. To compensate for working memory issues, evaluators are encouraged to make sure the test taker understands all the questions they are answering and not rush between questions and answers. In other words, they go slowly. The use of visual aids are included as a supplement to the written material since those with developmental disabilities often benefit from visual aids in comprehending or understanding material. Blasingame *et al.* have taken into account the tendency for the individual to want to please authority, and have modified oral questions in the interview accordingly to mitigate against that. The evaluator also makes sure there is sufficient time for breaks and extends the evaluation over several days, if the situation necessitates. The reading comprehension level for the written questionnaire in the ABID is at a second grade level to ensure adequate reading comprehension. According to Blasingame *et al.* the ABID instrument has a high internal consistency rating for individuals using it. Anecdotally, I do know a few ASD individuals who have taken the ABID and whose test scores have indicated that they do not have pedophile tendencies. This, of course, if true for a particular defendant in question, is extremely helpful and useful information to be able to give to a prosecutor. However, the ABID still uses the principle of visual reaction time, which involves visual spatial processing, motor skills impairments, prolonged attention to a visual stimulus, all of which are documented features of autism in the literature. Therefore, a defense attorney might want to inquire about the ABID as opposed to the Abel for their ASD client, keeping in mind that the actual test to measure sexual attraction involves visual reaction time for both exams.

Which now brings us to the polygraph, also used by prosecutors as a tool to gauge truthfulness as to one's past sexual history. Most readers will be somewhat familiar with what the polygraph does and what it purports to measure. As of this writing, there is a stunning dearth of research with regards to the efficacy of polygraphs on autistic individuals. However, we are left with some clues. In one study, researchers (Sasikumar & Adalarasu, 2015) measured blood flow states in 40 neurotypical children and 40 autistic children between the ages of 8 and 13 using photo plethysmography. Photo plethysmography is a noninvasive method to measure the arterial and venous blood volume changes near the surface of the skin such as in the finger and the earlobe. The same study also measured the galvanized skin responses of both groups (galvanized skin responses are used in conjunction with heart rate to measure stress levels on the polygraph). The study found that the galvanic skin response of autistic children is unpredictable—it was unable to determine when a child is stressed and when a child is relaxed. It also showed that the heart rate of the autism group was higher than the control group due to higher stress levels (*ibid.*). Other studies showed inconsistent heart arousal patterns in autistic individuals, whereas more typical patterns were demonstrated in neurotypical individuals (Goodwin *et al.*, 2006; Groden *et al.*, 2005). Ming *et al.* (2005) remark that autistic individuals have reduced parasympathetic nervous system activity, meaning that there are signs of autonomic dysfunction. Hirstein, Iversen and Ramachandran (2001) state that autistics do not have normal baseline activity in their galvanic skin responses. Another study showed elevated heart rate and blunted phasic electrodermal activity in people with ASDs when movie watching compared with a control group (Kushki *et al.*, 2013). Furthermore, interrogation tools are often used in conjunction with the polygraph (Chaffin, 2011), often leading to false confessions when the results are inconclusive or indicate deception (Iacono, 2009) in neurotypical offenders. I wrote earlier in the book about the fact that autistic people tend to want to please authority and that there are many false confessions on record for individuals with developmental disabilities. The use of the polygraph for this population should be avoided in establishing someone's level of risk or dangerousness for the reasons already expressed.

Relying on attraction measures or polygraphs to determine eligibility for a diversion program, or, worse, using charge bargaining and upping the charges, is a huge mistake for a prosecutor to make in relation to an autistic defendant.

To summarize, it is imperative that the second forensic expert and the ASD expert work in tandem, using appropriate instruments and interviewing techniques, to present a united front of information to the prosecutor's office. There should be as few discrepancies in the two reports as possible.

The Argument for Diversion

Armed with both reports and a clear foundational history of the autistic defendant, the aim is to ask a prosecutor to consider a pretrial diversion program. The history of pretrial diversion dates back to 1947 in the United States. In that year, the judicial conference recommended that "deferred prosecution" be offered to juvenile offenders who seemed to have the capacity to be rehabilitated (Ulrich, 2002). This program placed the youthful offenders under the watch of a probation officer for a definite period of time, and at the end of the supervision, if the person met the conditions of their diversion successfully, the charges would be dropped. In 1967, the Johnson Administration followed recommendations from the commission on law enforcement and juvenile justice and adopted diversion as a mainstream practice for juveniles. Diversion emerged as a major strategy to deal with crime in the 1970s (National Association of Pretrial Services Agencies, 2019). Some of the benefits that arose from pretrial diversion were a conservation of the court's time and resources, an opportunity for rehabilitation without permanently stigmatizing someone, and reducing the risk of someone becoming a repeat offender (Rackmill, 1996). This is because when someone has a criminal record, they have less to lose and less incentive to stay clean.

Under the jail diversion model (which was meant to keep offenders out of jail), there was a surge of community-based treatment for offenders with mental disabilities in the late 1990s and early 2000s (Heilbrun & Griffin, 1998; Steadman, Davidson & Brown, 2001; Wexler & Winick, 1996). Traditional eligibility for diversion programs, not surprisingly, used risk factors to exclude certain individuals based upon certain issues, like potential substance abuse difficulties, level of social support available to help the individual succeed, history of juvenile offending, and general criminogenic factors, such as whether one has offended previously or on multiple occasions (Fisher, Wolff & Roy-Bujnowski, 2003). Also, not surprisingly, sex offenders were and are traditionally excluded for consideration when it comes to pretrial diversion (Steadman, 2007). Traditional sex offender literature suggests that offenders often use denial, minimalism, and manipulation, and continue to reoffend (Pratley & Goodman-Delahunty, 2011), which most of the prosecutorial community believes is true. Contrast this to recidivism studies, which show that 0.2 percent of child pornography users in general recidivate for actual hands-on, contact sex offenses (Goller *et al.*, 2016). A meta-analysis from other authors found that out of 1247 child pornography offenders, the number was a little higher, though still only 2 percent (Seto, Hanson & Babchishin, 2011). The Bureau of Justice Statistics found that 5.3 percent of all registrants recidivated within three years, whereas 68 percent of non-sex offenders reoffended within three years (Bureau of Justice Statistics, 2003). Furthermore, as I have previously mentioned, *antisociality* is the major risk factor in sexual offending against children (Hanson & Bussière, 1998; Quinsey, 1986; Seto, 2008, 2013), a trait not commonly found in those on the autism spectrum (as opposed to social awkwardness, which is found in those on the spectrum). The gap between what is believed by the prosecutorial community and by the social science researchers is vast. It suggests that members of the autism community who are being charged with a sex crime are not necessarily bad candidates for diversion.

Specialty courts can sometimes be the midwives of a good diversion program. Two things helped to facilitate these courts coming into being. The first is that the opening up of psychiatric hospitals in the 1960s with the passing of the Community Mental Health Centers Act (Feldman, 2003) led to the unintentional transferring of patients from inpatient settings to prisons and jails (Farmer *et al.*, 2017; Hnatow, 2015; Shenson, Dubler & Michaels, 1990; Torrey *et al.*, 2014). And second, the war on drugs has exacerbated this problem (Hafemeister & George, 2012; Torrey, 1997; Walsh & Holt, 1999). Thus, we have created mental health courts, drug courts, veterans' courts (for those suffering from wartime PTSD), and juvenile diversion programs, each as a kind of specialty court designed to steer these specific individuals out of the criminal justice system and give them community support. The use of drug courts began with a single judge who ordered Miami, Florida, defendants to receive treatment for their drug use in lieu of jail (Fulkerson, 2009). By 2001, there were already more than 700 drug courts being used throughout the United States (Harrison & Scarpitti, 2002). Veterans' treatment courts are also a relatively new invention, with the first one coming into existence in 2004 during the time of the Iraq War (Baldwin, 2016). And mental health courts, which began in Broward County, Florida, in the late 1990s, have become commonplace. As of 2010, there were already 200 mental health courts operating throughout the United States (Fisler, 2015; Hughes & Peak, 2012). Bold, innovative ideas can be thought up and implemented within relatively short periods of time if enough stakeholders are motivated.

Two approaches to specialty courts predominate and, in my mind, are not mutually exclusive. One is the school of therapeutic jurisprudence, which sees the court process as taking the most non-adversarial route possible to help the offender psychologically and, in the process, contribute to the best interests of society (Haley, 2016). Typically, this philosophy is used in drug possession cases that might be considered a victimless crime. The second philosophy is called restorative justice. Restorative justice seeks to reconcile the harm done by the offender to their community by an act of rectification to restore both the offender and the harmed party and make them as whole as possible. Courts typically allow a combination of therapeutic intervention, vocational training, mediation between the parties, and accountability of the individual (Centre for Justice & Reconciliation, 2017; Haley, 2016). The belief here is that both parties, along with society, can be made whole without using entirely punitive means.

We are taking baby steps towards being where we should be in implementing diversion or specialty courts for autistic individuals. The only autism court for juveniles that exists in the United States as of the date of this writing is in Las Vegas, Nevada. Judge Soonhee Bailey (also known as "Sunny") set up her court for autistic children charged with domestic battery charges, or battery on a school teacher/employee. These are charges that might otherwise be felonies or serious juvenile offenses requiring prolonged detention in a state-run facility. Autistic courts give autistic youth an alternative to that fate (de Leon, 2019). Presumably, charges involving battery are listed because they are likely to occur during a meltdown. Detention Alternative for Autistic Youth (DAAY) seeks to screen autistic children into the program before they enter the juvenile justice system. Once it is determined that a child is on the spectrum, they end up in Judge Bailey's court or DAAY. Judge Bailey believes that her court helps autistic youth to become successful so that they don't end up in the adult criminal justice system. DAAY staff believe that autistic children do not get their needs met in a mental health service or a juvenile delinquency program.

There is no diversion court in America for autistic adults, in spite of the fact that many specialty courts rightfully exist for other adult populations in state courts. Why is the autism population currently excluded? Part of the reason I wrote this book was to highlight the absence of such a program. Pretrial diversion could be implemented on a wide scale for autistic adults if plans were put into place to follow through with it. In the federal system, United States attorneys are actually permitted to offer pretrial diversion for most crimes but rarely do this when it comes to a possession of child pornography crime.

Let me illustrate by quoting their own guidelines. According to the U.S. Department of Justice's guidelines for diversion, United States attorneys are theoretically given tremendous latitude. These are the requirements that a defendant must meet to be eligible for a pretrial diversion program:

> The U.S. Attorney, in his/her discretion, may divert any individual against whom a prosecutable case exists and who is not:
>
> 1. Accused of an offense which, under existing Department guidelines, should be diverted to the State for prosecution;
>
> 2. A person with two or more prior felony convictions;
>
> 3. A public official or former public official accused of an offense arising out of an alleged violation of a public trust; or
>
> 4. Accused of an offense related to national security or foreign affairs. (U.S. Department of Justice, 2015b)

As you can see from reading the above, crimes related to the possession of child pornography are *not* excluded for consideration of diversion by rules that govern United States attorneys. Yet in reality, pretrial diversion is rarely, if ever, offered to a defendant for the crimes that an autistic defendant might get arrested for in the federal system.

Furthermore:

> A. Divertees are initially selected by the U.S. Attorney based on the eligibility criteria stated in JM 9-22.100:
>
> 1. At the pre-charge stage; or
>
> 2. At any point (prior to trial) at which a PTD (pretrial diversion) agreement is effected.
>
> B. Participation in the program by the offender is voluntary:
>
> 1. The divertee must sign a contract agreeing to waive his/her rights to a speedy trial and presentment of his/her case within the statute of limitations;
>
> 2. The divertee must have advice of counsel, and if he/she cannot afford counsel, one will be appointed for him/her upon his/her application to the Chief Pretrial Services Officer (or Chief Probation Officer). Appointment of Counsel will be made through the United States Magistrate. Inquiries by magistrates should be directed to the Criminal Justice Act Division, Administrative Office of the United States Courts, (202) 727-2800, for expenditure authorizations.

C. All information obtained in the course of making the decision to divert an offender is confidential, except that written statements may be used for impeachment purposes. *See* USA Form 185, Letter to Offender, this Manual at 713.

D. Upon determining eligibility of an offender for PTD, the U.S. Attorney should refer the case along with the investigative agent's report to either the Chief Pretrial Services Officer or the Chief Probation Officer for a recommendation on the potential suitability of the offender for supervision. *See* USA Form 184, this Manual at 714.B814. The Chief Pretrial Services Officer (or the Chief Probation Officer) may make preliminary recommendations to the U.S. Attorney. As part of the background investigation, Pretrial Services will arrange with the United States Marshal's Office to have the divertee fingerprinted and to have such fingerprints submitted to the FBI on card FD-249. At the same time Pretrial Services should request notification of any prior record on the divertee from the FBI Identification Division Records.

E. If it is determined that PTD is appropriate for an offender, supervision should be tailored to the offender's needs and may include employment, counseling, education, job training, psychiatric care, etc. Many districts have successfully required restitution or forms of community service as part of the pretrial program. Innovative approaches are strongly encouraged.

The program of supervision which is recommended is outlined in the PTD Agreement, agreed upon by all parties, and administered by Pretrial Services.

F. *The Pretrial Diversion Agreement.* The diversion period begins upon execution of a Pretrial Diversion Agreement. The Agreement (USA Form 186, Criminal Resource Manual at 715) outlines the terms and conditions of supervision and is signed by the offender, his/her attorney, the prosecutor, and either the Chief Pretrial Services Officer or the Chief Probation Officer. The offender must acknowledge responsibility for his or her behavior, but is not asked to admit guilt.

G. *Successful completion of program/termination from program. The U.S. Attorney will formally decline prosecution upon satisfactory completion of program requirements.* Notice of satisfactory completion will be provided to the U.S. Attorney by either the Chief Pretrial Services Officer or the Chief Probation Officer. In addition, the Chief Pretrial Services Officer (or the Chief Probation Officer) will file an FBI Disposition Form R-84 so that the record will indicate successful completion/charges dropped.

H. *Breach of Agreement.* Upon breach of conditions of the Agreement by the divertee, the Chief Pretrial Services Officer (or the Chief Probation Officer) will so inform the U.S. Attorney, who, in his/her discretion, may initiate prosecution. When prosecution is resumed, the U.S. Attorney must furnish the offender with notice.

The decision to terminate an individual from continuing to participate in pretrial diversion based upon breach of conditions rests exclusively with the U.S. Attorney, with advice from either the Chief Pretrial Services Officer or the Chief Probation Officer. (U.S. Department of Justice Archives, 2015)

I want to call your attention to this key sentence from the above quotation: "Divertees are initially selected by the U.S. Attorney based on the eligibility criteria stated in JM 9-22.100" (*ibid.*). The reason that this chapter has focused so much on persuading prosecutors who typically remain skeptical about diversion is that prosecutors are the only ones who can facilitate diversion. Prosecutors are the gatekeepers. A judge has to approve the diversion deal should the prosecutor initiate one, but no one on the judiciary can implement diversion on their own.

A summary of the arguments for diversion when a deserving autistic defendant is charged is now given.

- Since the late 1940s, diversion has been a recognized principle of our justice system, acknowledging that certain juveniles who can be rehabilitated deserve an alternative to a permanent criminal record.

- We recognize that some juveniles deserve diversion because their brains (particularly frontal lobes) have not fully developed.

- Autistic individuals have incredibly uneven development. While many have extremely high IQ, the same individuals often lag behind in their emotional and adaptive development, sometimes having the adaptive age of a child, as can be seen on Vineland test scores.

- Autistic individuals are not, on the whole, prone to antisociality or psychopathy and thus tend not to be dangerous.

- Autistic individuals have trouble finding employment, so a way to bypass a permanent criminal record for a low-risk individual benefits the entire community and the individual.

- An autistic individual might have lacked full appreciation as to the nature of their crimes when they committed them because of their uneven development.

- Unlike some individuals with mental illness who might have the benefit of a mental health court, autistic individuals' development was affected from the time they were infants, and there is no equivalent court for them.

- Autistic people are likely to be rule followers and, thus, good candidates for diversion programs.

- United States attorneys are not prohibited from offering pretrial diversion to individuals convicted of a child pornography crime. Individuals who commit sex offenses generally have very low rates of recidivism. This should also be kept in mind at state court levels.

- If a person violates the diversion agreement, the charges get reinstated.

- Diversion can be considered a deterrent for autistic people who, as part of the program, would still have to go through extensive supervision for a prolonged period of time.

- As of this date, the Virginia Legislature has a bill pending that would permit autistic individuals to be granted diversion under appropriate circumstances. The idea is slowly gaining traction.

Lesser Included Offenses or Reduction of Charges

Diversion is an ideal outcome that won't happen in the vast majority of cases, even with the best of reasons and evidence that it should. The next best thing to diversion is a sentence that doesn't include incarceration or sex offender registration. In the next chapter, I will discuss in detail the catastrophic effects that jails and prisons have on the autistic population. Right now, I want to explore a few ways to get prosecutors to consider lesser included offenses that don't involve jail time or registration.

I spoke earlier about how prosecutors may (and may not) consult with the victims of a case when trying to determine the charges and punishment of a defendant. But it would do us all well to remember that in the United States, the victim is not actually the official "victim" in any given case. The state or the government is technically the victim (McBarnet, 1983). People might simply assume that all victims of crime would want complete retribution if that were possible but, counterintuitively, that does not seem to be true all of the time. One study of crime victims in Britain showed that over 40 percent surveyed said that they would have accepted an opportunity to meet their offender, and close to 60 percent of victims said that they would be willing to accept a reparative activity from their offender (Strang & Sherman, 2003). Another study of 34 crime victims in Canada said that the majority of victims were satisfied with their experience in a restorative justice program, which gave the victim and offender professionally guided mediation (van Camp & Wemmers, 2013). One meta-analysis taken from 22 studies and 35 restorative justice programs showed that victims were more satisfied with a restorative justice approach than the more traditional criminal justice approach (Latimer, Dowden & Muise, 2001). Another meta-analysis of findings from several studies showed that restorative justice programs had a 7 percent reduction on the rate of recidivism than purely punitive forms of justice (Bonta *et al.*, 2006). Punitive forms of justice are not the only tools that the justice system has to help society to reduce crime. Based on the evidence from studies over the years, many scholars believe that the restorative model is as efficacious and possibly superior to the punitive approach to crime (Dancig-Rosenberg & Gal, 2012). Unfortunately, excessive prosecutorial loads mean that sometimes offices are so busy that they don't have the time or resources to let victims know that the defendant has made bail or keep them posted as to the status of their victimizer's case (Gershowitz & Killinger, 2011). This implies that the victim's perspective or wishes can occasionally be ignored.

But what if the wishes of the victim were taken into consideration? Would victims be more receptive to defendants if they knew that they had an autism spectrum disorder and perhaps lacked the level of criminal intent that most defendants have? We don't know. We do know that many victims did not realize that their victimizer had a disorder at the time that the crime happened. Sometimes, the defendants themselves have not even been diagnosed with autism pre-adjudication. However, evidence taken over the course of several decades has shown that when push comes to shove, the general public tends to be more sympathetic to individuals with disabilities who have committed crimes than to their neurotypical counterparts (Garvey, 1998; Gibbons, Gibbons & Kassin, 1981).

When we speak of autism specifically, opinions may vary as to whether crime victims would have a better understanding of their victimizer's intentions with an autism diagnosis present or whether it might work against a defendant. After all, there have been plenty of negative media portrayals and there is plenty of stigma with regards to autistic individuals who have committed violent crimes (Brewer, Zoanetti & Young, 2017), such as Elliot Rodger, Adam Lanza, and Dylann Roof. However, one recent study involving 160 participants showed that mock jury participants were more favorable to a person *after* finding out about his autism diagnosis (Maras, Marshall & Sands, 2019). Participants were divided into two groups: one group who was told about a defendant's ASD and the other who was not. Both groups of participants read a vignette involving a 27-year-old male who was arrested on a charge of assault and battery of a police officer. It stated that the defendant behaved aggressively when the officer tried to restrain him.

When the officer tried to place cuffs on him, the defendant became violent and struck the officer. In court, the fictitious defendant presented with all the usual symptoms that one might expect of an autistic person, such as high anxiety, poor eye contact, and repetitive behaviors. Not surprisingly, the group who did not know that the defendant had ASD thought he appeared suspicious, rude, aggressive, and dishonest, and lacked remorse, was unhelpful, was off-putting, possessed aggressive tendencies, and should take responsibility for his actions. On the other hand, the ones who knew that he had ASD felt he was honest, rude but sympathetic, and displayed excessive candor, believed his ASD was responsible for the assault and battery, and saw him as overwhelmed and anxious. In other words, both groups were presented with the same set of facts but had completely different opinions of this fictitious person based on whether they knew he had an ASD diagnosis.

Crime victims may not be as forgiving. But then again, there has never been an attempt to use restorative justice with autistic defendants and their victims. I believe that a specialization in court mediation when it comes to restorative justice needs to come into existence for the autism population. More specifically, for the specific goal of asking a prosecutor to reduce the charges to a lesser included offense, it would be extremely helpful to have a victim's blessing (this would certainly not guarantee that outcome, but it might help). Until there is court mediation in place for autistic people in lieu of sentences that favor incarceration, defense attorneys will have to go through prosecutor's offices or the victim's personal attorney and delicately and sensitively explain the situation to see if a victim might be flexible and agree to a non-incarceration charge and/or sentence. As we have seen from the aforementioned studies, many crime victims have historically been open to forms of restorative justice in which the defendant and victim of a crime can be made whole. If that has happened in the past, why would it not be possible for individuals with developmental disabilities? A strong argument could be made to the prosecutor that if the victim is okay with a sentence of non-incarceration, the government should not object either.

Some prosecutors will also look at their own jurisdiction's history or other jurisdictions to see whether a similar sentence has ever been given under comparable circumstances. After all, most prosecutors don't want to be "the first" to offer a lenient sentence for an otherwise serious crime. While we normally consider assessing sentencing disparities in fashioning an appropriate sentence to be a function that the judge will handle (Yang, 2015), prosecutors also want to make sure that they are not giving unequal treatment. To that end, below are some cases where autism was considered and this resulted in a non-incarceration sentence. In all the federal cases involving child pornography, the autistic defendants were originally charged with receipt and sometimes distribution, subsequently having those more serious charges dropped by the prosecutor and the lesser included charge of possession of child pornography as the charge to which they all pled guilty. Because of mandatory minimums, a sentence of non-incarceration would not have been possible without the receipt and distribution charges being dropped first by the prosecutor.

- In United States v. Blattner (2008), an 18-year-old with a developmental disability was charged with having explosives in his college dorm and at his parents' home. The sentencing guidelines called for 24–30 months' imprisonment. He got five years' probation.

- In United States v. Carlsson (2016), an autistic man pled guilty to possession of child pornography. Two forensic psychologists examined him and opined that his ASD played a substantial role in the commission of the offense and said he was a low-risk individual. The sentencing guidelines called for 78–97 months' imprisonment. He received ten years of supervised release (the equivalent of probation).

- In United States v. Carpenter (2009), a 41-year-old autistic man pled guilty to possessing child pornography. Forensic psychologists said that he lacked the appreciation of the harm that possessing the images had on the victims. He was also deemed a low risk by forensic psychologists to reoffend. The sentencing guidelines called for 51–63 months' imprisonment. He received up to five years' probation.

- In United States v. Danaher (2010), an autistic defendant was charged with having just one image on his computer. A forensic evaluation determined that he had limited cognitive decision-making and social skills. He pled guilty. Unbelievably, for just one image, the sentencing guidelines called for 97–121 months in prison. He received ten years of supervised release, or probation.

- In United States v. DeHaven (2009), an autistic defendant pled guilty to possession of child pornography. The sentencing guidelines called for 78–97 months in prison. He received one day time served.

- In State of Nebraska v. Getzfred (2010), a 22-year-old autistic defendant was charged in state court with eight counts of possessing child pornography and three counts of delivery of child pornography. The presentence report noted that numerous experts had offered written testimony as to the debilitating effect that prison would have on this individual, stating that he would not survive the experience.

The sentencing guidelines called for 12–240 months in prison. He received eight years' probation.

- In United States v. Joy (2008), an autistic defendant pled guilty to possession of child pornography. Two experts offered testimony. The sentencing guidelines called for 57–71 months in prison. He received time served (no prison).

- In Commonwealth v. Kelmar (2010), a 19-year-old autistic defendant was charged with carnal knowledge of a child of 13 years of age. A psychologist evaluated him and determined that he had ASD. The sentencing guidelines called for ten years' imprisonment. He was sentenced to ten years' probation with restitution to his victim.

- In United States v. Keskin (2017), a 31-year-old autistic defendant pled guilty to child pornography. The sentencing guidelines called for 97–121 months in prison. He received 15 years of supervised release, or probation, with individualized therapy designed for his autism.

- In United States v. Meiller (2009), an autistic defendant pled guilty to possession of child pornography. He had a high-school grade-point average of 1.05 and the psychologist evaluating him thought that he was at low risk of reoffending. The sentencing guidelines called for 57–91 months in prison. He received 30 years' supervised release, or probation.

- In United States v. Munson (2009), an autistic defendant pled guilty to possession of child pornography. The sentencing guidelines called for 51–63 months. He received three months in jail and a mental health treatment program focused specifically on Asperger's Syndrome (as it was called at the time).

- In United States v. Peterson (2016), a 25-year-old autistic man was charged with enticing a minor into sexual activity by sending lewd texts to an undercover officer. Four evaluations took place and he immediately sought treatment for what he did, which was tailored to his ASD. The sentencing guidelines called for 15–21 months in prison. He received four years' probation.

- In United States v. Rodriguez (2014), charges were dismissed without prejudice due to the defendant's incompetency to stand trial. He was charged with receipt and possession of child pornography. The sentencing guidelines called for up to 240 months in prison.

- In United States v. Wilson (2012), an 18-year-old autistic defendant pled guilty to transportation of obscene material (the lesser included charge of possession, receipt, and distribution of child pornography). He voluntarily checked himself into a rehabilitation clinic and was seen by three forensic experts, who felt that the defendant was a low risk to reoffend and was not likely to engage in a hands-on offense. They also felt that his level of sexual awkwardness due to his autism made it difficult to explore his sexuality in the real world. The sentencing guidelines called for 78–97 months in prison. He received one year of supervised release and was not required to register as a sex offender.

- My own case. I pled guilty to possession of child pornography in federal court. The sentencing guidelines called for ten years in prison. I received five years of supervised release and was required to register.

The case of United States v. Wilson (2012) is particularly illustrative. Wilson's defense attorneys were able to negotiate a plea with the prosecutors for charges that did not require sex offender registration—transportation of obscene material as opposed to possession of child pornography. If, by statute, he had been required to plead guilty to possession of child pornography, no judge could have taken him off the registry at sentencing. Perhaps the fact that this defendant was only 18 (a very young age to be charged in the federal system) was part of why he was afforded the opportunity to plead to a non-registrable offense. However, this shows that, ultimately, the charges that a prosecutor—and only a prosecutor—decides to bring against an individual can make the difference between incarceration and non-incarceration, and registry and no registry. It also underscores the importance of a defense attorney fighting to get their client to plead guilty to a charge that doesn't require incarceration or registration, if they are forced by a prosecutor to plead guilty. If the prosecution insists upon a guilty plea, a defense attorney representing an autistic client needs to try to get the prosecutor to agree to let the client plead to a crime that does not carry a mandatory minimum and automatic sex offender registration so that the judge has more discretion!

Unfortunately, these relatively favorable outcomes that are mentioned above are not typical among ASD defendants in the criminal justice system. They are outliers and are favorable only in comparison to most other adjudications seen across the board. But they are provided here to show that there are informal, non-binding precedents that exist where prosecutors and judges considered a defendant's ASD based upon expert witnesses, and it resulted in vast departures from the prescribed legislative sentencing guidelines.

Guilty Plea

In the United States, a guilty plea must be made voluntarily and intelligently (Minix, 2017) in order to be considered valid. Defendants are supposed to understand that they are waiving the future right to appeals, right to a jury trial, confrontation of witnesses at trial, loss of the right to vote, loss of the privilege against self-incrimination, and other constitutional rights that are lost with a criminal conviction. Defendants are also supposed to be aware of all the *possible* consequences they face if they choose to plead guilty. It is the judge's job at the plea hearing to make sure that a defendant understands this and to preserve it for the record, so a guilty plea cannot be appealed. Judges will frequently ask if a person is intoxicated or took drugs the night before the plea hearing. They do this to make sure that a defendant is completely cognizant of what they are doing. The word "voluntary" might seem a bit peculiar given that most plea bargaining tends to be coercive by nature, but it is a very loose standard. In the 1970 Supreme Court case Brady v. United States, the court ruled that even though the defendant was facing the death penalty (which could be seen by laypeople as not being a voluntary plea), the Justices had no reason to believe that his plea of guilt wasn't voluntary, intelligently made, and truthful (Minix, 2017). They reasoned that his plea was voluntary because at his plea hearing the judge: asked and made sure that he was not threatened with physical harm or coercion (other than death); made sure that he was appointed competent counsel; questioned him about his acts before accepting his plea. Such relaxed application of the word "voluntary" might explain why many factually innocent defendants do indeed plead guilty (Blume & Helm, 2014) and never get their convictions overturned. Only rarely does someone get a guilty plea vacated. In one case, a defendant said at his plea hearing: "I broke into an elderly lady's house and robbed her and forced her to have sex with me" (Shechtman & Cohn, 2014, p.5). But this statement was entirely untrue. This defendant pled guilty to this crime because his plea agreement was time limited (meaning it could be withdrawn if not accepted immediately) and he was told by his attorney that a future offer would be worse. Neither the lawyer nor the client knew that exculpatory DNA evidence had not been turned over, which allowed the defendant to appeal his conviction to the West Virginia Supreme Court 13 years later and have it vacated (Redlich *et al.*, 2017).

For a plea to be made intelligently, the person must possess an understanding of the elements deemed critical to the particular offense to which they are pleading guilty. A 1976 Supreme Court case, Henderson v. Morgan, illustrates this requirement. It involved a cognitively impaired 19-year-old who was indicted for first-degree murder but pled guilty to second-degree murder (Minix, 2017). He appealed, saying he did not understand the nature of the charges that he had pled guilty to, because second-degree murder involves an element of purposefully causing someone's death, which he did not know existed with a second-degree charge. Since he had made no admission of the fact that he killed with intent and his defense counsel did not agree that he had the requisite intent, it was not considered an "intelligent" plea and was therefore set aside.

I am aware of an autistic individual who swears that his guilty plea was not made intelligently. He says that he was held in jail for almost a year before his trial and was so disoriented that he had no understanding of what was really taking place. He says that there was a minimal amount of contact between him and his public defender, and that his attorney worked out a plea agreement without him being part of the discussion or negotiation. By the time he pled guilty in open court, he didn't know what the charge was that he was pleading guilty to and what the consequences would be. He was simply parroting back "yes" answers to the judge so that he could move on with his life, even though he lacked the understanding of what he was saying "yes" to. The judge accepted the plea, and this young man claims that the lack of understanding at his plea hearing ruined his life.

Another instance is in Commonwealth v. Kelmar (2010), a case mentioned earlier in which an autistic defendant filed a writ of habeas corpus to the appellate court in Virginia, claiming ineffective assistance of counsel. This autistic defendant argued that he would never have taken the guilty plea had he known at the time of his plea hearing that this would make him a registered sex offender for the rest of his life. His appeal was denied both at the appellate level and by the Supreme Court of Virginia. The defendant's father said that the family was not made aware of this crucial fact until after sentencing. To quote the defendant's father:

> This was absolutely devastating and the consequences last a lifetime. This punishment will limit his ability to be employed, where he or our family can live, where he can travel to visit family members or even his future family (if they are under 18). He can't even travel to see his own grandmothers now because of the laws affecting travel between states. This whole experience has been like a slow, agonizing psychological death sentence for him, and for our entire family. (The Arc, 2016)

I know for a fact that certain defendants are put at a disadvantage at plea hearings. One study looked at individuals with traumatic brain injuries (Wszalek & Turkstra, 2019). It compared 19 adults with moderate and severe head trauma with 21 adults without any traumatic brain injuries. Both groups were given what was called the "plea colloquy stimuli," which was done by taking the Wisconsin Waiver of Rights Form/Plea Questionnaire on which dialogues between judges and defendants are based regarding losing one's rights at plea hearings. After filling out the questionnaire, participants completed an altered, manipulated form with word substitutions from transcripts of 40 plea hearings. The third form given to participants was yet another altered, manipulated form, this time with simplified syntax. Participants were given forced-choice answers, as in a multiple-choice test based on simple language comprehension. The two altered forms (the ones that were not the actual Wisconsin Waiver of Rights Form) were randomized for every category across participants, so the experiments could not be interpreted with bias. Researchers found differences on the effect of comprehension accuracy and response times. It suggested that those with traumatic brain injuries were more likely to have poorer, slower comprehension of legal language and be at risk of misunderstanding language within legal contexts. This could negatively affect legal outcomes and convictions. Researchers attributed many of these differences to problems with working memory, which can also present issues for ASD individuals (Silk *et al.*, 2006).

Two important points arise from this information. The first point is that most defense attorneys are non-specialists when it comes to the sex offender registry. It is highly unlikely that a judge and a defense attorney will adequately explain every collateral consequence and obligation that arises from a criminal conviction that places an individual on the sex offender registry, even though this is, technically, the job of a defense attorney before a plea hearing and a judge at the plea hearing. Therefore, it is incumbent upon caretakers, spouses, and siblings to ask as many questions as possible and do research into these matters on their own. Their attorney will likely not have all the answers.

Second, defense lawyers are extremely accustomed to going over the waiver of rights form with their clients before their clients plead guilty at plea hearings. But they probably need to spend extra time with their autistic clients, making sure that the client understands everything before the judge asks them the same questions in open court. In the case of autistic individuals, this should be done before an individual decides to take a guilty plea. According to one study, 72 percent of defense attorneys wait until after their client has decided to plead guilty to perform this important step (Fountain, 2017), which could cause a huge surprise and shock to a population that does not tolerate changes or surprises well. Furthermore, attorneys must walk a delicate balance between realism and assurance before a plea hearing. If their autistic client has been out of bond before the plea, there is a small chance that there may be a change imposed between the plea and sentencing, such as electronic monitoring or, in rare instances, being remanded in custody.

Lawyers should take autistic behaviors into consideration and try to modify them into brief, succinct answers for the judge through rehearsal with their clients. For example, the autistic client should be told that if a judge asks a question pertaining to their guilt, they should answer that question very briefly, with no elaboration, unless they are asked for further clarification. Lastly, if a prosecutor agrees, defense counsel should ask for an informal conference in chambers with the judge (with the prosecutor present) to explain why certain behaviors at the plea hearing may be different from what they are used to in order to minimize the risk for misinterpretation of the ASD client's perceived rude behavior.

Presentence Report (PSR)

Once the defendant and their attorney have negotiated the best possible plea offer that they are likely to receive, and that assuming a defendant does not go to trial (trials are beyond the scope of this book), a plea agreement is drawn up. Once a guilty plea takes place in open court, a presentence investigation commences. Presentence investigations and reports are among the least understood aspects of the whole criminal justice system process. They are also perhaps some of the most consequential parts, and they can undo the progress made by favorable forensic evaluations.

Presentence investigations, which are solidified into reports after they are completed, are done by probation officers at the behest of the court. Probation officers are considered the eyes and ears of the court (Kyle Cook, 2014). Their job in this capacity is to perform an investigative function for the court and make sentencing recommendations to the judge based on both the guidelines that they calculate and on what they consider to be pertinent information about a defendant and their life history. In the federal system, a presentence report determines what security level the Federal Bureau of Prisons will place the defendant into upon arrival, which can be the difference between a prison camp and a maximum-security facility. Probation officers are considered to be a neutral party that is best situated to provide information to a judge regarding sentencing analysis (Kelch, 2011). In the vast majority of cases, a court will accept the presentence report's sentencing guideline range (Heaney, 1991), giving this report supreme importance. A presentencing report is extremely extensive. It covers, but is not limited to, the following.

- Adult record/probation/parole history

- Victim-impact statement

- Gang affiliation
- Pretrial service officer recommendations and probation officer recommendations
- Background and ties to the community
- Substance abuse history and mental health
- Juvenile record (in federal cases)
- Employment
- Plea bargain made
- Custody status (if the person was jailed before the plea or after)
- Financial circumstances
- Physical health
- Marital history
- Military record
- Level of remorse shown. (Fiftal Alarid & Montemayor, 2010)

The report is both investigatory and done by way of interviews with the convicted defendant. Berman (2002) notes that the best defense attorneys not only try to influence the way the presentence report is shaped, they are also present for the interview. They also try to prepare the defendant to offer whatever information the probation officer will most likely want to see and to present that information favorably.

This last point by Berman cannot be underscored enough, especially for the autistic population. I participated in two presentence interviews after I pled guilty in 2013, one at the courthouse and one at my home. They were two of the most frightening experiences of my life. I learned what a presentence interview was immediately after pleading guilty, so I had very little time to prepare for it. The probation officer asks numerous questions about who you are (your life history) and the nature of your offense, and you must answer those questions with complete candor. If not, that is noted in the report. The interview can last for many hours. I did not feel particularly well prepared for mine, even though my attorney was present for the first meeting, because I was not educated on its function nor how much was truly at stake. But looking back, it was by far the most important interview of my life—much more important than any job interview. This is because the probation officer's impression of the individual forms a large basis of the report, which is sent directly to the judge. Autistic adults notoriously struggle with job interviews, but research shows that, with preparation, they do better (Morgan *et al.*, 2014). The same would probably be true in my case. Autistic defendants should be told that this is like an interview with a forensic psychologist who is interested in every aspect of their life but it will be even more probing. Furthermore, when necessary, the attorney should make every attempt to convey to the officer that the defendant has a communication disorder called autism and that they are earnestly trying to answer the questions to the best of their ability. This should occur before or at the time of the interview. The officer should not take the autistic individual's lack of affect or eye contact as a lack of remorse.

Acclaimed best-selling author Michael Santos (2007) wrote a fascinating insider's look at life in prison and now runs a consulting agency where he advises defendants on their strategy of navigating the time between lodging a guilty plea and sentencing. In a 2012 publication, Santos discusses what can go wrong with a poor presentence report. The consequences include being ineligible for programs that could lead to early release from prison, serving time in higher security facilities, having less access to telephone/visitors, and being misclassified. On his website (which is a terrific resource), Santos (2018) says that it is not uncommon for everyone in a defendant's life to be contacted by the probation officer who is conducting the investigation. He recommends getting character reference letters lined up in advance of the interview, along with a written statement of remorse and commitment to change by the defendant. Santos says that, at the interview, questions can be wide ranging. With regards to someone's background, they can ask about their family, where they grew up, the type of neighborhood it was, every city they have ever lived in, and their current living situation, among many other topics. As far as someone's family is concerned, Santos says they can ask about every family member's contact information, each parent's occupation, the type of relationship they have with their parents, whether there were any domestic disturbances growing up, siblings and their availability to be interviewed, spouses, and children. When it comes to the defendant's physical conditions, questions can be about tattoos and the meaning or significance of each tattoo, and their medical conditions, attending a physician, treatment plan, medications, etc. (*ibid.*). The probation officer will also ask a wide variety of questions related to someone's mental health history, including who their treatment providers are, what medications they take, who prescribes them, etc. The probation officer will also ask a series of substance-abuse questions along with another series of questions on educational, vocational, and special skills. Finally, the officer will take a very detailed inventory of the person's assets and savings, requiring them to disclose information about their personal accounts (*ibid.*). Then, they will likely undergo a drug test.

As stated before, the interview would be overwhelming for a neurotypical. For an autistic, it is much more challenging. Even if the autistic person knows the answer to every question, the questions can feel intrusive or irrelevant. The autistic individual's executive functioning can be challenged in being asked so many questions in rapid fire succession. An attorney should be there to help the autistic individual to answer the questions, fill in the gaps, and explain communication differences. Before the interview, the attorney should also explain that the autistic individual has to answer the questions politely unless the attorney objects, meaning that the defense lawyer deems the question being asked by the probation officer to be irrelevant. Attorneys may also try to have the most favorable passages of forensic reports highlighted in the presentence report.

Once the probation officer compiles all the information from both the interviews and their own investigations, they determine the sentencing guidelines and make recommendations to the judge in the form of a lengthy presentence report. While sentencing guidelines are in part formulaic, they still involve subjective judgments on the part of the probation officer (Berman, 2002). Defense lawyers are entitled and expected to challenge what they believe to be a misapplication of the guidelines towards their clients, if they see fit. Most autistic individuals who have never been in trouble with the law and show remorse will receive lower guidelines than career criminals. However, many crimes begin with extremely high base sentencing levels (the level where one starts, with all things being equal) (Stabenow, 2011). Possession of child pornography is an example of such a crime at the federal level. Both the defense attorney and the prosecutor can make challenges to the presentence report once it is disclosed to both parties (Drake Law School Legal Clinic, 2011). It is extremely important that the defense lawyer and the autistic client and their caretakers go over the report to ensure complete accuracy before it is sent to the judge. I have heard of many instances where factual errors in presentence reports ended up hurting autistic defendants and negatively affecting their sentences. This is completely preventable.

The sentencing guidelines are only advisory, and a judge is not bound by them (Yang, 2014), at least not in the federal system. In certain states, the guidelines are mandatory, whereas in other states, they are advisory, as with the federal system (Mitchell, 2017). For judges to depart from the guidelines, however, there generally needs to be strong mitigating factors. Some states and the federal systems have not codified autism as a mitigating factor that would lead to a downward departure from the guidelines (going lower than the guidelines would suggest) (Cea, 2014). As I have noted in a previous section, judges have considered autism as a mitigating factor in certain cases and have dramatically departed from the guidelines. This is most likely due to the fact that judges can take "diminished mental capacity" into consideration as a reason to depart from the guidelines (*ibid.*).

Sentencing

Before sentencing, both the prosecutor assigned to the case and the defense attorney prepare sentencing memorandums for the judge. A sentencing memorandum summarizes what each side would like the judge to do. Before a plea is made, the prosecutor and defense attorney negotiate for the best possible plea, but when it comes to sentencing, the process shifts into being completely adversarial in nature. Depending on the case and the individual circumstances, most prosecutors will at least argue that the judge should sentence the defendant towards the middle to high end of the sentencing guidelines in a case that involves a serious crime. Conversely, defense attorneys will argue that judges should sentence a defendant either at the low end of the guidelines or, in extraordinary circumstances, depart from the guidelines altogether and give a sentence of non-incarceration. A defense attorney's strategy will vary considerably depending on the judge who is overseeing sentencing. If a judge has the reputation of never giving defendants a break, a defense attorney may look to cut their losses and argue at the low end of the guidelines, rather than risk alienating the judge by asking for something "unreasonable" or unattainable. On the other hand, if the judge has a reputation of being open and flexible, the defense attorney may be more aggressive in what they argue. Neither side can pick their judge of choice. Judges are assigned at random (Hall, 2010). And even if the prosecutor and defense attorney agreed to a no-prison plea agreement for a defendant, there is theoretically no guarantee that any judge will accept the plea agreement (McConkie, 2015); it can be rejected.

What can be done about the prosecutor's memorandum? Very little. Unfortunately, the prosecutor's memorandum is beyond an autistic defendant's control. By this stage of the proceedings, the negotiations have ceased between the two parties and both sides present their best arguments to the judge. In contrast, with a plea agreement that occurs before a defendant pleads guilty in the pretrial phase, a prosecutor and defense lawyer negotiate and come to some resolution or agreement. They may agree to no prison for the defendant, may ask for prison time, or may leave it up to the judge and take no position. Likewise, some plea agreements allow defendants to withdraw their guilty pleas if the court does not accept the agreement, while other plea agreements do not allow for this (Federal Rules of Criminal

Procedure, 2020). Some plea agreements allow the defendant to plead guilty to lesser included offenses that allow for no prison time, while others don't. Ultimately, though, a defendant and their attorney would hope that the prosecutor would agree to a sentence of non-incarceration where there is no mandatory minimum and stipulate to it in the plea agreement.

But things change dramatically after a guilty plea. The memorandum is at the punishment phase, which is post-trial. At this point, what matters is what the judge thinks. What the prosecution is going to be arguing for as a punishment at sentencing has already been established. Like the presentence report, the judge receives both of these memoranda before sentencing. They also receive character reference letters that people typically submit to the judge on behalf of the defendant.

Judges who make these "life-and-death" decisions about what should happen to defendants rely on a variety of factors. They look to precedent. In other words, they look to see if a sentence of non-incarceration is even possible. They also consider whether a binding precedent for a defendant's particular guilty plea made in a state or federal circuit court makes such a sentence prohibited and appealable. Additionally, they look to see whether there are mandatory minimums that prescribe a sentence of incarceration for a particular crime to which the defendant has pled guilty, in which case they would have no choice but to pass a sentence of incarceration. Furthermore, they look at the characteristics of the offender, situational factors surrounding the offense, relationship between victim and offender, victim characteristics, type of harm, and level of harm caused (Knapp & Hauptly, 1991). But at the center of every judge's decision, there are five factors.

- Making sure there is some form of retribution.

- Making sure there is deterrence. This is to say, that by giving a particular sentence, others in the community would be deterred from committing the same crime.

- Making sure there is some incapacitation: Whether one is in prison, on house arrest, or on probation.

- Making sure the offender is rehabilitated by the sentence.

- Making sure there is equity in sentencing. In other words, reducing sentencing disparities between similarly situated defendants. (Cappellino & Meringolo, 2013)

Going from the general to the specific, how do judges view autistic defendants? There is a dearth of research addressing this question. A couple of studies, however, might give us a clue. One study specifically looked at judicial attitudes and perceptions towards individuals with high-functioning autism (HFA) (Berryessa, 2016). It surveyed 21 criminal court trial judges from the California Superior Court who regularly sentenced defendants to prison. The judges were randomly sampled and not targeted towards one party affiliation or the other. Nine judges talked about autism being a mitigating factor, and the majority of the 21 judges felt that autism could potentially be a mitigating factor if the defendant's criminal intent was influenced by the symptoms of their autism. Three of the judges talked about the possibility of viewing autism as an aggravating factor, saying that if the autism prevented an individual from controlling their own behavior, it could contribute to the individual reoffending or having problems with impulse control. Most of the judges agreed that incarceration was not a good setting for HFA individuals and that they would not want to incarcerate these defendants. Judges expressed the desire for alternative sentences to prison or jail but conceded that the criminal justice system may not have the tools to provide these desired alternatives. One judge interviewed expressly said he would prefer treatment to prison, if he had a choice.

Another study conducted two years earlier by Berryessa (2014) randomly sampled another set of 21 criminal court trial judges from the California Superior Court. The themes that emerged from those judges regarding their perceptions of defendants were as follows.

- HFA individuals viewed the world inherently differently. Because of their genetic roots, they possibly had problems with impulse control. One judge said: "It hurts them because they could be more dangerous than someone with impulse control" (p.8). Another judge said, with regards to impulse control, that it "may make you [the HFA person] more prone to violent behavior if it's not controlled" (p.8). Impulse control was a dual-edged sword. Another judge said that an HFA individual "was less culpable as someone who had better mental health and better impulse control, better judgment" (p.8).

- Some HFA individuals might not be malleable enough for treatment. One judge said: "You can't tell him [an autistic person] that he's wrong because that is the way he thinks it is" (p.7).

- Perhaps, in many cases, HFA individuals lacked the mens rea (or guilty mind) when they committed the crime, which many considered a mitigating factor (Weiss, 2011).

The biggest concern that I have from this last study is that many judges were under the impression that autistic individuals lack impulse control across the board. This has negative repercussions when it comes to sentencing, but the same judges felt that many of the defendants were not as blameworthy, which has positive repercussions. So perhaps the feelings of some of these judges with regards to impulse control are balanced out by their understanding of lesser blameworthiness.

A defense attorney who is representing an autistic person must realize that there is a decent chance that the judge they are appearing before may not know that much about autism. The defense attorney may want to make the argument in their memorandum that their client's needs are sui generis (i.e., extremely unique). Defense attorneys also may find it necessary to reassure the court that there can be strong community protection without a sentence of incarceration for the autistic defendant. In other words, it is important to show that autism is not an aggravating factor for the defendant in question, because a judge may believe that to be the case. In my view, which is that of a non-lawyer, the sentencing memorandum should recapitulate every point made in the defense forensic psychologists' reports, because we know that judges can be strongly influenced by what these professionals say. (These professionals may have to testify at the sentencing hearing and hold up under cross-examination.) The attorney might feel free to quote liberally the most favorable parts of these reports in the memorandum. Furthermore, in my view, there is a great need for defense attorneys to emphasize how autism is a congenital condition that affects one's development from the day of birth, as opposed to a mental illness that manifests later in life. This would, ideally, be seen by the judge as a mitigating factor from the vantage point of diminished capacity. In most sentencing memoranda I have read, the defense counsel of autistic defendants argues that their client would not survive in a jail or prison setting. This is a valid argument from my perspective, and completely true for many autistic individuals. It is especially true if the defendant has a younger emotional or social age and cannot pick up on the social cues necessary in the jail or prison setting in order to survive. There cannot be rehabilitation (a judge's fourth goal) if a defendant is completely incapacitated and unable to recover. According to the *U.S. Sentencing Guidelines Manual* (Cappellino & Meringolo, 2013), a judge is supposed to look at the different types of sentences available. In this spirit, if a non-incarceration sentence is available because there is no mandatory minimum, and if the judge is able to depart from the guidelines, it should be strongly argued that this action be taken.

If the person is a low-risk individual, all evidence can be put forth in the memorandum as to why and how this was determined, perhaps with an emphasis on high impulse control, if this is the case for that person. If it is a child pornography case, again, all the evidence of the person's actual low risk of harming a child can be put forth from the reports and life history. Similarly, research cited throughout this book regarding the propensity of most ASD people to be adherent rule followers and conscientious individuals can be connected to both the diagnosis of autism and the individual's life history in relation to why the defendant is likely not to recidivate.

To avoid sentencing disparities, defense attorneys might choose to search their jurisdiction or nearby jurisdictions to find informal precedent for non-incarceration sentences for the same crime with which the autistic defendant is charged. Cases with the most similar circumstances make the strongest arguments for judges. Additionally, a defense attorney may cite appellate cases that support non-incarceration sentences for autistic individuals or those with developmental disabilities where the guidelines were given less weight than usual.

Defense attorneys can also argue that a sentence of supervision outside of the jail or prison setting would result in deterring a criminal conviction, possible attendant sex offender status, and the burdens of intense supervision. Attorneys may also want to argue in support of house arrest in lieu of prison. In instances where disabilities such as autism compromise daily living to an extreme and it is difficult for the person to take care of themselves, a sentence of probation, house arrest, or supervised release reflects the seriousness of the offense, promotes respect for the law, and provides just punishment. Defense attorneys may want to argue at sentencing that certain conditions of supervision post-release (or as part of probation) should be tailored and individualized for the person on the autism spectrum. For example, if traditional sex offender treatment programs (SOTPs) are prescribed according to the offense, the judge can tailor the therapy for an individualized setting and with a therapist who is knowledgeable about ASD rather than a group setting with a court-contracted social worker. For reasons mentioned earlier related to polygraphs and Abel Assessment testing, at sentencing, defense lawyers may or may not want to express concern about these conditions, which are often imposed as part of a SOTP.

In addition to gathering character reference letters from individuals who know the defendant, one other strategy that families who have the resources may consider before sentencing is the making of a mitigation video (Austin, 2014). There are professionals who help to make mitigation videos for a living. They can be made for a judge when the defendant is seeking a downward departure or full departure from the guidelines. According to Austin (2014), a good mitigation video includes sight and sound footage of the defendant's early childhood difficulties through interviews and photos, followed by what might have led them to break the law, the introspection gained from going through the criminal justice process, and, finally, the growth and change of the individual. They are usually five to eight minutes long and are intended to supplement all other existing documentation. I believe that an effectively produced mitigation video could give life to certain elements of living with autism that no written report could ever do justice to. By employing sight and sound to give life to a defendant's life with autism, their life experiences, and their difficulties, judges may be moved by the mitigating circumstances. However, depending on the jurisdiction, there can be evidentiary hurdles to getting these videos in front of a judge. Some judges are willing to view them, while others will not. Sometimes, family members or other people who appear in the video may be subjected to cross-examination at sentencing (*ibid.*), and they may not want to appear in the videos under those conditions. These are issues that a defense attorney would need to investigate before encouraging a family to pursue this course of action.

The day of sentencing happens after the judge reviews the presentence report and the memorandums. Defense attorneys will prepare their clients for whatever may happen. Attorneys of autistic defendants may rehearse ways to come across as sincerely remorseful in court with the client. The lawyers will make oral arguments to the judge. If there are direct victims and they choose to testify, victim impact statements are made. Family members of the defendant can ask for leniency. The defendant can choose to make a statement to the court or remain silent. The judge then pronounces the sentence. After the judge does this and lists the conditions after release—and assuming that probation is not given—the attorney can ask the judge to let the client self-surrender instead of being taken into custody on that day. They may also try to get the ASD defendant classified into a lower security facility.

Conclusion

This chapter does not end on a happy note. As mentioned earlier, once an individual on the autism spectrum has landed in the criminal justice system, a tragedy has begun to unfold—one that in all likelihood is irreparable. The genie has been summoned from the bottle and it cannot be placed back in.

In the next chapter, I will describe the aftermath of this crisis and present suggestions for more effective strategies to use with the ASD population post-sentencing.

CHAPTER 4

The Aftermath

I am fortunate because I have not spent any time in a custodial setting. But I have talked to many individuals on the autism spectrum who have. It is a harrowing experience for anyone, but arguably, at least in my opinion, it's a human rights violation for individuals on the spectrum who do not present a danger to the community.

Take one common incident among many that happen to autistic people in custody. An autistic man was written up in prison for complaining about a board game being played in the common area because the players were noisier than he could tolerate. The inmate apparently picked up the board game in an attempt to get the other inmates to stop playing. The corrections officer told the autistic inmate to drop the board game and remarked that he was not acting logically. The officer told him that this was not a hotel and other inmates could be as loud as they wanted to be. The autistic inmate said: "I know this isn't a f*cking hotel." For that, he lost visiting privileges for 90 days and was given time in solitary confinement. I wrote about Vineland testing earlier and how it can affect daily living skills. It appears that the ASD man's extreme sensory sensitivities, combined with a lower age of social and emotional functioning, set him up for the "perfect storm" of punishment.

This was only the beginning of his troubles. Getting basic medications was an ordeal for the ASD inmate. He was told to wait near the door at certain times, but on many occasions either the prison medical personnel would not come or he could not hear them, so he went without his medications. He claimed that staff completely ignored him for two months. Getting accurate information about when the pill line was in operation was almost impossible for him. He was told to wait in the pill line between 6 a.m. and 10 a.m., and, if he didn't receive his medication at that time, to wait there again from 5 p.m. to 9 p.m. It was often a physical impossibility for him to wait in the pill line at these times due to a cell count, lockdown, or job obligations in the prison throughout the day. As a result of not getting his medications, he spent a lot of time in solitary confinement. He has said he had learned a lot in prison and that his rights were being violated by the prison not following the Rehabilitation Act and not providing accommodations for his disability. An example of that is not providing earplugs for excessive noise and sunglasses for bright lights. He was roughhoused by other inmates, beaten up, taken advantage of, and blackmailed, had commissary money stolen, and had to be taken into protective custody due to scary situations.

Americans with Disabilities Act (ADA) and the Rehabilitation Act

I wrote earlier in this book about Title II of the ADA, which passed in 1990 and was signed by President George H. W. Bush. This was established to provide accommodations to individuals with disabilities and was affirmed to apply to prisoners in the 1998 Supreme Court case of Pennsylvania Department of Corrections v. Yeskey (Ginsberg, 2009). However, states have been able to shield themselves from lawsuits against prisoners because of the Eleventh Amendment, which provides states and governments with sovereign immunity.

The predecessor of the ADA is Section 504 of the Rehabilitation Act, which poses fewer sovereign immunity obstacles (Public Law 93-112, 1973, codified 2006). Under 504, disability discrimination is prohibited by any agency receiving federal funding (29 U.S. Code § 794(a)) and all state and federal corrections receiving federal assistance. Yet, with Title II, a disability can be a motivating factor for discrimination in order to be valid, whereas with 504, it must be the sole basis for discrimination (Ginsberg, 2009). But unlike the Eighth Amendment (cruel and unusual punishment is prohibited) where inmates must prove that corrections officers had specific intent to deny them accommodations (deliberate indifference), intent does not have to be proven when claims are brought against prisons under Section 504 and Title II. When a jail or prison is being sued, qualified immunity does not apply to them as it only applies to individual people (Owen v. City of Independence, 1980). Regulations on expert fees differ between 504 and Title II, as well as attorney's fees. But the bottom line is that very few cases see the light of day. In 1996, the Prison Litigation Reform Act was passed to reduce frivolous litigation of prisoners by adding an administrative fee for indigent defendants (Ginsberg, 2009). To exhaust administrative remedies is to risk retaliation by prison staff. So, fighting mistreatment in prison on account of a disability is an uphill battle.

Lawsuits are filed against prisons that are accused of violating the ADA and 504 all the time, and the ACLU is often involved in these suits for the plaintiffs, or disabled inmates. For example, an autistic inmate was having a grand mal seizure while being improperly restrained, and the man bit the corrections officer in the midst of the seizure (Ciaramella, 2019). As punishment, for seven months the autistic man was placed in a cell that regularly flooded with raw sewage. The Florida Department of Corrections denied the man's allegations, claiming he was probably having an adverse reaction to synthetic marijuana. Body-camera footage (which is required during use-of-force incidents) was turned off until 38 minutes into the altercation. This is a common though tragic and horrifying story. One can Google "disabilities," "lawsuits," and "prisons" and find a plethora of these types of lawsuits.

Autism and Incarceration

Jails and prison are places where privacy is extremely limited, hierarchy dictates prisoner subculture, and bullying and victimization are the absolute norm (Ashkar & Kenny, 2008; Doyle, 2003; Ireland, 2000; South & Wood, 2006). I wrote a book about autism and bullying (Dubin, 2007) in which I highlighted the ways that autistic children are vulnerable to being bullied; this vulnerability has a much higher magnitude in prison. Ostracism, theft, sexual assault, and blackmail are common ways that inmates are victimized in prison (Banbury, 2004; Connell & Farrington, 1996; de Viggiani, 2006; Edgar, 2005; Ireland & Archer, 1996; Nagi, Browne & Blake, 2006; O'Donnell & Edgar, 1998; Wolff & Shi, 2009).

Bullying, social isolation, and altercations with other inmates are quite common for the autistic population in prison due to ASD inmates' literalism, obsessions, compulsions, and problems communicating with others (Allely, 2015). Joining gangs or being left without any sort of protection is often a common dilemma. In jails or prisons there are unwritten rules between members within a subculture, gang, or race of individuals, and autistic people are often unaware of what these unwritten rules are unless they are told (Michna & Trestman, 2016). Understandably, autistic individuals experience higher levels of anxiety, have less ability to cope, and derive fewer benefits from attempts at rehabilitation in an incarcerated setting (Lewis et al., 2015). Researchers also have observed that autism is actually a risk factor for encountering less empathy among correctional staff due to ASD inmates' inherent communication challenges (Glaser & Deane, 1999; Shively, 2004).

Newman, Cashin and Waters (2015) did a hermeneutic phenomenological examination of the lived experience of incarceration for those with autism.

This simply means that they wanted to understand how autistic people feel about the experience and not what third-party observers might think. Themes ran along several different lines.

- Constantly being in an unpredictable environment

- Being deprived of the ability to regain control of one's world

- Strangeness and incomprehension of prison routines and rules

- Negotiating the social world of prison

- Coping with social-related demands of prison through self-isolation and avoidance.

With regards to the first theme, there is much talk in the literature of prison providing rules and routines that could actually be beneficial for autistic individuals. But these people fail to realize that these "rules and routines" are ever-changing in prison and can shift on a moment's notice. Prisoners can sometimes be transferred from one prison to another in the middle of the night without receiving any kind of warning (Jefferis & Godfrey, 2018). Guards change shifts and old correctional staff are replaced with new staff over time. Wardens come and go, cellmates and bunkmates change, and both formal and informal rules can be rewritten. Along these lines, one autistic participant in Newman *et al.*'s study (2015) said about prison transfers:

> It's like if I'm settling in and I've got to move it upsets me a lot and really annoys me because I've just settled in, and getting settled, you know, and getting into my routine. (p.634)

Participants tried to achieve sameness in an unpredictable environment by cleaning their jail cells all day long at the expense of participating in programs. One autistic inmate stayed away from others by writing books in his cell all day long. He said:

> ...in the mornings I get a coffee and then get on the phone, try to get into the library...every day is the same...too many files to read, too many things to write. (p.635)

The second theme that autistic prisoners cited in Newman *et al.*'s study (2015) was the lack of an ability to feel in control of their world. Unexpected changes would occur with no notice and would greatly disrupt the autistic inmates. One participant said:

> ...those one-off things that come out of the blue, that upsets my whole day or my whole week and then I have to change things around. (p.635)

Another autistic inmate spoke about how his need for sameness through routines was taken advantage of by correctional staff. His anxieties manifested as a need to clear his cell all day long, so staff would simply move him from cell to cell without any notice:

> What they do is move me to a cell, I clean it all top to bottom, next day they tell me to move again so then I got to do it again and again and again. I spend all the time washing these new cells. (p.635)

Correctional staff would make him do all the cleaning work, which included general cleaning for everyone else on the wing.

The third theme in Newman *et al.*'s study (2015) about autistic prisoners had to do with the strange feeling of being unable to comprehend prison rules and routines. Since prison logic differs so much to logic in the outside world, autistic inmates struggled to make the necessary adjustments. Some people on the autistic spectrum couldn't make sense of the seemingly illogic bureaucratic procedures that they had to follow. One autistic inmate talked about the experience of being transferred from prison to court, when the two were in such close proximity. He spoke about how this procedure did not make sense to him:

> I mean it's across the road. It's literally 10 minutes...and all you do is just sit in a cage for four hours for no reason at all, you know, and then there's a truck that picks you up and drives five metres, going through a whole lot of security checks – you know, guns and things and all that – handcuffs – the whole experience – and it's (really)...10 minutes – you know, that just sums up the whole – the way it works. It's just unnecessary. (p.635)

Because autistic prisoners had difficulty with what they perceived to be incomprehensible rules, they had trouble following them. I found this alarming. Sometimes prison staff would take disciplinary action against an entire unit without an autistic individual understanding why. In one case, a fight broke out within the unit and everyone was locked down. The autistic inmate didn't understand why and he experienced great distress because of it. He said:

> Someone was having a go at someone else, and I got locked in with everyone else in the [unit]. [It was] uncomfortable [because I was] just thinking of why we were locked in...to begin with [I didn't understand why]. (p.635)

The fourth theme of Newman *et al.*'s study (2015) had to do with negotiating the social world of prison. Autistic inmates talked about how being socially aloof made them prime targets for abuse. One said:

> I don't do that [socially mix]...that makes you aloof and consequently a victim of abuse and target for, you know, everything else...by being an oddity. (p.636)

Another autistic inmate said:

> [Prison is] real hard [because of] prisoners standing over me and bashing me up all the time. (p.636)

They spoke about how they experienced excessive name calling from other inmates and how their reactions to these provocations were not always under control.

The final theme of Newman et al.'s study (2015) was the way that autistic individuals coped with the social demands of prison by isolating themselves. There is no social distancing in prison. Even so, autistic prisoners in this study tried their best to achieve such a result. Some of them tried to live in their own head completely, which is arguably regressive. One individual said:

> People call it aloof, but it's not aloof. It's – you're in your head and you're thinking about something and you're not wondering about which path you've cut across or what – you know, you're just not focused. (p.636)

But wanting to be alone is actually quite logical for autistic prisoners in this setting, given what they have to contend with. These autistic inmates wanted to avoid overcrowding, bullying, and complex social scenarios. One autistic inmate asked to be housed in segregation, which was normally viewed as a punishment. He said:

> [I] wanted to be by myself...and they ended up just throwing me in solitary confinement by myself for nothing when I hadn't done anything wrong. (p.636)

Even some autistic inmates who tried to make social overtures every once in a while felt rejected. One of the autistic inmates said:

> I try to [get to know other prisoners] but sometimes they don't want to get to know me...because they think I'm a retard...I like to keep to myself. (p.636)

Prison, and more specifically solitary confinement, arguably increases autistic symptoms in some neurotypical individuals. Men housed in solitary confinement over a period of time displayed symptoms that involved increased hypersensitivity to environmental stimuli, becoming easily overloaded, and becoming extremely stressed by noise coming from adjacent cells (Grassian, 2006; Haney & Lynch, 1997). Reports say that prolonged time in solitary confinement can result in hyposensitivities to pain (Smith, 2006). I know that pain thresholds among some autistic individuals are high and certain autistic people cannot feel pain. This is a documented concern throughout the literature (Yasuda *et al.*, 2016). Individuals who have difficulties with understanding the social hierarchies of life and accepting unfamiliar rituals and routines often end up in solitary confinement (Michna & Trestman, 2016). Autistic individuals can sometimes be desperate to enter solitary confinement. Mesibov and Sreckovic (2017) tell of an autistic individual who was sexually assaulted on a daily basis and started a fire just so he could be put into solitary confinement. Assuming that certain aspects of prison, like solitary confinement, make neurotypicals start exhibiting autistic features, just imagine the kind of regression that autistic individuals might have in the same setting.

In my opinion, there are better and more humane ways to treat this population. Let me name a few:

- House arrest, home detention, or curfews in lieu of incarceration when possible and appropriate. This can be accomplished through the use of electronic monitoring (Larsen, 2017).

- Probation or diversion should be given in lieu of custody when possible, as has been stressed throughout the book. If a suspect needs to be apprehended and taken into custody in a jail because they are a clear and present danger, diagnostic protocol for possible autism needs to be implemented upon intake.

- If autistic individuals must be incarcerated for whatever reason, standard screening protocols must be universally implemented in jails and prisons for the autistic population (McKenzie *et al.*, 2012; Robinson *et al.*, 2012). If a person has autism, they should be placed in a high-care facility, but not necessarily a higher security facility. With one in 54 individuals being on the autism spectrum (CDC, 2020), resources should be dedicated to separate autistic people from the general population to ensure their safety. Similarly, autistic individuals who are sex offenders should never be housed with the general population.

- Regular mandated training should be given to corrections officers on developmental disabilities and autism.

Sex Offender Registry

It is beyond the scope of this book to give a written history of the sex offender registry in America, or my opinion of it. But I want to describe how it would affect an autistic person, after serving a sentence in jail or prison or during their term of probation. I also want to give suggestions to remedy this dramatic problem.

If you are an autistic person who has been convicted as a sex offender, most states will require that you have a place to live outside of a residency restriction (sometimes 1000 feet from a school, church, park, or daycare center) before they approve your release from prison (Carlson, Clark & Hinchcliffe, 2012; Lussier & Mathesius, 2019). If your parents live within a residency-restriction zone, and you plan to live with them after release from prison, they have to move to a different address or you must stay in prison. If you have a cousin, sibling, or friend who lives in a residency-restriction zone, you can't move in with them. You will have to stay in prison until you provide an acceptable address. I know an autistic young man who is stuck at a halfway house because his parents have not yet found a home outside of a residency-restriction zone. And if you believe that automatic release is a given if you have a place to live outside of a residency-restriction zone, please consider this: the federal government and many states commit those with "mental disorders" and autistic individuals to mental facilities indefinitely if they believe that there is a good chance that they will recidivate (Kellaher, 2015). This is known as civil commitment, and the usual procedural safeguards associated with criminal trials are absent. One case that involved civil commitment involved a man who drew pictures of children in his cell (Aviv, 2013) and ended up being civilly committed after his sentence, presumably for the rest of his life.

Shifting perspectives, let's assume that the autistic person with sex offender status now wants to find somewhere to live on their own so they can get out of prison. This may be next to impossible, as most apartment complexes refuse to rent to those on the sex offender registry (and can legally do so) (Frankel, 2019; Hamilton-Smith, 2020; Kunstler & Tsai, 2020). According to Frankel (2019), people often go past their release dates before they are put on a shelter waitlist. No doubt, this is due to some registrants not being notified that this is a legal requirement beforehand. If the autistic person on the registry tries to get federal assistance for housing, they will be denied, as sex offender registration disqualifies one from Section 8 housing (McPherson, 2016). If the autistic person on the registry planned on living in a group home, that also may be off limits, as many group homes deny access to registrants (Ramage, 2019). On a related note, many nursing homes deny elderly registrants from living there (Frankel, 2019). It is frightening to consider autistic registrants as being "legislated into homelessness" as Levenson (2018, p.1) puts it, but this happens more often than we want to acknowledge. An infamous example is the Julia Tuttle Causeway in Miami, Florida, where 140 registrants live in perpetual exile because the whole city of Miami falls within a residency restriction. Many homeless shelters turn registrants away (Rolfe, Tewksbury & Schroeder, 2017). As a harrowing example in Michigan, a sex offender who was denied access to several home shelters was found dead in the snow during a furious blizzard (Michels, 2009).

We know that individuals on the autism spectrum struggle to maintain employment and are vastly underemployed (Hendricks, 2010; Müller et al., 2003; Scott et al., 2019; Taylor & Seltzer, 2011; Whitehouse et al., 2009). Paroles, probationers, and those released from prison are often required to maintain employment, or they risk being violated and sent back to prison (Vance, 2017). Finding employment, though, is not easy for anyone on the registry—let alone for an autistic registrant. A 2009 survey (Levenson & Tewksbury, 2009) of 584 family members of registrants found that 82 percent of them reported facing financial hardships due to the registrant family member not being able to find employment. Unemployment numbers for sex offenders can be anywhere from 57 to 79 percent (Levenson, D'Amora & Hern, 2007; Suresh et al., 2010; Tewksbury, 2005). Finding employment as a registrant is always an uphill battle (Reed, 2017; Rydberg, 2018; Winters et al., 2017), and it is probably much higher for those who are on both the spectrum and the registry. Difficulties arise because employers use the sex offender registry to screen people out and because many jobs involve direct contact with children. But also, the Adam Walsh Child Protection and Safety Act mandates that people give to the police information that is publicly available on the sex offender registry website, such as the address of their employer (Wright, 2014). Most employers who are cognizant that a candidate's address is going to appear on the registry will not take a chance by hiring even a potentially good employee. Furthermore, many registrants are fired once a customer or co-worker finds out about their inclusion on the registry.

What about autistic registrants who come from homes with enough resources that they can be taken care of and not have to worry about work? Life is still hard. Across the United States, community notification (Sample, Evans & Anderson, 2011) involves officers going door to door to let neighbors know of a sex offender registrant's presence within a given radius, signs on trees about where they live, clubhouse meetings, ads in newspapers, town-hall meetings, sometimes mandatory signs on their own lawn or door installed by a sheriff's deputy (KFOR-TV and Querry, 2015), and gossip on social media (Harris, Lobanov-Rostovsky & Levenson, 2015). This makes any caregiver living with the autistic registrant, such as parents, as well as the registrant, the target of vigilantism and crimes. Sociologists refer to this type of "guilt by association" stigma as "courtesy stigma," or secondary stigma (Furst & Evans,

2014). Family members of registered citizens have been harassed, threatened, assaulted, and injured, and had their personal property damaged (Levenson & Cotter, 2005; Mercado, Alvarez & Levenson, 2008).

Can an autistic sex offender attend church if they happen to be religious? Sometimes, but there will often be many restrictions on where they can be in the church and what times of the day they can visit (Chammah, 2015). Other times, local sheriffs, mostly in small communities, will take it upon themselves to simply ban registrants from religious communities altogether (*ibid.*). Research shows that not all religious communities are necessarily welcoming towards registrants who attempt to join their communities (Dum *et al.*, 2019). If registrants are banned from church or other places of worship, where can they go? The answer is, not many places. Many states have what are called "presence restrictions," which prohibit registrants from entering McDonald's if there is a play structure, as well as libraries, schools, parks, playgrounds, or any other place where children are likely to congregate (Calaway, 2018). It is very easy to find stories online of people on the sex offender registry going into restricted places and getting into trouble. In 2019, an offender stepped foot on library property but did not go in and was arrested by police (Mercado, Alvarez & Levenson, 2008). A similar incident occurred at an Iowa library (Grant, 2019). Even when the authorities cannot legally remove a registrant from a given area, that does not mean that other people will not put pressure on the person to leave. A community might try to stop a person from swimming in a community pool (Moran, 2017). Individual jurisdictions might pass laws independent of the state, unbeknownst to the registrant, at any given time. In Huntington Beach, California, for example, it is a crime for a registrant to go to a city beach (Greenberg & Greenberg, 2013). But how would someone who lives in nearby Los Angeles know that if they went to Huntington Beach? What if the autistic registrant wants to visit Grandpa Jack in Florida? Each state has its own requirements as to how many days the registrant can be there before registering, and the onus is on the registrant to know these requirements— not the state to inform that person (Rolfe, 2019).

How long is a person on the registry? It varies, but usually between 15 years and their whole life, with their whole life being the most common result (Zgoba & Ragbir, 2016).

This discussion is not aimed around sex offenders, however. Sex registry laws are beyond the scope of this book. I am instead aiming to describe how the sex offender registry would apply to a low-risk, autistic sex offender who, in my opinion, has no business being on such a registry. Autism is already a significant disability. Imposing a further life-denying civil disability on top of autism on a person who is at low risk of reoffending is a truly cruel act. It consigns these autistic people to a life of being banished from society (Zgoba, 2011) and living on the margins, where finding social acceptance and financial stability becomes nearly impossible. It imposes on autistic people a byzantine patchwork of confusing laws, and if the individual makes just one mistake, they risk going back to jail or prison. For the non-dangerous, autistic registrant, it is most likely impossible to comprehend the daily hate, exclusion, repulsion, and disgust that most people have towards them—since harming people is not the intention of most autistic people. When prosecutors insist that autistic people who are at low risk of sexually harming another individual plead guilty to crimes that involve mandatory sex offender registration, I want them to know that this is the life that is ahead for these individuals.

I belong to a listserv of parents whose autistic children are on the sex offender registry. Most have never had a partner and did not have any involvement with the criminal justice system before their offense. Here are some of the direct quotes I have heard over the years; each quote represents a separate parent.

- "My 31-year-old son had to leave our home where I could take care of him because of children in the house."

- "He needs supervision with every aspect of life. DD Medicaid waiver. My son cannot get housing vouchers nor live in a group support home."

- "We had to sell our home due to residency restrictions."

- "He cannot take care of himself, much less understand the restrictions, and is not capable of reporting when required without help."

- "He will never be allowed to be in any type of residential home after we die."

- "He cannot attend functions that might help him learn social skills or help him find employment."

- "For the disability services here in [one of the 50 states], under the DD Medicaid waiver someone on the registry cannot get housing vouchers nor live in a group support home. Most rentals will not let them rent a place because he is on the list. So without family support he will end up homeless."

- "My ASD son has been on the registry now for 4.5 years. He has to be on it for 15 years. He cannot live by himself. I am retired and his dad is disabled. Soon we will have to move for financial reasons. We don't know if he will be able to live with us then, or where he can live when we cannot take him any longer."

- "He lost a previous job at a car wash, even though he was the top employee, when the national chain did a background check on him. Even though his offense was only a misdemeanor they fired him two days before Christmas 2016. He found another car-wash job within a week and has been there more than a year—again the top employee. But we are very worried about what his and our future will hold, and feel helpless to affect the outcome."

And these quotes are from three autistic people on the registry.

- "I just recently had a psychologist group tell me that I was not allowed to go for treatment because of me being on the registry. When I tried to check myself into hospitals when having a panic attack and major suicidal tendencies, they told me it was normal for me to feel that way and sent me out."

- "I cannot get hired for any employment."

- "I got kicked out of two synagogues after they found out about me."

At the beginning of the book, I highlighted how laws of the past tended to either separate disabled people from the rest of society or place them in institutions far away from the general population. When we decontextualize first-time, non-dangerous autistic offenders during their sex offender registration period and the result is that these autistic people become isolated from society, we are doing the same thing today.

Sex offender laws are not going away anytime soon. Some sex offenders have committed serious crimes and may do so again given the chance. However, the mainstream media has discovered in the past few years that there is a serious problem with low-risk autistic people getting caught up in the criminal justice system as sex offenders (Eisner, 2019; Pasha, 2017; Robison, 2013; Rubin, 2017; Sunderland, 2017). What can be done about it in the current climate?

- Create an exclusive law-enforcement registry for first-time registrants who are autistic, are intellectually disabled, or have a developmental disability. These individuals should be determined low risk by at least two experts. Do not allow their address, car, or license plate to be listed on the public registry so as to eliminate the chance of them becoming a victim of vigilantism.

- Create legislation that allows for removal from the registry after a certain number of years with no reoffending. Allow the autistic registrant to petition the court for removal.

- Exempt autistic individuals from the penalties that come with not complying with the registry, especially because any non-compliance may simply be lack of understanding. Failure to register is not associated with sexual recidivism in general (Zgoba & Levenson, 2012) and one would strongly speculate that this would be especially true for this population.

- Allow Section 8 housing, Medicaid waivers, and other governmental services that would be denied because of sex offender status.

- Eliminate residency restrictions for autistic individuals who are low risk, as homelessness is likely for this population who cannot financially support themselves.

- Allow professional advocacy groups to act as disability advocates who can help the autistic individual to navigate the registry when an immediate family member is not available. Let these professionals help to register individuals and make whatever changes to their registration that are necessary, with the cooperation of the police. Have them help autistic individuals to keep track of the rules and changes.

- Create emotional and informational support groups for parents and autistic registrants within major autism organizations so that these people and families do not feel so alone.

Autism and Sex Offending

Preliminary studies suggest that there could be an overrepresentation of autistic individuals who are identified as sex offenders. Sutton and colleagues (2013) found that 60 percent of juveniles in a Pennsylvania facility who were being treated for perpetrating sexual offenses met the criteria for an ASD. Byers and Nichols (2014) examined 205 ASD adults who were in a relationship for at least three months. Participants with more autistic symptoms reported lower sexual satisfaction scores with their partners and lower scores on an instrument called the Interpersonal Exchange Model of Sexual Satisfaction (IEMSS). Mehzabin and Stokes (2011) showed that autistic individuals have lower levels of sexual experiences and of sexual and social behavior.

What can look like a paraphilia (a condition characterized by abnormal sexual desires, typically involving extreme or dangerous activities) in those with developmental disabilities can in fact be a function of social disadvantage or lack of developmental maturity (Hingsburger, Griffiths & Quinsey, 1991). The term used to describe this is "counterfeit deviance." Its definition is just as the name suggests—specifically, behavior that seems deviant is really more of a function of lack of experience, developmental maturity, emotional regulation capacities, and/or overall daily functioning. Autism is on a spectrum and, as I have emphasized throughout the book, there is usually a strong gap between someone's IQ and their adaptive functioning. Autistic individuals consistently exhibit lower levels of adaptive functioning on tests such as the Vineland test (Charman *et al.*, 2016). Freeman and colleagues (1999) point out that scoring low on the social skills portion of the Vineland test is not necessarily related to IQ. Furthermore, Magiati and colleagues (2016) showed that a higher IQ for autistic people does not necessarily indicate better overall functioning than in those with lower levels of cognitive functioning (Howlin *et al.*, 2004). In other words, certain behaviors that appear to be criminal can be explained by counterfeit deviance in some individuals on the autism spectrum who may be "higher functioning." This is critical to consider when someone with ASD becomes involved in the criminal justice system for certain offending behaviors (e.g., child pornography).

Given this, it is important to consider whether the services that are applied to the general sex offender population would be effective for individuals with ASD. Currently, there is no empirical research that has investigated this (see also Higgs & Carter, 2015). However, the literature can act as a guide for future research into this important question.

Issues of Treatment

There is an urgent need for research to identify the specific needs of sexual offenders with ASD to inform the development and implementation of an appropriate treatment strategy (Sutton *et al.*, 2013). There is also a need for a systematic study to investigate to what extent one of the core features of ASD, namely circumscribed interests, is associated with different offending behaviors that may lead an individual to become involved in the criminal justice system (Allely & Creaby-Attwood, 2016; Creaby-Attwood & Allely, 2017).

If a deserving ASD defendant is given diversion, what kind of psychological care should they receive? What kind of care should they receive if they didn't receive diversion but are either on probation or released from prison? To address this issue, we need to start by describing sex offender treatment programs (SOTPs) and how they generally work. In the United

States, sex offenders are subject to what is called the "containment model" (English, 1998), also known as the risk-need model. Almost all 50 states and the federal government use this model in working with sex offenders. The containment model takes an aggressive approach in working with sex offenders under the belief that sex offenders are at a high risk to reoffend. It involves a close collaboration between the probation officer, a polygraph examiner who routinely administers tests for sexual history and compliance, the therapist who conducts group therapy, and members of the community (perhaps neighbors and family). The aim is to keep the offender completely accountable at all times and under complete surveillance, sometimes utilizing GPS anklets to monitor the person's whereabouts 24 hours a day, seven days a week. According to English (1998), who created this model, the five distinct components of containment are a victim-centered philosophy, multidisciplinary collaboration, specific management tools, consistent multi-agency policies and protocols, and program quality-control mechanisms.

Group therapy is the method of choice for agencies across the board who work with sex offenders (Jennings & Sawyer, 2003). The containment model sees group therapy as part of a trifecta: in other words, it is given approximately one-third of the importance in determining whether an individual is making progress, along with the polygraph and the probationer's compliance under conditions given by the court. A common maxim of group therapy under the containment model is that denials (in general) are to be judged as a red flag of treatment (Levenson & Macgowan, 2002). Because there is no confidentiality in group therapy under the containment model, any "suspicious" behavior (which could include denials or selective mutism) would be relayed back to the probation officer. Frequent and intense communication between the probation officer and the therapist is considered absolutely essential under the containment model (Newstrom *et al.*, 2018). Another maxim is that engagement in group therapy is correlated with optimal treatment progress (Levenson & Macgowan, 2002). The more that one actively engages in treatment and interacts with fellow group members and the therapist, the more progress one is said to be making. Disclosure is required and oftentimes group members are pressured to confront one another to disclose all of their sexual misdeeds in the name of keeping the probationer "accountable." Additionally, it is not unusual for a probation officer supervising sex offenders to occasionally sit in on a given session or even come regularly to their probationers' sessions (Marino, 2009).

Additionally, Lacombe (2007) has observed that the treatment of sex offenders in prison and group settings often assumes that sex offenders are a "species" that is other than human. In other words, some officials working in the prison setting and beyond believe that sex offenders are monsters that must be contained, like a virus. Lacombe compares this kind of treatment to how the disease of diabetes is treated, highlighting the metaphoric connection between chronic illness and the perceived "incurable illness" that sex offenders possess. Douard (2009) also sees a parallel between the medicalization of sex offenders and branding of them as monsters, both in treatment and in contemporary society. This is ironic, considering that sex offenders literally have the lowest recidivism findings than any other category of criminal. A meta-analysis of 73 studies involving 19,267 participants found that the sexual recidivism rate was 13.7 percent (Hanson & Morton-Bourgon, 2005). A study conducted by the Department of Justice (Langan, Schmitt & Durose, 2009) showed that within three years of 9691 sexual offenders being released from prison, 5.3 percent had reoffended. Furthermore, Barbaree and colleagues (2001) found in their meta-analysis that only an antisocial personality exhibited by a sexual offender predicted recidivism. As stated earlier, Baron-Cohen (2012) views ASD and psychopathy/anti-social personality as opposite ends of a spectrum. Hence, it is likely that the reoffence rate is even lower for autistic offenders.

Other tests such as the Abel Assessment mentioned earlier in this book (Osborn, Abel & Warberg, 1995), and the penile plethysmograph (PPG), attempt to measure sexual attraction to children through visual reaction time testing and genital arousal, respectively. I have already stated my concerns about the Abel Assessment. I also talked about my concerns about the polygraph, which is routinely used on sex offender probationers or those who have been released from prison and are under officer supervision. Sugrue (2017) believes that polygraph testing on individuals with ASD would be ineffective due to hypersensitivities to loud sounds, bright lights, and touch aversion. He also notes the strong conscience that ASD individuals have and the tendency for false positives to arise due to their nature of being "guilt grabbers." If this is true, it would render a third of the containment model ineffective for the autism population.

Is the containment model the best approach for individuals on the autism spectrum? While no specific research has been conducted on this question, I can speculate about the answer based on what I know about both autism and the model. I can also name and discuss why an alternative existing model may be more appropriate for this population. First, let us analyze why I do not consider the containment model to be the best approach for ASD individuals. This analysis is confined to individuals with ASD and not the broader sex offender population. The top priority is, of course, public safety and particularly the protection of children. It would stand to reason that the interventions we use on offenders would further promote that goal rather than run counter to it. My view is that containment would be contraindicated for the goals of public safety for the ASD population. One reason for this is the different way in which autistic individuals experience empathy and the challenge of targeting interventions to this specific difference. It is a mistake when treating offending ASD individuals to assume that they experience empathy in the same way as the general population. ASD individuals need to feel that they are in a nurturing and safe environment to benefit from treatment. This begins with a clinician not assigning undue blame to a client who may not understand the goal of treatment due to the blame they have received for perpetrating sexual offenses.

As mentioned earlier, there are two ways of measuring empathy in a person: the cognitive and affective approaches (Baron-Cohen & Wheelwright, 2004). Affective empathy is the vicarious sharing of emotions. It is the emotional response we have towards other people's emotions. When we feel "something" if another person displays an emotion, our affective empathy is at work. Cognitive empathy, on the other hand, is "meta-emotional" in that it hypothesizes what others may be feeling (Kozéki & Berghammer, 1992). It involves higher-order thinking and a certain amount of abstraction. While a person with affective empathy "sees an" emotion in another person and reacts accordingly, cognitive empathy in a person requires the person to *understand* how one would feel in a certain situation. To the extent that theory of mind and cognitive empathy rely on perspective taking and "putting oneself in another person's shoes," the two terms can be used interchangeably. Tests can measure both affective and cognitive empathy. Affective empathy can be measured simply by observing changes in physiology using heart rate and galvanic skin responses, while tests for cognitive empathy focus on having the person verbalize an understanding of the emotions in others using tests that measure perspective taking, empathic accuracy, and theory of mind (Batson *et al.*, 1997). The empathy quotient (EQ) also measures general levels of empathy in a person.

Some studies have shown that individuals with ASD do not differ in affective empathy but are significantly deficient in cognitive empathy when compared with controls. When a group of 21 ASD adults was matched with 21 controls using tests that measure both cognitive and affective empathy, the ASD group scored lower than the control group on tests that involved theory of mind but scored no differently on "empathetic concern." Notably, they scored even higher than the control group on personal distress (Rogers *et al.*, 2007). Another study measured groups of boys with psychopathic tendencies and problems with perspective taking. Not surprisingly, the boys with psychopathic issues had trouble with affective empathy (Jones *et al.*, 2010). They felt *nothing* when others were distressed. In contrast, the boys with ASD were compromised in their ability to take the perspectives of others but reported emotional experiences that were in line with a control group. They had appropriate affective empathy but lacked cognitive empathy. The authors concluded that psychopathic tendencies are far different from ASD in that psychopathy is associated with difficulties in resonating with people's distress whereas ASD is characterized by difficulties in knowing what other people think. It is not surprising that people with weak cognitive empathy would struggle with the components that make up their socio-sexuality (Wlodarski, 2015) or their psychosexual development.

These studies indicate that the containment model makes assumptions about some individuals with ASD who have offended sexually that simply are not the case. Standard sex offender treatment assumes that these offenders had cognitive empathy when they offended. Perhaps the offender compartmentalized their thinking in order to put out of their mind why an offense against a child was wrong, according to common thinking. Or perhaps the typical offender habitually rationalizes their criminal behavior. It follows that the ongoing goal of treatment would be to get them to give up all of their habitual rationalizations and denials. However, as we have seen, individuals with ASD tend to have adequate affective empathy and weak cognitive empathy. For some individuals with ASD, this goes beyond mere compartmentalization and falls within the realm of not accepting criminal responsibility. It is plausible that an individual does not understand why looking at illegal images is wrong/illegal or why touching someone without consent is sexual assault (see Allely & Creaby-Attwood, 2016; Allely & Dubin, 2018; Creaby-Attwood & Allely, 2017). Once someone with ASD learns that another person is in distress, they are incredibly caring and empathetic. However, this needs to be explained and taught to the ASD individual like a second language. Thus, when group sex offender treatment heavily relies on confrontation between group members and aggressiveness between the treatment provider and the probationer, I would argue that this is extremely counterproductive in preventing recidivism and would actually be harmful for the ASD population. Many autistic people do not set out to break the law and should not be shamed. We should assume that some of the information that the ASD individual is learning in treatment is being acquired for the first time. Scolding them for lacking empathy or asking them to "spill the beans" to make more self-disclosures is likely to be confusing and harmful.

There are other problems with the containment model as it applies to ASD individuals. Group therapy with neurotypical offenders would be problematic for this population who have their own targeted set of needs. Bleil Walters *et al.* (2013) cite research to suggest that programs should target the specific needs of each ASD offender, such as social skills training, empathy training, detailed identification of biological anatomy, psychosexual education, and the progression of how healthy relationships usually develop. ASD presents with a unique set of communication issues that would not play out well in a heterogeneous group setting (Melvin, Langdon & Murphy, 2017). One of those issues is selective mutism, which is an anxiety disorder where a person who can normally speak proficiently literally cannot speak in certain situations and to certain people. Selective mutism is often comorbid with developmental disabilities (Kristensen, 2000). One study examining 97 people with selective mutism showed that 63 percent met a diagnosis for ASD (Steffenburg *et al.*, 2018). What would happen if a group therapist mistook silence for defiance, denials, or rationalizations? It is easy to imagine scenarios where this could result in big trouble for the probationer with ASD. The author of this book is familiar with one specific instance where this has happened.

It is also well documented that autistic individuals experience disproportionately high anxiety levels in general (e.g., Kim *et al.*, 2000). Indeed, numerous studies have found that there is a strong comorbidity between ASD and anxiety (e.g., Zaboski & Storch, 2018). South and Rodgers (2017) have attributed this to atypical sensory functioning, alexithymia (difficulty labeling one's own emotions, or finding the right words to describe them), and the intolerance of uncertainty. They suggest that the biological basis of anxiety for ASD individuals is the disrupted integration between the medial prefrontal cortex and the limbic and insula-based networks within the brain. Group environments that thrive on confrontation and unpredictability to keep the probationer off-guard in order to forcibly ensure compliance would most likely be contraindicated for this population. Probation officers routinely show up and conduct unannounced visits to a sex offender's residence and/or place of work. I would suggest that the unpredictability associated with these visits would also exacerbate the extreme anxiety that ASD individuals already feel. Mark Mahoney (2009) gives an example of a young man with ASD who was mandated to attend group sex offender therapy:

> As a condition of his probation that young man was ordered to attend a traditional SOTP. He has said that the stories he hears at his group treatment make him feel nauseous. He does not understand how or why the others in the treatment program did what they did, and he believes that everything that is said as part of his SOTP is the opposite of what he is told by his private psychologists. Overall, he seems to find the traditional SOTP unhelpful and upsetting. Instead of helping him learn appropriate behavior, it is confusing him and placing him in contact with individuals who actually are sexual predators. (p.57)

Although the literature is sparse in the area of treatment success and failure with ASD individuals charged with crimes, there are some examples. In one study where group therapy was utilized, some recidivism was displayed by ASD group participants (Griffin-Shelley, 2010). In another study where individual therapy was used because the participant found group work difficult, individual psychoeducational therapy was employed and there was no recidivism (Radley & Shaherbano, 2011). Another study focused on an autistic young man admitted to the hospital after multiple counts of sexual assault. His treatment involved group work but it also incorporated social skills training, CBT, occupational therapy, and relapse-prevention training. No recidivism was reported (Kelbrick & Radley, 2013). Another study for juveniles with ASD aged 14–17 focused on naming emotions (alexithymia), working on expanding cognitive flexibility, and identifying triggers. Recidivism was varied in this study (Ray et al., 2004). The generalizability of these studies is unknown since factors such as substance abuse, terms of incarceration, and history of abuse are missing, as is other pertinent information.

It is important to highlight that conventional sex offender treatment is predominantly based on group therapy. In these group sessions, there is a focus on the individual's understanding of their offending pattern, learning about thought errors, practicing empathetic responses to the victims, and stopping deviant thoughts and fantasies. Sugrue (2017) has argued that this approach in treatment (which can be effective with neurotypicals) is not appropriate for individuals with ASD (Griffiths & Fedoroff, 2009; Ray et al., 2004). A more effective approach for individuals with ASD would be a tailored treatment consisting of very explicit sex education, which also has a focus on learning "specific responses to specific situations" (Griffiths & Fedoroff, 2009). Another feature needed for such an ASD treatment program is content repetition due to the difficulty that some ASD individuals tend to have in understanding and appreciating abstract concepts (Klin et al., 1995).

Should treatment for an autistic offender be different than for a neuro-typical one? Based on the literature, my opinion is yes. I suggest a model of habilitating autistic individuals when it comes to psychosexual issues rather than rehabilitating them. Cognitive empathy is a skill that this population needs to acquire. It is not innate among them. I further suggest a model that that is trauma-informed (can treat trauma-based issues), one that mixes CBT to strengthen cognitive empathy with relapse prevention and psychoeducational programming, the aforementioned being effective treatment modalities for this population (Kose, Fox & Storch, 2018; Smith et al., 2012). If group therapy is used, I suggest it be employed by a person specifically trained in ASD and homogenized for the ASD population.

I also call for further research to explore effective treatment modalities for this unique issue.

I argue that the Good Lives Model (GLM) is appropriate for individuals with ASD to augment the aforementioned treatment modalities. The GLM is a strength-based rehabilitation/habilitation theory that focuses on a person developing life goals and fulfillments in order to erase the need to criminally offend (Ward, Yates & Long, 2006; Yates & Ward, 2008; Yates, Prescott & Ward, 2010). Treatment emphasis is on the attainment of goals as opposed to strictly avoiding certain behaviors. Instead of "overcoming intimacy deficits," for example, primary relationship skills are taught in the first place (Yates & Ward, 2008). The GLM works towards helping a person to develop an intrinsic acceptance of self, learn important life skills, and find basic happiness, inner peace, and community involvement.

The GLM would be a great supplement to and augmentation of other treatment modalities for a few reasons. First, in order for the quality of life of individuals on the autism spectrum to be improved, they have to acquire basic life skills or adaptive functioning. Unlike neurotypicals who may have attained these skills, such as knowing how to cook, balancing a budget, and so forth, many autistic adults have not, as shown by Vineland test scores. Feeling productive and caring for oneself would probably lead to improvements in all areas of life and would very likely reduce the need to reoffend. The GLM would include a module on sex education tailored to meet the specific needs of the probationer who might lack basic psychosexual knowledge. Second, the GLM does not make assumptions that offenders have a predilection to offend that needs to be under constant surveillance or control. As noted earlier, counterfeit deviance for an autistic individual is the commission of a criminal act without the intent or understanding of why the act was wrong or illegal. While other treatment modalities would help to identify cognitive thinking errors and monitor relapse prevention, the GLM would augment those approaches by focusing on the habilitation of the individual. Griffiths and Fedoroff (2009) note that traditional sex offender treatment that is rehabilitative in nature seeks to return sexual expression to a state of dignity. Habilitative therapy seeks to "establish that state of dignity" in the first place. Bolton (2018) notes that classifying ASD individuals as deviant and attempting to remedy the deviance within this medicalized framework would miss the mark. Instead, Bolton recommends an educational approach with very implicit sex education as well as behavioral therapy tailored to the individual. Additionally, Ray and colleagues (2004) feel that traditional group sex offender treatment that requires the probationer to replace "deviant" behaviors with prosocial ones is inappropriate and often harmful, despite its well-intentioned nature. They noted problems in adolescents with ASD in adapting to this treatment, including aversive reactions to the treatment. Instead, they recommend providing information in a piecemeal fashion, making use of visual aids, and creating long-term goals, which the GLM utilizes. The GLM provides a sense of structure, which appeals to the sensibilities of those on the autism spectrum. Lastly, because the GLM is strength based, it would tap into the special interests that individuals with ASD naturally have (Winter-Messiers *et al.*, 2007). It would ideally help ASD individuals to acquire socially appropriate special interests, or further develop the ones they already have, to gain more enjoyment out of life. While models of containment and risk/need focus exclusively on ascertaining whether the individuals pose a threat to the community, the GLM is individualistic, humanistic, and holistic, and is applicable to all areas of life. It measures treatment success not just on lack of recidivism, but also on helping the autistic individual to attain broader goals in life.

One other program, which I believe has utility and applicability for the autistic population, is the Circles of Support and Accountability program (COSA) (Wilson, McWhinnie *et al.*, 2007). No effective treatment program is complete unless it helps to ensure that an individual remains accountable for their continued behavior, and COSA does this in a humane way that is responsible in terms of both the community and the offender. Interestingly, the program started because of a "slightly intellectually disabled" person who committed several sex offenses in the past (Höing, 2015, p.15). When the disabled individual was released from prison, he had no one to look out for him. A local church member who had known the young man for a while decided to start a support group just for him, modeled on the idea of wraparound care. After the police informed neighbors of this young man's presence in the neighborhood, there was an uproar, to such an extent that police had to patrol his home 24/7. The young man's circle of support helped him to get through the experience. The group members advocated for him to make sure he was able to access the benefits he was entitled to, helped him manage his outbursts and the anxiety associated with anger from neighbors, walked him through emergencies, mediated landlord conflicts, and celebrated anniversaries and every success he had towards reintegration into society. After a while, the uproar died down and police became supportive of what the circle of support was doing as they witnessed the young man's success. With the success of this case, the COSA concept of working with sex offenders took off across Canada and Europe, thanks to Mennonite and Quaker communities that promoted the program.

A typical COSA program consists of three to six community volunteers who pass a careful selection and training program and are then paired with the offender and the professionals designated to oversee them, such as a probation officer and therapist (*ibid.*). In order to qualify, program volunteers must demonstrate a supportive attitude towards restorative justice, must be empathetic to the "core member" (offender), must be willing to communicate and cooperate with other volunteers, and must also monitor risks that the core member faces. Community volunteers (like the church members in the disabled individual's case) meet face to face at least weekly and are available on a 24/7 basis for the core member. These circles can be thought of as a "surrogate social network" (*ibid.*, p.86) in which the core member is provided a safe space to learn new behaviors that are adaptable and promote success. A circle coordinator (such as a case manager) records the minutes for each meeting, and community members can report recidivism concerns to the circle coordinator at any time (Bates, Saunders & Wilson, 2007). Circles usually last one to one-and-a-half years, but can often go on for longer (Bates *et al.*, 2014). COSA's philosophy is to help the core member reduce isolation and emotional loneliness, model appropriate relationships, and demonstrate humanity and care of the individual (Wilson & Saunders, 2003). It also properly monitors the individual to protect the public and keep the person accountable.

COSA works well with autistic individuals and the developmentally disabled because it tailors its curriculum to fit the unique needs of the individual. A case in point is a 17-year-old adolescent named "Gary", who had been referred to the UK's Respond Circle of Support and Accountability group (Respond, 2020). Gary grew up in an abusive household, experienced severe neglect and had a dual diagnosis of autism and ADHD. After some troubling incidents involving sexual behavior and a risk assessment performed at his school that indicated he needed intervention, Gary was referred to the program—presumably in lieu of involvement in the criminal justice system. Gary's core group members were all informed about his traumatic life circumstances, behaviors, and were regularly in contact with the COSA coordinator, his headteacher, social worker, and psychiatrist.

Group members went out of their way to create a non-judgmental space for Gary. They quickly intuited that they were not going to make progress the traditional way with Gary through CBT or aversion therapy. So they began at a simple starting place: playing interactive games with Gary. It worked! Interacting in a way that Gary felt comfortable with helped build his trust with interpersonal relationships, developing his communication skills and increasing his confidence. In time, Gary felt more comfortable talking about the reason why he was in the program to begin with—learning about sex, relationships, and friendships. For the first time, Gary learned how his behavior impacted others and gained insight into it. Gary learned how to avoid risky situations and thereby probably helped him stay out of more legal jeopardy, too. The volunteers created a visual chart for his bedroom in the form of an "easy read", presumably to help him identify his triggers and stay emotionally regulated (Respond, 2020).

Gary made remarkable progress in his 18 months at this COSA group. He experienced a sense of companionship, and a feeling that he deserved friendships and relationships outside of the group, this was a first for Gary (Respond, 2020). He was acquiring skills he did not have before entering the group. Most importantly, the group went out of its way to mimic a typical social group, ensuring Gary was not the center of attention or a specimen to be focused upon. The groups are, of course, designed to make the client feel as if they genuinely belong.

I can see why this approach could be effective with autistic people. It focuses on educating the individual, rather than rehabilitating them. It keeps a person accountable, rather than solely focusing on keeping them contained and sealed off from the rest of society. And the research also supports its efficacy with the general population. One study (Duwe, 2018) from Minnesota Circles of Support and Accountability (MnCOSA), a sex offender reentry program implemented by the Minnesota Department of Corrections in 2008, suggested that the offense rate would lower by 88 percent for a new sex offense by implementing the program. Another study found an 83 percent reduction for a new sex offense (Wilson, Picheca & Prinzo, 2007).

Conclusion

This book has explored new ways of looking at an old problem that, up until now, simply has not been addressed. I have tried to synthesize the literature into a cohesive whole in order to provide a potential roadmap for the future. I have emphasized the importance of prevention as the primary way to avoid the nightmare of autistic individuals facing the criminal justice system in Chapter 1. But, in the case of the tragedy unfolding, I have laid out alternative strategies based on the literature that contrast with what is currently being employed. It is my wish that, in the years to come, this topic reaches the audience it needs to. I would like to see change at all levels of society—starting with state legislators who propose and vote on laws, those who develop prosecutorial policies, judges who consider autistic defendants who appear before them in court, and finally, professionals who can establish therapeutic and habilitative methods to help to prevent ASD individuals becoming involved in the criminal justice system—so that these tragic, nightmare scenarios do not unfold in the first place.

May we choose the road less traveled and be better for it. May we have fewer victims, fewer prosecutions, more diversions, fewer autistic sex offender registrants, and better aftercare for ASD individuals who do end up in the criminal justice system.

References

18 U.S. Code § 17 (2020). *Insanity Defense*. Accessed on 23/11/2020 at www.law.cornell.edu/uscode/text/18/17.

29 U.S. Code § 794(a) (2006). *Nondiscrimination Under Federal Grants and Programs*. Accessed on 23/11/2020 at www.law.cornell.edu/uscode/text/29/794.

42 U.S. Code § 12132 (1990). *Discrimination*. Accessed on 23/11/2020 at www.law.cornell.edu/uscode/text/42/12132.

Abramov, E. (2017). 'An autistic man lives here cops no excuses... Oh yes he is black too.' *Cognitive Disability, Race and Police Brutality in the United States* (Master's Thesis, Columbia University).

Abrams, D. (2013). 'Putting the trial penalty on trial.' *Duquesne University Law Review 51*, 777–785.

Al-Rousan, T., Rubenstein, L., Sieleni, B., Deol, H., & Wallace, R. B. (2017). 'Inside the nation's largest mental health institution: A prevalence study in a state prison system.' *BMC Public Health 17* (1), 871–881.

Allely, C. & Creaby-Attwood, A. (2016). 'Sexual offending and autism spectrum disorders.' *Journal of Intellectual Disabilities and Offending Behaviour 7* (1), 35–51.

Allely, C. S. (2015). 'Experiences of prison inmates with autism spectrum disorders and the knowledge and understanding of the spectrum amongst prison staff: A review.' *Journal of Intellectual Disabilities and Offending Behaviour 6* (2), 55–67.

Allely, C. S. (2018). 'Sexual offending behaviours: Urgent need for "autism sensitive risk assessment guide".' *Gillberg's Blogs*. Accessed on 23/11/2020 at https://gillberg.blogg.gu.se/en/2018/02/27/725.

Allely, C. S. (2019). 'Firesetting and arson in individuals with autism spectrum disorder: A systematic PRISMA review.' *Journal of Intellectual Disabilities and Offending Behaviour 10* (4), 89–101.

Allely, C. S. & Dubin, L. (2018). 'The contributory role of autism symptomology in child pornography offending: Why there is an urgent need for empirical research in this area.' *Journal of Intellectual Disabilities and Offending Behaviour 9* (4), 129–152.

Allely, C. S. & Faccini, L. (2017). '"Path to intended violence" model to understand mass violence in the case of Elliot Rodger.' *Aggression and Violent Behavior 37*, 201–209.

Allely, C. S. & Faccini, L. (2019). 'Clinical profile, risk, and critical factors and the application of the "path toward intended violence" model in the case of mass shooter Dylann Roof.' *Deviant Behavior 40* (6), 672–689.

Allely, C. S., Wilson, P., Minnis, H., Thompson, L., Yaksic, E., & Gillberg, C. (2017). 'Violence is rare in autism: When it does occur, is it sometimes extreme?' *The Journal of Psychology 151* (1), 49–68.

Allen, D., Evans, C., Hider, A., Hawkins, S., Peckett, H., & Morgan, H. (2008). 'Offending behaviour in adults with Asperger syndrome.' *Journal of Autism and Developmental Disorders 38* (4), 748–758.

Allen, R. & Heaton, P. (2010). 'Autism, music, and the therapeutic potential of music in alexithymia.' *Music Perception: An Interdisciplinary Journal 27* (4), 251–261.

Allen, S. (2015). 'Police were called to take Teresa Sheehan to a hospital. Instead, they shot her seven times.' *BuzzFeed News*. Accessed on 23/11/2020 at www.buzzfeednews.com/article/sandraeallen/the-trials-of-teresa-sheehan-how-america-is-killing-its-ment.

Ambler, P. G., Eidels, A., & Gregory, C. (2015). 'Anxiety and aggression in adolescents with autism spectrum disorders attending mainstream schools.' *Research in Autism Spectrum Disorders 18*, 97–109.

American Psychiatric Association (2013). *Diagnostic and Statistical Manual of Mental Disorders* (5th ed.). Washington, DC: American Psychiatric Association.

Anderson, K. A., McDonald, T. A., Edsall, D., Smith, L. E., & Taylor, J. L. (2016). 'Postsecondary expectations of high-school students with autism spectrum disorders.' *Focus on Autism and Other Developmental Disabilities 31* (1), 16–26.

Anderson, K. A., Shattuck, P. T., Cooper, B. P., Roux, A. M., & Wagner, M. (2014). 'Prevalence and correlates of postsecondary residential status among young adults with an autism spectrum disorder.' *Autism 18* (5), 562–570.

Ania, F., Breetvelt, E., Vorstman, J., Chow, E., *et al.* (2018). 'F72: Neurocognition and adaptive functioning in the 22q11.2 deletion syndrome model of schizophrenia.' *Schizophrenia Bulletin 44* (Suppl 1), S247–S247.

Anthony, L. G., Kenworthy, L., Yerys, B. E., Jankowski, K. F., *et al.* (2013). 'Interests in high-functioning autism are more intense, interfering, and idiosyncratic than those in neurotypical development.' *Development and Psychopathology 25* (3), 643–652.

Arnett, J. J. (1998). 'Learning to stand alone: The contemporary American transition to adulthood in cultural and historical context.' *Human Development 41* (5–6), 295–315.

Ashkar, P. J. & Kenny, D. T. (2008). 'Views from the inside: Young offenders' subjective experiences of incarceration.' *International Journal of Offender Therapy and Comparative Criminology 52*, 584–597.

Asperger, H. (1991). '"Autistic Psychopathy" in Childhood.' In U. Frith (ed.) *Autism and Asperger Syndrome* (pp.37–92). Cambridge: Cambridge University Press.

Associated Press. (2018). 'Video shows off-duty Chicago police officer shooting unarmed autistic man.' *The Guardian*. Accessed on 23/11/2020 at www.theguardian.com/us-news/2018/oct/17/video-shows-chicago-police-officer-shoot-unarmed-autistic-man.

Atkins v. Virginia [2002]. 536 U.S. 304, 122 S. Ct. 2242, 153 L. Ed. 2d 335.

Atladóttir, H. Ó., Thorsen, P., Østergaard, L., Schendel, D. E., *et al.* (2010). 'Maternal infection requiring hospitalization during pregnancy and autism spectrum disorders.' *Journal of Autism and Developmental Disorders 40* (12), 1423–1430.

Attwood, T., Hénault, I., & Dubin, N. (2014). *The Autism Spectrum, Sexuality and the Law: What Every Parent and Professional Needs to Know*. London: Jessica Kingsley Publishers.

Aunos, M. & Feldman, M. A. (2002). 'Attitudes towards sexuality, sterilization and parenting rights of persons with intellectual disabilities.' *Journal of Applied Research in Intellectual Disabilities 15* (4), 285–296.

Austin, R. (2014). '"Not just a common criminal": The case for sentencing mitigation videos.' *University of Pennsylvania Law School, Public Law Research Paper*, 14–19.

Autistic Self Advocacy Network. (2011). Homepage. *Autistic Self Advocacy Network*. Accessed on 23/11/2020 at https://autisticadvocacy.org.

Aviv, R. (2013). 'The science of sex abuse.' *The New Yorker*. Accessed on 23/11/2020 at www.newyorker.com/magazine/2013/01/14/the-science-of-sex-abuse.

Bacon, S. L. (2010). 'A distinction without a difference: Receipt and possession of child pornography and the double jeopardy problem.' *University of Miami Law Review 65*, 1027–1058.

Baer, R. A., Smith, G. T., Hopkins, J., Krietemeyer, J., & Toney, L. (2006). 'Using self-report assessment methods to explore facets of mindfulness.' *Assessment 13* (1), 27–45.

Bagenstos, S. (2000). 'Subordination, stigma, and "disability".' *Virginia Law Review*, 397–534.

Bailey, A. & Sines, D. (1998). 'Significance of the attitudes of police and care staff toward sex and persons who have a learning disability.' *Journal of Intellectual Disabilities 2* (3), 168–174.

Baldwin, J. M. (2016). 'Investigating the programmatic attack: A national survey of veterans treatment courts.' *Journal of Criminal Law and Criminology 105*, 705–751.

Baldwin, S., Costley, D., & Warren, A. (2014). 'Employment activities and experiences of adults with high-functioning autism and Asperger's disorder.' *Journal of Autism and Developmental Disorders 44* (10), 2440–2449.

Ballaban-Gil, K., Rapin, I., Tuchman, R., & Shinnar, S. (1996). 'Longitudinal examination of the behavioral, language, and social changes in a population of adolescents and young adults with autistic disorder.' *Pediatric Neurology 15* (3), 217–223.

Ballan, M. S. (2012). 'Parental perspectives of communication about sexuality in families of children with autism spectrum disorders.' *Journal of Autism and Developmental Disorders 42*, 676–684.

Ballan, M. S. & Freyer, M. B. (2017). 'Autism spectrum disorder, adolescence, and sexuality education: Suggested interventions for mental health professionals.' *Sexuality and Disability 35* (2), 261–273.

Banbury, S. (2004). 'Coercive sexual behaviour in British prisons as reported by adult ex-prisoners.' *Howard Journal 43*, 113–130.

Barbaree, H. E., Seto, M. C., Langton, C. M., & Peacock, E. J. (2001). 'Evaluating the predictive accuracy of six risk assessment instruments for adult sex offenders.' *Criminal Justice and Behavior 28* (4), 490–521.

Barnett, J. P. & Maticka-Tyndale, E. (2015). 'Qualitative exploration of sexual experiences among adults on the autism spectrum: Implications for sex education.' *Perspectives on Sexual and Reproductive Health 47* (4), 171–179.

Baron-Cohen, S. (2012). *The Science of Evil: On Empathy and the Origins of Cruelty*. New York, NY: Basic Books.

Baron-Cohen, S. & Wheelwright, S. (2004). 'The empathy quotient: An investigation of adults with Asperger syndrome or high functioning autism, and normal sex differences.' *Journal of Autism and Developmental Disorders 34* (2), 163–175.

Baron-Cohen, S., Ashwin, E., Ashwin, C., Tavassoli, T. & Chakrabarti, B. (2009). 'Talent in autism: Hyper-systemizing, hyper-attention to detail and sensory hypersensitivity.' *Philosophical Transactions of the Royal Society B: Biological Sciences 364* (1522), 1377–1383.

Barry-Walsh, J. B. & Mullen, P. E. (2004). 'Forensic aspects of Asperger's syndrome.' *Journal of Forensic Psychiatry and Psychology 15* (1), 96–107.

Bates, A., Saunders, R., & Wilson, C. (2007). 'Doing something about it: A follow-up study of sex offenders participating in Valley Circles of support and accountability.' *British Journal of Community Justice 5* (1), 19–42.

Bates, A., Williams, D., Wilson, C., & Wilson, R. J. (2014). 'Circles South East: The first 10 years 2002–2012.' *International Journal of Offender Therapy and Comparative Criminology 58* (7), 861–885.

Bath, C., Bhardwa, B., Jacobson, J., May, T., & Webster, R. (2015). 'There to help: Ensuring provision of appropriate adults for mentally vulnerable adults detained or interviewed by police.' *Irish Journal of Learning Disabilities 44* (3), 213–224.

Batson, C. D., Polycarpou, M. P., Harmon-Jones, E., Imhoff, H. J., *et al.* (1997). 'Empathy and attitudes: Can feeling for a member of a stigmatized group improve feelings toward the group?' *Journal of Personality and Social Psychology 72* (1), 105–118.

Baude, W. (2018). 'Is qualified immunity unlawful?' *California Law Review 106* (1), 45–90.

Becker-Weidman, A. (2009). 'Effects of early maltreatment on development: A descriptive study using the Vineland Adaptive Behavior Scales-II.' *Child Welfare 88* (2), 137–161.

Beddows, N. & Brooks, R. (2016). 'Inappropriate sexual behaviour in adolescents with autism spectrum disorder: What education is recommended and why.' *Early Intervention in Psychiatry 10* (4), 282–289.

Belardinelli, C., Raza, M., & Taneli, T. (2016). 'Comorbid behavioral problems and psychiatric disorders in autism spectrum disorders.' *Journal of Childhood and Developmental Disorders 2* (11), 275–266.

Bellin, J. (2019). 'The power of prosecutors.' *New York University Law Review 94*, 171–212.

Bellini, S. & Hopf, A. (2007). 'The development of the Autism Social Skills Profile: A preliminary analysis of psychometric properties.' *Focus on Autism and Other Developmental Disabilities 22* (2), 80–87.

Berger v. United States [1935]. 295 U.S. 78, 55 S. Ct. 629, 79 L. Ed. 1314.

Berman, D. A. (2002). 'From lawlessness to too much law: Exploring the risk of disparity from differences in defense counsel under guidelines sentencing.' *Iowa Law Review 87*, 435–463.

Berry, K. (2015). 'How judicial elections impact criminal cases.' *Brennan Center for Justice*. Accessed on 23/11/2020 at www.brennancenter.org/our-work/research-reports/how-judicial-elections-impact-criminal-cases.

Berryessa, C. M. (2014). 'Judiciary views on criminal behaviour and intention of offenders with high-functioning autism.' *Journal of Intellectual Disabilities and Offending Behaviour 5* (2), 97–106.

Berryessa, C. M. (2016). 'Brief report: Judicial attitudes regarding the sentencing of offenders with high functioning autism.' *Journal of Autism and Developmental Disorders 46* (8), 2770–2773.

Bertilsdotter-Rosqvist, H. (2019). 'Knowing what to do: Exploring meanings of development and peer support aimed at people with autism.' *International Journal of Inclusive Education 23* (2), 174–187.

Bettelheim, B. (1959). 'Feral children and autistic children.' *American Journal of Sociology 64* (5), 455–467.

Bhakare, P. & Vinchurkar, A. (2015). 'Study of visual reaction time in autism.' *Indian Journal of Medical Research and Pharmaceutical Sciences 2* (7), 49–51.

Bharara, P. & Kennedy, D. (2015). *Williams v. City of N.Y., 12 Civ. 6805 (VEC) (S.D.N.Y.). Statement of Interest to the United States of America.* Accessed on 23/11/2020 at www.ada.gov/williams_new-york_soi.pdf.

Biller v. State [2013]. 109 So. 3d 1240 (Fla. Dist. Ct. App. 2013).

Bird, G., Press, C., & Richardson, D. C. (2011). 'The role of alexithymia in reduced eye-fixation in Autism Spectrum Conditions.' *Journal of Autism and Developmental Disorders 41*, 556–564.

Blair, R. J. R. (2005). 'Responding to the emotions of others: Dissociating forms of empathy through the study of typical and psychiatric populations.' *Consciousness and Cognition 14*, 698–718.

Blair, R. J. R. (2008). 'Fine cuts of empathy and the amygdala: Dissociable deficits in psychopathy and autism.' *The Quarterly Journal of Experimental Psychology 61* (1), 157–170.

Blasingame, G. D., Abel, G. G., Jordan, A., & Wiegel, M. (2011). 'The utility and psychometric properties of the Abel-Blasingame assessment system for individuals with intellectual disabilities.' *Journal of Mental Health Research in Intellectual Disabilities 4* (2), 107–132.

Bleil Walters, J., Hughes, T. L., Sutton, L. R., Marshall, S. N., *et al.* (2013). 'Maltreatment and depression in adolescent sexual offenders with an autism spectrum disorder.' *Journal of Child Sexual Abuse 22* (1), 72–89.

Blume, J. H. & Helm, R. K. (2014). 'The unexonerated: Factually innocent defendants who plead guilty.' *Cornell Law Review 100*, 157–192.

Bolger, P., Kremser, J., & Walker, H. (2019). 'Detention or diversion? The influence of training and education on school police officer discretion.' *Policing: An International Journal 42* (2), 255–269.

Bolton, A. & KUSA (2014). 'Misunderstanding leads to suspicion of DUI.' *KUSA.* Accessed on 27/9/2019 at www.9news.com/article/news/local/9news-evenings/misunderstanding-leads-to-suspicion-of-dui/249453143.

Bolton, W. (2018). 'Developmental Theory and Developmental Deficits: The Treatment of Sex Offenders with Asperger's Syndrome.' In *Sex, Mind, and Emotion* (pp.41–61). London: Routledge.

Bond, C. F., Jr. & DePaulo, B. M. (2006). 'Accuracy of deception judgments.' *Personality and Social Psychology Review 10*, 214–234.

Bonta, J., Jesseman, R., Rugge, T., & Cormier, R. (2006). 'Restorative Justice and Recidivism: Promises Made, Promises Kept?' In D. Sullivan & L. Tifft (eds) *Handbook of Restorative Justice: A Global Perspective* (pp.108–120). Abingdon: Routledge.

Booth, R. D. & Happé, F. G. (2018). 'Evidence of reduced global processing in autism spectrum disorder.' *Journal of Autism and Developmental Disorders 48* (4), 1397–1408.

Brace, P., Hall, M. G., & Langer, L. (1999). 'Judicial choice and the politics of abortion: Institutions context, and the autonomy of courts.' *Albany Law Review 62* (2), 1265–1303.

Bradley, R. J. (2017). *"Why Single Me Out"? Peer Mentoring, Autism and Inclusion in Mainstream Schools* (Doctoral Dissertation, University of Birmingham).

Brady v. United States [1970]. 397 U.S. 742, 90 S. Ct. 1463, 25 L. Ed. 2d 747.

Brewer, N., Zoanetti, J., & Young, R. L. (2017). 'The influence of media suggestions about links between criminality and autism spectrum disorder.' *Autism 21*, 117–121.

Brewer, R. J., Davies, G. M., & Blackwood, N. J. (2016). 'Fitness to plead: The impact of autism spectrum disorder.' *Journal of Forensic Psychology Practice 16* (3), 182–197.

Broekman, B. F., Olff, M., & Boer, F. (2007). 'The genetic background to PTSD.' *Neuroscience and Biobehavioral Reviews 31* (3), 348–362.

Bronsard, G., Botbol, M., & Tordjman, S. (2010). 'Aggression in low functioning children and adolescents with autistic disorder.' *PLOS ONE 5* (12).

Bronson, J. & Berzofsky, M. (2017). 'Indicators of mental health problems reported by prisoners and jail inmates, 2011–12.' *Bureau of Justice Statistics*, 1–16.

Brosnan, M. & Gavin, J. (2015). 'Are Friends Electric? Why Those with an Autism Spectrum Disorder (ASD) Thrive in Online Cultures but Suffer in Offline Cultures.' In L. D. Rosen, N. Cheever, & L. M. Carrier (eds) *The Wiley Handbook of Psychology, Technology, and Society First Edition* (pp.108–120). Chichester: Wiley.

Brown, K. W. & Kasser, T. (2005). 'Are psychological and ecological well-being compatible? The role of values, mindfulness, and lifestyle.' *Social Indicators Research 74* (2), 349–368.

Brown-Lavoie, S. M., Viecili, M. A., & Weiss, J. A. (2014). 'Sexual knowledge and victimization in adults with autism spectrum disorders.' *Journal of Autism and Developmental Disorders 44* (9), 2185–2196.

Brucker, D. L. (2015). 'Perceptions, behaviors, and satisfaction related to public safety for persons with disabilities in the United States.' *Criminal Justice Review 40* (4), 431–448.

Bryen, D. N. & Wickman, C. H. (2011). 'Ending the silence of people with little or no functional speech: Testifying in court.' *Disability Studies Quarterly 31* (4).

Bureau of Justice Statistics (2003). *Recidivism of Sex Offenders Released from Prison in 1994*. Washington, DC: U.S. Department of Justice.

Buron, K. D. & Curtis, M. (2003). *The Incredible 5-Point Scale: Assisting Students with Autism Spectrum Disorders in Understanding Social Interactions and Controlling their Emotional Responses.* Shawnee, KS: AAPC Publishing.

Byers, E. S. & Nichols, S. (2014). 'Sexual satisfaction of high-functioning adults with autism spectrum disorder.' *Sexuality and Disability 32* (3), 365–382.

Byers, E. S., Nichols, S., & Voyer, S. D. (2013). 'Challenging stereotypes: Sexual functioning of single adults with high functioning autism spectrum disorder.' *Journal of Autism and Developmental Disorders 43* (11), 2617–2627.

Cabrera, K. & Rice, L. (2019). 'For those with autism and other disabilities, new law could prevent miscommunication with police.' *The Texas Tribune.* Accessed on 23/11/2020 at www.texastribune.org/2019/08/29/autism-new-law-police.

Cage, E., Di Monaco, J., & Newell, V. (2018). 'Experiences of autism acceptance and mental health in autistic adults.' *Journal of Autism and Developmental Disorders 48* (2), 473–484.

Calaway, W. R. (2018). 'Sex offenders, custody and habeas.' *St. John's Law Review 92*, 755–795.

Capozzi, S., Barmache, D., Cladis, E., Peña, E. V., & Kocur, J. (2019). 'The significance of involving nonspeaking autistic peer mentors in educational programs.' *Autism in Adulthood 1* (3), 170–172.

Cappadocia, M. C., Weiss, J. A., & Pepler, D. (2012). 'Bullying experiences among children and youth with autism spectrum disorders.' *Journal of Autism and Developmental Disorders 42* (2), 266–277.

Cappellino, A. & Meringolo, J. (2013). 'The federal sentencing guidelines and the pursuit of fair and just sentences.' *Albany Law Review 77*, 771–824.

Carlson, K., Clark, G., & Hinchcliffe, K. (2012). 'Attorneys: Sex offenders face dilemma when finding housing.' *WRAL.com.* Accessed on 24/11/2020 at www.wral.com/attorneys-sex-offenders-face-dilemma-when-finding-housing/11436830.

Carpenter, C. L. (2006). 'The constitutionality of strict liability in sex offender registration laws.' *Boston University Law Review 86*, 295–369.

Cashin, A. & Yorke, J. (2016). 'Overly regulated thinking and autism revisited.' *Journal of Child and Adolescent Psychiatric Nursing 29* (3), 148–153.

Cassidy, M., Thompson, R., El-Nagib, R., Hickling, L. M., & Priebe, S. (2019). 'Motivations and experiences of volunteers and patients in mental health befriending: A thematic analysis.' *BMC Psychiatry 19* (1), 116.

CBS News (2017). 'John Benjamin Haygood: 10-year-old student with autism handcuffed in disturbing video.' *CBS News.* Accessed on 23/11/2020 at www.cbsnews.com/news/john-benjamin-haygood-disturbing-video-shows-10-year-old-with-autism-arrested-at-school.

CDC (2020). *Data and Statistics on Autism Spectrum Disorder.* Accessed on 23/11/2020 at www.cdc.gov/ncbddd/autism/data.html.

Cea, C. N. (2014). 'Autism and the criminal defendant.' *St. John's Law Review 88*, 495–530.

Centre for Justice and Reconciliation (2017). 'Lesson 1: What is restorative justice?' *Centre for Justice and Reconciliation.* Accessed on 23/11/2020 at http://restorativejustice.org/restorative-justice/about-restorative-justice/tutorial-intro-to-restorative-justice/lesson-1-what-is-restorative-justice.

Chaffin, M. (2011). 'The case of juvenile polygraphy as a clinical ethics dilemma.' *Sexual Abuse: A Journal of Research and Treatment 23* (3), 314–328.

Chammah, M. (2015). 'Barred from Church.' *The Marshall Project.* Accessed on 23/11/2020 at www.themarshallproject.org/2015/03/11/barred-from-church.

Chang, Y. C. & Locke, J. (2016). 'A systematic review of peer-mediated interventions for children with autism spectrum disorder.' *Research in Autism Spectrum Disorders 27*, 1–10.

Charman, T., Pickles, A., Simonoff, E., Chandler, S., Loucas, T., & Baird, G. (2011). 'IQ in children with autism spectrum disorders: Data from the Special Needs and Autism Project (SNAP).' *Psychological Medicine 41* (3), 619–962.

Charman, T., Young, G. S., Brian, J., Carter, A., *et al.* (2016). 'Non-ASD outcomes at 36 months in siblings at familial risk for autism spectrum disorder (ASD): A baby siblings research consortium (BSRC) study.' *Autism Research: Official Journal of the International Society for Autism Research 10* (1), 169–178.

Chatham, C. H., Taylor, K. I., Charman, T., Liogier D'Ardhuy, X., *et al.* (2018). 'Adaptive behavior in autism: Minimal clinically important differences on the Vineland-II.' *Autism Research 11* (2), 270–283.

Chawarska, K., Macari, S., & Shic, F. (2013). 'Decreased spontaneous attention to social scenes in 6-month-old infants later diagnosed with autism spectrum disorders.' *Biological Psychiatry 74* (3), 195–203.

Cheely, C. A., Carpenter, L. A., Letourneau, E. J., Nicholas, J. S., Charles, J., & King, L. B. (2012). 'The prevalence of youth with autism spectrum disorders in the criminal justice system.' *Journal of Autism and Developmental Disorders 42* (9), 1856–1862.

Chess, S. (1976). 'Autism in children with congenital rubella.' *Journal of Autism and Childhood Schizophrenia 1* (1), 33–47.

Chevallier, C., Kohls, G., Troiani, V., Brodkin, E. S., & Schultz, R. T. (2012). 'The social motivation theory of autism.' *Trends in Cognitive Sciences 16* (4), 231–239.

Chiang, H. M., Cheung, Y. K., Hickson, L., Xiang, R., & Tsai, L. Y. (2012). 'Predictive factors of participation in postsecondary education for high school leavers with autism.' *Journal of Autism and Developmental Disorders 42* (5), 685–696.

Chien, Y. L., Gau, S. S. F., Chiu, Y. N., Tsai, W. C., Shang, C. Y., & Wu, Y. Y. (2014). 'Impaired sustained attention, focused attention, and vigilance in youths with autistic disorder and Asperger's disorder.' *Research in Autism Spectrum Disorders 8* (7), 881–889.

Chown, N. (2010). '"Do you have any difficulties that I may not be aware of?" A study of autism awareness and understanding in the UK police service.' *International Journal of Police Science and Management 12* (2), 256–273.

Christopher, M. S. & Gilbert, B. D. (2010). 'Incremental validity of components of mindfulness in the prediction of satisfaction with life and depression.' *Current Psychology 29* (1), 10–23.

Church, B. A., Rice, C. L., Dovgopoly, A., Lopata, C. J., *et al.* (2015). 'Learning, plasticity, and atypical generalization in children with autism.' *Psychonomic Bulletin and Review 22* (5), 1342–1348.

Church, C., Alisanski, S., & Amanullah, S. (2000). 'The social, behavioral, and academic experiences of children with Asperger syndrome.' *Focus on Autism and Other Developmental Disabilities 15* (1), 12–20.

Ciaramella, C. J. (2019). 'Lawsuit: Florida inmate thrown in solitary for biting guard while having seizure.' *Reason.* Accessed on 23/11/2020 at https://reason.com/2019/08/22/lawsuit-florida-inmate-thrown-in-solitary-for-biting-guard-while-having-seizure.

Cimera, R. E., Burgess, S., & Bedesem, P. L. (2014). 'Does providing transition services by age 14 produce better vocational outcomes for students with intellectual disability?' *Research and Practice for Persons with Severe Disabilities 39* (1), 47–54.

City and County of San Francisco, California, et al., petitioners, v. Teresa Sheehan [2015]. 135 S. Ct. 702, 190 L. Ed. 2d 434, Supreme Court of United States. Accessed on 23/11/2020 at www.supremecourt.gov/opinions/14pdf/13-1412_0pl1.pdf.

Clayton, J., Donovan, C., & MacDonald, S. J. (2016). 'A critical portrait of hate crime/incident reporting in North East England: The value of statistical data and the politics of recording in an age of austerity.' *Geoforum 75*, 64–74.

Clements, J. & Zarkowska, E. (2000). *Behavioral Concerns and Autistic Spectrum Disorder: Explanations and Strategies for Change.* London: Jessica Kingsley Publishers.

Commonwealth v. Kelmar [2010]. CR-11000231 (Cir. Court Hanover Cty).

Compton, M. T., Esterberg, M. L., McGee, R., Kotwicki, R. J., & Oliva, J. R. (2006). 'Crisis intervention team training: Changes in knowledge, attitudes, and stigma related to schizophrenia.' *Psychiatric Services 57* (8), 1199–1202.

Connell, A. & Farrington, D. P. (1996). 'Bullying among incarcerated young offenders: Developing an interview schedule and some preliminary results.' *Journal of Adolescence 19*, 75–93.

Conner, C. M., White, S. W., Beck, K. B., Golt, J., Smith, I. C., & Mazefsky, C. A. (2019). 'Improving emotion regulation ability in autism: The Emotional Awareness and Skills Enhancement (EASE) program.' *Autism 23* (5), 1273–1287.

Connolly, J., Furman, W., & Konarski, R. (2000). 'The role of peers in the emergence of heterosexual romantic relationships in adolescence.' *Child Development 71* (5), 1395–1408.

Contreras, M. J., Silva, E., & Manzanero, A. L. (2015). 'Evaluation of capacities to testify in victims with intellectual disabilities.' *Yearbook of Legal Psychology 25*, 87–96.

Copenhaver, A. & Tewksbury, R. (2019). 'Interactions between autistic individuals and law enforcement: A mixed-methods exploratory study.' *American Journal of Criminal Justice 44* (2), 309–333.

Corbett, B. A., Schupp, C. W., Simon, D., Ryan, N., & Mendoza, S. (2010). 'Elevated cortisol during play is associated with age and social engagement in children with autism.' *Molecular Autism 1* (1), 1–12.

Cordell-Whitney, D. (2017). 'Federal judge OKs autistic inmate's claims of abuse.' *Courthouse News Service.* Accessed on 23/11/2020 at www.courthousenews.com/judge-oks-autistic-inmates-claims-abuse.

Corner, E., Gill, P., & Mason, O. (2016). 'Mental health disorders and the terrorist: A research note probing selection effects and disorder prevalence.' *Studies in Conflict and Terrorism 39* (6), 560–568.

Corrigan, P., Markowitz, F. E., Watson, A., Rowan, D., & Kubiak, M. (2003). 'An attribution model of public discrimination towards persons with mental illness.' *Journal of Health and Social Behavior 44* (2), 162–179.

Courchesne, E., Karns, C. M., Davis, H. R., Ziccardi, R., et al. (2001). 'Unusual brain growth patterns in early life in patients with autistic disorder: An MRI study.' *Neurology 57* (2), 245–254.

Courchesne, E., Mouton, P. R., Calhoun, M. E., Semendeferi, K., et al. (2011). 'Neuron number and size in prefrontal cortex of children with autism.' *JAMA 306* (18), 2001–2010.

Craft, A. (ed.) (1994). *Practice Issues in Sexuality and Learning Disabilities.* London: Routledge.

Craig, L. A., Lindsay, W. R., & Browne, K. D. (eds) (2010). *Assessment and Treatment of Sexual Offenders with Intellectual Disabilities: A Handbook.* Chichester: John Wiley & Sons.

Crane, L. & Maras, K. (2018). 'General Memory Abilities for Autobiographical Events in Adults with Autism Spectrum Disorder.' In *The Wiley Handbook of Memory, Autism Spectrum Disorder, and the Law* (pp.146–178). Hoboken, NJ: John Wiley & Sons.

Crane, L., Maras, K. L., Hawken, T., Mulcahy, S., & Memon, A. (2016). 'Experiences of autism spectrum disorder and policing in England and Wales: Surveying police and the autism community.' *Journal of Autism and Developmental Disorders 46*, 2028–2041.

Creaby-Attwood, A. & Allely, C. S. (2017). 'A psycho-legal perspective on sexual offending in individuals with Autism Spectrum Disorder.' *International Journal of Law and Psychiatry 55*, 72–80.

Criminal Justice Policy Foundation (2014). *Mandatory Minimums and Sentencing Reform.* Silver Spring, MD: Criminal Justice Policy Foundation.

Cuddeback, G. S. (2019). 'Jails and prisons caring for those with complex needs.' *North Carolina Medical Journal 80* (6), 357–358.

Cutler, B., Findley, K. A., & Loney, D. (2014). 'Expert testimony on interrogation and false confessions.' *UMKC Law Review 82*, 3–36.

Dalton, K. M., Nacewicz, B. M., Johnstone, T., Schaefer, H. S., et al. (2005). 'Gaze fixation and the neural circuitry of face processing in autism.' *Nature Neuroscience 8* (4), 519–526.

Daly, A., Heah, R., & Liddiard, K. (2019). 'Vulnerable subjects and autonomous actors: The right to sexuality education for disabled under-18s.' *Global Studies of Childhood 9* (3), 235–248.

Dancig-Rosenberg, H. & Gal, T. (2012). 'Restorative criminal justice.' *Cardozo Law Review 34*, 2313–2346.

Davies, C. & Dubie, M. (2011). *Intimate Relationships and Sexual Health: A Curriculum for Teaching Adolescents/Adults with High-Functioning Autism Spectrum Disorders and Other Social Challenges.* Shawnee, KS: AAPC Publishing.

Davis, A. J. (2007). *Arbitrary Justice: The Power of the American Prosecutor.* Oxford: Oxford University Press.

Davis, M. H. (1980). 'A multidimensional approach to individual differences in empathy.' *JSAS Catalog of Selected Documents in Psychology 10*, 85.

Dawson, G. & Watling, R. (2000). 'Interventions to facilitate auditory, visual, and motor integration in autism: A review of the evidence.' *Journal of Autism and Developmental Disorders 30*, 415–421.

Day, K. (1997). 'Clinical Features and Offence Behaviour of Mentally Retarded Sex Offenders: A Review of Research.' In R. J. Fletcher & D. Griffiths (eds) *Congress Proceedings: International Congress II on the Dually Diagnosed* (pp.95–99). New York, NY: NADD.

de Leon (2019). 'Nation's only court for kids with autism is in Nevada.' *Las Vegas.* Accessed on 16/5/2020 at www.fox5vegas.com/news/nations-only-court-for-kids-with-autism-is-in-nevada/article_fff5638e-5ca8-11e9-a8fd-275bab42b1be.html.

de Viggiani, N. (2006). 'Surviving prison: Exploring prison social life as a determinant of health.' *International Journal of Prisoner Health 2*, 71–89.

De Vignemont, F. & Frith, U. (2008). '5.3: Autism, morality, and empathy. *Moral Psychology 3*, 273–280.

Debbaudt, D. (2002). *Autism, Advocates and Law Enforcement Professionals: Recognizing and Reducing Risk Situations for People with Autism Spectrum Disorders.* London: Jessica Kingsley Publishers.

Debbaudt, D. (2004). *Beyond Guilt or Innocence.* Worcester, MA: Autism New Zealand Inc.

Debbaudt, D. & Brown, M. (2006). 'The Autism Response Team: A concept whose time has come.' *Autism Spectrum Quarterly* (Spring), 7–10.

Decety, J. & Meyer, M. (2008). 'From emotion resonance to empathic understanding: A social developmental neuroscience account.' *Development and Psychopathology 20*, 1053–1080.

DeGue, S., Fowler, K. A., & Calkins, C. (2016). 'Deaths due to use of lethal force by law enforcement: Findings from the National Violent Death Reporting System, 17 US states, 2009–2012.' *American Journal of Preventive Medicine 51* (5), S173–S187.

Demetral, D. G. (1981). 'Does ignorance really produce irresponsible behavior?' *Sexuality and Disability 4*, 151–160.

Dennis, A. L. (2007). 'Reining in the minister of justice: Prosecutorial oversight and the superseder power.' *Duke Law Journal 57*, 131–162.

DePaulo, B. M., Lindsay, J. J., Malone, B. E., Muhlenbruck, L., Charlton, K., & Cooper, H. (2003). 'Cues to deception.' *Psychological Bulletin 129*, 74–112.

Dewinter, J., Van Parys, H., Vermeiren, R., & Van Nieuwenhuizen, C. (2017). 'Adolescent boys with an autism spectrum disorder and their experience of sexuality: An interpretative phenomenological analysis.' *Autism 21* (1), 75–82.

Dewinter, J., Vermeiren, R., Vanwesenbeeck, I., Lobbestael, J., & Van Nieuwenhuizen, C. (2015). 'Sexuality in adolescent boys with autism spectrum disorder: Self-reported behaviours and attitudes.' *Journal of Autism and Developmental Disorders 45* (3), 731–741.

Dewinter, J., Vermeiren, R., Vanwesenbeeck, I., & Van Nieuwenhuizen, C. (2013). 'Autism and normative sexual development: A narrative review.' *Journal of Clinical Nursing 22* (23–24), 3467–3483.

Dewinter, J., Vermeiren, R., Vanwesenbeeck, I., & Van Nieuwenhuizen, C. (2016). 'Parental awareness of sexual experience in adolescent boys with autism spectrum disorder.' *Journal of Autism and Developmental Disorders 46* (2), 713–719.

Dezember, A. & Redlich, A. D. (2019). 'Plea Bargaining in the Shadow of the Trial.' In *Handbook on Sentencing Policies and Practices in the 21st Century* (pp.168–187). London: Routledge.

Di Giulio, G. (2003). 'Sexuality and people living with physical or developmental disabilities: A review of key issues.' *The Canadian Journal of Human Sexuality 12*, 53–68.

Dietz, D. (2015). *The Wallet Card.* Accessed on 23/11/2020 at https://vimeo.com/117175394.

Dir, A. L., Cyders, M. A., & Coskunpinar, A. (2013). 'From the bar to the bed via mobile phone: A first test of the role of problematic alcohol use, sexting, and impulsivity-related traits in sexual hookups.' *Computers in Human Behavior 29* (4), 1664–1670.

Ditterline, J., Banner, D., Oakland, T., & Becton, D. (2008). 'Adaptive behavior profiles of students with disabilities.' *Journal of Applied School Psychology 24* (2), 191–208.

Dixon, D., Granpeesheh, D., Smith, M., & Teagardin, J. (2012). 'Randomized trial of law enforcement training on autism spectrum disorders.' *Research in Autism Spectrum Disorders 6* (3), 1113–1118.

Doak, J. & Doak, L. (2017). 'Non-verbal victims in the adversarial criminal process: Communication, competency, and credibility.' *Northern Ireland Legal Quarterly 68* (4), 451–468.

Doley, R., Dickens, G., & Gannon, T. (eds) (2015). *The Psychology of Arson: A Practical Guide to Understanding and Managing Deliberate Firesetters*. London: Routledge.

Donaldson, E. (2013). 'Raising Cubby: A Father and Son's Adventures with Aspergers, Trains, Tractors and High Explosives, by John Elder Robison: Review.' Accessed on 23/11/2020 at www.thestar.com/entertainment/books/2013/04/07/raising_cubby_a_father_and_sons_adventures_with_aspergers_trains_tractors_and_high_explosives_by_john_elder_robison_review.html.

Donovan, P. (1998). 'School-based sexuality education: The issues and challenges.' *Family Planning Perspectives 30*, 188–193.

Douard, J. & Schultz, P. (2017). 'Asperger's Syndrome and Downloading Child Pornography.' In L. Dubin & E. Horowitz, *Caught in the Web of the Criminal Justice System: Autism, Developmental Disabilities, and Sex Offenses* (pp.305–329). London: Jessica Kingsley Publishers.

Dourd, J. (2009). 'Sex offender as scapegoat: The monstrous other within.' *NYLS Law Review 53* (1), 31–52.

Doyle, J. (2003). 'Custody and caring: Innovations in Australian correctional mental health nursing practice.' *Contemporary Nurse 14* (3), 305–311.

Drake Law School Legal Clinic (2011). *Federal Criminal Law and Procedure, Spring 2012*. Accessed on 23/11/2020 at https://citeseerx.ist.psu.edu/viewdoc/download?doi=10.1.1.732.1836&rep=rep1&type=pdf.

Drayton, L. A., Santos, L. R., & Baskin-Sommers, A. (2018). 'Psychopaths fail to automatically take the perspective of others.' *Proceedings of the National Academy of Sciences 115* (13), 3302–3307.

Dubbelin, L. M., Scheeren, A. M., Lever, A.G., & Geurts, H. M. (2016). '2016 International Meeting for Autism Research: Two validation studies of a performance validity test for autism spectrum disorder.' *International Society for Autism Research*. Accessed on 23/11/2020 at https://insar.confex.com/insar/2016/webprogram/Paper21170.html.

Dubin, N. (2007). *Asperger Syndrome and Bullying: Strategies and Solutions*. London: Jessica Kingsley Publishers.

Duffy, K. (2019). 'Student accused of attacking teacher to go before judge.' *CBS News*. Accessed on 23/11/2020 at https://cbs12.com/news/local/student-accused-of-attacking-teacher-to-go-before-judge.

Dum, C. P., Socia, K. M., Long, B. L., & Yarrison, F. (2019). 'Would God forgive? Public attitudes toward sex offenders in places of worship.' *Sexual Abuse*. DOI: 10.1177/1079063219839498.

Duncan, A. W. & Bishop, S. L. (2015). 'Understanding the gap between cognitive abilities and daily living skills in adolescents with autism spectrum disorders with average intelligence.' *Autism 19* (1), 64–72.

Duwe, G. (2018). 'Can circles of support and accountability (CoSA) significantly reduce sexual recidivism? Results from a randomized controlled trial in Minnesota.' *Journal of Experimental Criminology 14* (4), 463–484.

Dziobek, I., Preissler, S., Grozdanovic, Z., Heuser, I., Heekeren, H. R., & Roepke, S. (2011). 'Neuronal correlates of altered empathy, and social cognition in borderline personality disorder.' *Neuroimage 15*, 539–548.

Dziobek, I., Rogers, K., Fleck, S., Bahnemann, M., *et al.* (2008). 'Dissociation of cognitive and emotional empathy in adults with Asperger syndrome using the Multifaceted Empathy Test (MET).' *Journal of Autism and Developmental Disorders 38* (3), 464–473.

Eadens, D. M., Cranston-Gingras, A., Dupoux, E., & Eadens, D. W. (2016). 'Police officer perspectives on intellectual disability.' *Policing: An International Journal of Police Strategies and Management 39* (1), 222–235.

Egen-Jones, P. (2019). 'Jones on cultural sensitivity training for police officers.' *New Jersey Assembly Democrats*. Accessed on 23/11/2020 at www.assemblydems.com/jones-on-cultural-sensitivity-training-for-police-officers.

Edelson, M. G. (2010). 'Sexual abuse of children with autism: Factors that increase risk and interfere with recognition of abuse.' *Disability Studies Quarterly 30* (1), 1–16.

Edgar, K. (2005). 'Bullying, victimization and safer prisons.' *Probation Journal 52*, 390–400.

Eisner, C. (2019). 'When people with intellectual disabilities are punished, and parents pay the ultimate price.' *The Marshall Project*. Accessed on 23/11/2020 at www.themarshallproject.org/2019/09/13/when-people-with-intellectual-disabilities-are-punished-parents-pay-the-price.

Emerson, R. W., Adams, C., Nishino, T., Hazlett, H. C., *et al.* (2017). 'Functional neuroimaging of high-risk 6-month-old infants predicts a diagnosis of autism at 24 months of age.' *Science Translational Medicine 9* (393).

English, K. (1998). 'The containment approach: An aggressive strategy for the community management of adult sex offenders.' *Psychology, Public Policy, and Law 4* (1–2), 218–235.

Epstein, L. (2016). 'Some thoughts on the study of judicial behavior.' *William & Mary Law Review 57* (6), 2017–2073.

Esbensen, A. J., Bishop, S., Seltzer, M. M., Greenberg, J. S., & Taylor, J. L. (2010). 'Comparisons between individuals with autism spectrum disorders and individuals with Down syndrome in adulthood.' *American Journal on Intellectual and Developmental Disabilities 115* (4), 277–290.

Estes, A., Zwaigenbaum, L., Gu, H., John, T. S., *et al.* (2015). 'Behavioral, cognitive, and adaptive development in infants with autism spectrum disorder in the first two years of life.' *Journal of Neurodevelopmental Disorders 7* (1), 24.

Eyal, G. (2013). 'For a sociology of expertise: The social origins of the autism epidemic.' *American Journal of Sociology 118* (4), 863–907.

Fabian, J. M. (2011). 'Assessing the sex offender with Asperger's disorder: A forensic psychological and neuropsychological perspective.' *Sex Offender Law Report 12* (5), 65–80.

Farley, M. A., McMahon, W. M., Fombonne, E., Jenson, W. R., *et al.* (2009). 'Twenty-year outcome for individuals with autism and average or near-average cognitive abilities.' *Autism Research 2* (2), 109–118.

Farmer, L., Davis, T., Richards, J., Fonseca, F., *et al.* (2017). 'Deinstitutionalization in Alabama: A mental health crisis.' *The Alabama Counseling Association Journal 41* (2), 82–103.

Federal Rules of Criminal Procedure (2020). *Rule 11: Pleas.* Accessed on 23/11/2020 at www.federalrulesofcriminalprocedure.org/title-iv/rule-11-pleas.

Feldman, G., Hayes, A., Lumar, S., Greeson, J., & Laurenceau, J.-P. (2007). 'Mindfulness and emotion regulation: The development and initial validation of the Cognitive and Affective Mindfulness Scale-Revised (CAMS-R).' *Journal of Psychopathology and Behavioral Assessment 29* (3), 177–190.

Feldman, S. (2003). 'Reflections on the 40th anniversary of the US Community Mental Health Centers Act.' *Australian and New Zealand Journal of Psychiatry 37*, 662–667.

Fesmire, S. (2003). *John Dewey and Moral Imagination.* Bloomington, IN: Indiana University Press.

Fiftal Alarid, L. & Montemayor, C. D. (2010). 'Attorney perspectives and decisions on the presentence investigation report: A research note.' *Criminal Justice Policy Review 21* (1), 119–133.

Finkenauer, C., Pollmann, M. M., Begeer, S., & Kerkhof, P. (2012). 'Brief report: Examining the link between autistic traits and compulsive internet use in a nonclinical sample.' *Journal of Autism and Developmental Disorders 42*, 2252–2256.

Fisher, W. H., Wolff, N., & Roy-Bujnowski, K. (2003). 'Community Mental Health Services and Criminal Justice Involvement.' In W. H. Fisher (ed.) *Community-Based Interventions for Criminal Offenders with Severe Mental Illness* (pp.25–51). Oxford: Elsevier.

Fisk, N. (2009). *Understanding Online Piracy: The Truth about Illegal File Sharing.* Santa Barbara, CA: Praeger.

Fisler, C. (2015). 'Toward a new understanding of mental health courts.' *Judges' Journal 54* (2), 8–13.

Fitzsimons, N. (2016). 'Justice for crime victims with disabilities in the criminal justice system: An examination of barriers and impetus for change.' *University of St. Thomas Law Journal 13* (1), 33–87.

Fleming, A. (2015). *Autism and Sexuality: Self Advocates Focus Groups* (Master's Thesis, Pennsylvania State University).

Fletcher-Watson, S., McConnell, F., Manola, E., & McConachie, H. (2014). 'Interventions based on the Theory of Mind cognitive model for autism spectrum disorder (ASD).' *Cochrane Database of Systematic Reviews* (3), 1–72.

Foley, A. (2001). 'Allegories of freedom: Individual liberty and social conformity in Ken Kesey's One Flew Over the Cuckoo's Nest.' *Journal of Literary Studies 17* (1–2), 31–57.

Forst, B. (2002). *Prosecution in James Q. Wilson and Joan Petersilia's Crime: Public Policies for Crime Control.* Oakland, CA: ICS Press.

Foster, W. L. (1897). 'Expert testimony, prevalent complaints and proposed remedies.' *Harvard Law Review 11*, 169–186.

Fountain, E. N. (2017). *Adolescent Plea Bargains: Developmental and Contextual Influences of Plea Bargain Decision Making* (Doctoral Dissertation, Georgetown University).

Fournier, K. A., Hass, C. J., Naik, S. K., Lodha, N., & Cauraugh, J. H. (2010). 'Motor coordination in autism spectrum disorders: A synthesis and meta-analysis.' *Journal of Autism and Developmental Disorders 40* (10), 1227–1240.

Fox, E., Amaral, D., & Van de Water, J. (2012). 'Maternal and fetal antibrain antibodies in development and disease.' *Developmental Neurobiology 72* (10), 1327–1334.

Francescani, C. & Margolin, J. (2019). 'This is what mental distress feels like: Experts.' *ABC News.* Accessed on 24/11/2020 at https://abcnews.go.com/GMA/News/virtual-reality-training-tech-takes-cops-directly-minds/story?id=63125741.

Frankel, A. (2019). 'Pushed out and locked in: The catch-22 for New York's disabled, homeless sex-offender registrants.' *The Yale Law Journal Forum*, 279–324.

Frase, R. S. (2000). 'Is guided discretion sufficient? Overview of the state sentencing guidelines.' *Saint Louis University Law Journal 44*, 425–449.

Freckelton, I. & List, D. (2009). 'Asperger's disorder, criminal responsibility and criminal culpability.' *Psychiatry, Psychology and Law 16* (1), 16–40.

Freeman, B. J., Del'Homme, M., Guthrie, D., & Zhang, F. (1999). 'Vineland Adaptive Behavior Scale scores as a function of age and initial IQ in 210 autistic children.' *Journal of Autism and Developmental Disorders 29* (5), 379–384.

Freeman-Loftis, S. (2016). 'The Autistic Victim.' In L. J. Davis (ed.) *The Disabilities Studies Reader* (5th ed., pp.470–480). New York, NY: Routledge.

Friedman, C., Arnold, C., Owen, A., & Sandman, L. (2014). '"Remember our voices are our tools": Sexual self-advocacy as defined by people with intellectual and developmental disabilities.' *Sex Disability 32*, 515–532.

Frith, U. & De Vignemont, F. (2005). 'Egocentrism, allocentrism, and Asperger syndrome.' *Consciousness and Cognition 14* (4), 719–738.

Fulero, S. M. & Everington, C. (1995). 'Assessing competency to waive Miranda rights in defendants with mental retardation.' *Law and Human Behavior 19*, 533–543.

Fulkerson, A. (2009). 'The drug treatment court as a form of restorative justice.' *Contemporary Justice Review 12*, 253–267.

Furfaro, H. (2018). 'Why police need training to interact with people on the autism spectrum.' *Spectrum Magazine.* Accessed on 24/11/2020 at www.spectrumnews.org/features/deep-dive/police-need-training-interact-people-spectrum.

Furst, T. & Evans, D. (2014). 'An exploration of stigma in the lives of sex offenders and heroin abusers.' *Deviant Behavior 36* (2), 130–145.

Gaigg, S. B., Gardiner, J. M., & Bowler, D. M. (2008). 'Free recall in autism spectrum disorder: The role of relational and item-specific encoding.' *Neuropsychologia 46*, 983–992.

Garcia, E. T., Ware, S. G., & Baker, L. J. (2019). 'Measuring presence and performance in a virtual reality police use of force training simulation prototype.' *Proceedings of the 32nd AAAI International Conference of the Florida Artificial Intelligence Research Society.*

Gardiner, F., Díaz, M., & Brown, L. X. Z. (2016). 'Charles Kinsey's story is about race. It's also about ableism.' *Sojourners.* Accessed on 24/11/2020 at https://sojo.net/articles/charles-kinseys-story-about-race-its-also-about-ableism.

Garvey, S. P. (1998). 'Aggravation and mitigation in capital cases: What do jurors think?' *Columbia Law Review 98*, 1538–1576.

George, R. & Stokes, M. A. (2018). 'Sexual orientation in autism spectrum disorder.' *Autism Research 11* (1), 133–141.

Georgia Commission on Feeblemindedness & Anderson, V. V. (1919). *Mental Defect in a Southern State: Report of the Georgia Commission on Feeblemindedness and the Survey of the National Committee for Mental Hygiene.* National Committee for Mental Hygiene.

Georgiades, S., Szatmari, P., & Boyle, M. (2013). 'Importance of studying heterogeneity in autism.' *Neuropsychiatry 3* (2), 123–125.

Geretsegger, M., Elefant, C., Mössler, K. A., & Gold, C. (2014). 'Music therapy for people with autism spectrum disorder.' *Cochrane Database of Systematic Reviews* (6).

Gerhardt, P. F. (2006). 'Sexuality instruction and autism spectrum disorders.' *Autism Asperger's Digest*, 44–46.

Gerouki, M. (2007). 'Sexuality and relationships education in the Greek primary schools—See no evil, hear no evil, speak no evil.' *Sex Education 7*, 81–100.

Gershman, B. L. (2011). 'The zealous prosecutor as minister of justice.' *San Diego Law Review 48*, 151–156.

Gershowitz, A. M. & Killinger, L. R. (2011). 'The state (never) rests: How excessive prosecutorial caseloads harm criminal defendants.' *Northwestern University Law Review 105*, 261–302.

Ghaziuddin, M. & Al-Owain, M. (2013). 'Autism spectrum disorders and inborn errors of metabolism: An update.' *Pediatric Neurology 49* (4), 232–236.

Ghaziuddin, M., Tsai, L., & Ghaziuddin, N. (1991). 'Brief report: Violence in Asperger syndrome, a critique.' *Journal of Autism and Developmental Disorders 21* (3), 349–354.

Gibbons, F. X., Gibbons, B. N., & Kassin, S. M. (1981). 'Reactions to the criminal behavior of intellectually disabled and nondisabled offenders.' *American Journal of Mental Deficiency 86*, 235–242.

Gibson, M. F. & Douglas, P. (2018). 'Disturbing behaviours: Ole Ivar Lovaas and the queer history of autism science.' *Catalyst: Feminism, Theory, Technoscience 4* (2).

Gillberg, C. (2007). 'The Autism Spectrum.' In J. W. Jacobson, J. A. Mulick, & J. Rojahn (eds) *Handbook of Intellectual and Developmental Disabilities* (pp.41–60). New York, NY: Springer Publishing Co.

Gillespie-Lynch, K., Kapp, S. K., Shane-Simpson, C., Smith, D. S., & Hutman, T. (2014). 'Intersections between the autism spectrum and the internet: Perceived benefits and preferred functions of computer-mediated communication.' *Intellectual and Developmental Disabilities 52*, 456–469.

Gilmour, L., Schalomon, P. M., & Smith, V. (2012). 'Sexuality in a community based sample of adults with autism spectrum disorder.' *Research in Autism Spectrum Disorders 6* (1), 313–318.

Gilotty, L., Kenworthy, L., Sirian, L., Black, D. O., & Wagner, A. E. (2002). 'Adaptive skills and executive function in autism spectrum disorders.' *Child Neuropsychology 8* (4), 241–248.

Ginevra, M. C., Nota, L., & Stokes, M. A. (2016). 'The differential effects of autism and Down's syndrome on sexual behavior.' *Autism Research 9*, 131–140.

Ginsberg, B. (2009). 'Out with the new, in with the old: The importance of Section 504 of the Rehabilitation Act to prisoners with disabilities.' *Fordham Urban Law Journal 36*, 713–746.

Glaser, W. & Deane, K. (1999). 'Normalisation in an abnormal world: A study of prisoners with an intellectual disability.' *International Journal of Offender Therapy and Comparative Criminology 43* (3), 338–356.

Gnaulati, E. (2014). 'The Isla Vista shooter: This is not the autism spectrum.' *The Atlantic*. Accessed on 24/11/2020 at www.theatlantic.com/health/archive/2014/05/the-isla-vista-shooter-suffered-from-pathological-narcissism-not-autism/371768.

Godsey, M. (2017). *Blind Injustice: A Former Prosecutor Exposes the Psychology and Politics of Wrongful Convictions*. Berkeley, CA: University of California Press.

Goldstein, G., Minshew, N. J., & Siegel, D. J. (1994). 'Age differences in academic achievement in high functioning autistic individuals.' *Journal of Clinical and Experimental Neuropsychology 16*, 671–680.

Goldstein, N. E., Condie, L. O., Kalbeitzer, R., Osman, D., & Geier, J. L. (2003). 'Juvenile offenders' Miranda rights comprehension and self-reported likelihood of offering false confessions.' *Assessments 10*, 359–369.

Goller, A., Jones, R., Dittmann, V., Taylor, P., & Graf, M. (2016). 'Criminal recidivism of illegal pornography offenders in the overall population—a national cohort study of 4612 offenders in Switzerland.' *Advances in Applied Sociology*, 48–56.

Golubchik, P., Sever, J., Katz, N., Shoval, G., & Weizman, A. (2012). 'Handshaking as a measure of social responsiveness in patients with autistic spectrum disorder.' *Comprehensive Psychiatry 53* (6), 805–808.

Goodley, D., Runswick-Cole, K., & Liddiard, K. (2016). 'The dishuman child.' *Discourse: Studies in the Cultural Politics of Education 37* (5), 770–784.

Goodwin, M. S., Groden, J., Velicer, W. F., Lipsitt, L. P., *et al.* (2006). 'Cardiovascular arousal in individuals with autism.' *Focus on Autism and Other Developmental Disabilities 21* (2), 100–123.

Gordo, S. & Kelley, E. (2019). 'The attorney client relationship: Bridging the gap between attorneys, clients with I/DD and their families.' *The Arc*. Accessed on 24/11/2020 at https://thearc.org/wp-content/uploads/forchapters/Webinar-Slides.pdf.

Gorner, J. (2019). 'Chicago police turn to virtual reality technology to train officers in how to deal with the mentally ill.' *Chicago Tribune*. Accessed on 24/11/2020 at www.chicagotribune.com/news/breaking/ct-met-chicago-police-virtual-reality-20190522-story.html.

Gougeon, N. A. (2009). 'Sexuality education for students with intellectual disabilities. A critical pedagogical approach: Outing the ignored curriculum.' *Sex Education 3*, 277–291.

Gougeon, N. A. (2010). 'Sexuality and autism: A critical review of selected literature using a social-relational model of disability.' *American Journal of Sexuality Education 5* (4), 328–361.

Gougeon, N. A. (2013). *Interest, Understanding, and Behaviour: Conceptualizations of Sexuality Education for Individuals with an Autism Spectrum Disorder Using a Socially Inclusive Lens* (Thesis, University of Ottawa).

Graham, M. H. (1999). 'The expert witness predicament: Determining reliable under the gatekeeping test of Daubert, Kumho, and proposed amended Rule 702 of the Federal Rules of Evidence.' *University of Miami Law Review 54*, 317–357.

Grandin, T. (2000). 'My mind is a web browser: How people with autism think.' *Cerebrum 2*, 14–22.

Grandin, T. & Barron, S. (2005). *Unwritten Rules of Social Relationships: Decoding Social Mysteries Through the Unique Perspectives of Autism*. Arlington, TX: Future Horizons.

Granpeesheh, D., Tarbox, J., Dixon, D. R., Peters, C. A., Thompson, K., & Kenzer, A. (2010). 'Evaluation of an eLearning tool for training behavioral therapists in academic knowledge of applied behavior analysis.' *Research in Autism Spectrum Disorders 4* (1), 11–17.

Grant, J. (2019). 'Sex offender reported at Sheldon library.' *N'West Iowa REVIEW*. Accessed on 31/5/2020 at www.nwestiowa.com/news/sex-offender-reported-at-sheldon-library/article_36494622-fa5a-11e9-b12d-33bb1f6eab48.html.

Grassian, S. (2006). 'Psychiatric effects of solitary confinement.' *Washington University Journal of Law and Policy 22* (1), 327–383.

Gray, S. R., Abel, G. G., Jordan, A., Garby, T., Wiegel, M., & Harlow, N. (2015). 'Visual Reaction TimeTM, as a predictor of sexual offense recidivism.' *Sexual Abuse: A Journal of Research and Treatment 27*, 173–188.

Green, F. (2020). 'Autism: Bills affect those in the legal system.' *Richmond-Times Dispatch*. Accessed on 24/11/2020 at www.pressreader.com/usa/richmond-times-dispatch-weekend/20200216/281582357643468.

Green, J., Gilchrist, A., Burton, D., & Cox, A. (2000). 'Social and psychiatric functioning in adolescents with Asperger syndrome compared with conduct disorder.' *Journal of Autism and Developmental Disorders 30*, 279–293.

Greenberg & Greenberg (2013). 'Huntington Beach proposes ban on beaches for sex offenders.' *Greenberg & Greenberg.* Accessed on 24/11/2020 at https://danielgreenberglaw.com/resources/articles/huntington-beach-proposes-ban-on-beaches-for-sex-offenders.

Greer, J. H. & Bellard, H. S. (1996). 'Sexual content induced delays in unprimed lexical decisions: Gender and context effects.' *Archives of Sexual Behavior 25,* 379–395.

Greer, J. H. & Melton, J. S. (1997). 'Sexual content-induced delay with double-entendre words.' *Archives of Sexual Behavior 26,* 295–316.

Greiert, B. (2016). 'Key components of successful sexuality education for high functioning students with autism spectrum disorder.' *Electronic Theses and Dissertations 1133.* Accessed on 24/11/2020 at https://digitalcommons.du.edu/cgi/viewcontent.cgi?article=2133&context=etd.

Griffin-Shelley, E. (2010). 'An Asperger's adolescent sex addict, sex offender: A case study.' *Sexual Addiction and Compulsivity 17* (1), 46–64.

Griffith, G. M., Totsika, V., Nash, S., & Hastings, R. P. (2012). '"I just don't fit anywhere": Support experiences and future support needs of individuals with Asperger syndrome in middle adulthood.' *Autism 16,* 532–546.

Griffiths, D. (2003). 'Sexuality and People who have Developmental Disabilities: From Myth to Emerging Practices.' In I. Brown & M. Percy (eds) *Developmental Disabilities in Ontario* (2nd ed., pp.677–690). Toronto: Ontario Association on Developmental Disabilities.

Griffiths, D. & Fedoroff, J. P. (2009). 'Persons with Intellectual Disabilities Who Sexually Offend.' In F. M. Saleh, A. J. Grudzinskas, J. M. Bradford, & D. J. Brodsky (eds) *Sex Offenders: Identification, Risk Assessment, Treatment and Legal Issues* (pp.353–378). New York, NY: Oxford University Press.

Griffiths, D., Quinsey, V., & Hingsburger, D. (1989). *Changing Inappropriate Sexual Behavior.* Baltimore, MD: Paul H. Brookes.

Griffiths, D. M., Richards, D., Fedoroff, P., & Watson, S. L. (2002). 'Sexuality and Mental Health Issues.' In D. M. Griffiths, C. Stavrakaki, & J. Summers (eds) *Dual Diagnosis: An Introduction to the Mental Health Needs of Persons with Developmental Disabilities* (pp.419–454). Sudbury, ON: Habilitative Mental Health Resource Network.

Groden, J., Goodwin, M. S., Baron, M. G., Groden, G., *et al.* (2005). 'Assessing cardiovascular responses to stressors in individuals with autism spectrum disorders.' *Focus on Autism and Other Developmental Disabilities 20* (4), 244–252.

Gu, J., Strauss, C., Bond, R., & Cavanagh, K. (2015). 'How do mindfulness-based cognitive therapy and mindfulness-based stress reduction improve mental health and wellbeing? A systematic review and meta-analysis of mediation studies.' *Clinical Psychology Review 37,* 1–12.

Gudjonsson, G. H., Sigurdsson, J. F., Brynjólfsdóttir, B., & Hreinsdóttir, H. (2002). 'The relationship of compliance with anxiety, self-esteem, paranoid thinking and anger.' *Psychology, Crime and Law 8,* 145–153.

Günal, A., Bumin, G., & Huri, M. (2019). 'The effects of motor and cognitive impairments on daily living activities and quality of life in children with autism.' *Journal of Occupational Therapy, Schools, and Early Intervention 12* (4), 1–11.

Hadden, S. (2001). *Slave Patrols: Law and Violence in Virginia and the Carolinas.* Cambridge, MA: Harvard University Press.

Hafemeister, T. L. & George, J. (2012). 'The ninth circle of hell: An eighth amendment analysis of imposing prolonged supermax solitary confinement on inmates with a mental illness.' *The Denver University Law Review 90,* 1–54.

Haley, M. J. (2016). 'Drug courts: The criminal justice system rolls the rock.' *Loyola Journal of Public Interest Law 17,* 183–214.

Hall, I., Clayton, P., & Johnson, P. (2005). 'Arson and Learning Disability.' In B. Swann, C. Swann, & T. Riding (eds) *The Handbook of Forensic Learning Disabilities* (pp.51–72). Oxford: Radcliffe.

Hall, M. (2010). 'Randomness reconsidered: Modeling random judicial assignment in the US courts of appeals.' *Journal of Empirical Legal Studies 7* (3), 574–589.

Hallmayer, J., Cleveland, S., Torres, A., Phillips, J., *et al.* (2011). 'Genetic heritability and shared environmental factors among twin pairs with autism.' *Archives of General Psychiatry 68* (11), 1095–1102.

Hamilton-Smith, G. P. (2020). 'The agony & the ecstasy of #MeToo: The hidden costs of reliance on carceral politics.' *Southwestern University Law Review 49,* 1–29.

Han, G., Helm, J., Iucha, C., Zahn-Waxler, C., Hastings, P. D., & Klimes-Dougan, B. (2016). 'Are executive functioning deficits concurrently and predictively associated with depressive and anxiety symptoms in adolescents?' *Journal of Clinical Child and Adolescent Psychology 45* (1), 44–58.

Hancock, G., Stokes, M. A., & Mesibov, G. (2020). 'Differences in romantic relationship experiences for individuals with an autism spectrum disorder.' *Sexuality and Disability 38* (2), 231–245.

Hand, L. (1901). 'Historical and practical considerations regarding expert testimony.' *Harvard Law Review 15,* 40–58.

Hannah, L. A. & Stagg, S. D. (2016). 'Experiences of sex education and sexual awareness in young adults with autism spectrum disorder.' *Journal of Autism and Developmental Disorders 46*, 3678–3687.

Haney, C. & Lynch, M. (1997). 'Regulating prisons of the future: A psychological analysis of supermax and solitary confinement.' *Review of Law and Social Change XXIII* (4), 477–510.

Hanson, R. K. & Bussière, M. T. (1998). 'Predicting relapse: A meta-analysis of sexual offender recidivism studies.' *Journal of Consulting and Clinical Psychology 66* (2), 348–362.

Hanson, R. K. & Morton-Bourgon, K. E. (2005). 'The characteristics of persistent sexual offenders: A meta-analysis of recidivism studies.' *Journal of Consulting and Clinical Psychology 73* (6), 1154–1163.

Haracopos, D. & Pedersen, L. (1992). *Sexuality and Autism: A Nationwide Survey in Denmark.* Unpublished manuscript.

Harden, K. P. (2014). 'A sex-positive framework for research on adolescent sexuality.' *Perspectives on Psychological Science 9* (5), 455–469.

Hardy, S., French, M., Johnston, J., & Streeton, R. (2016). 'Raising magistrates' awareness of vulnerable adults: A pilot.' *Journal of Mental Health Practice 20* (4), 19–23.

Harmon, A. (2014). 'Fearing a stigma for people with autism.' *The New York Times.* Accessed on 23/11/2020 at www.nytimes.com/2012/12/18/health/fearing-a-stigma-for-people-with-autism.html.

Harrington, J. F. (2013). *The Faithful Executioner: Life and Death, Honor and Shame in the Turbulent Sixteenth Century.* New York, NY: Farrar, Straus and Giroux.

Harrington, K. B. (2017). 'Policing reasonable accommodations for individuals with disabilities.' *UC Davis Law Review 50* (3), 1361–1394.

Harris, A. J., Lobanov-Rostovsky, C., & Levenson, J. S. (2015). *Law Enforcement Perspectives on Sex Offender Registration and Notification: Preliminary Survey Results.* Lowell, MA: University of Massachusetts Lowell.

Harrison, L. D. & Scarpitti, F. R. (2002). 'Introduction: Progress and issues in drug treatment courts.' *Substance Use and Misuse 37* (12–13), 1441–1467.

Haruvi-Lamdan, N., Horesh, D., & Golan, O. (2018). 'PTSD and autism spectrum disorder: Co-morbidity, gaps in research, and potential shared mechanisms.' *Psychological Trauma: Theory, Research, Practice, and Policy 10* (3), 290–299.

Hazlett, H. C., Poe, M., Gerig, G., Smith, R. G., *et al.* (2005). 'Magnetic resonance imaging and head circumference study of brain size in autism: Birth through age two years.' *Archives of General Psychiatry 62* (12), 1366–1376.

Heaney, G. W. (1991). 'The reality of guidelines sentencing: No end to disparity.' *Federal Sentencing Reporter 4* (3), 142–144.

Heeramun, R., Magnusson, C., Gumpert, C. H., Granath, S., *et al.* (2017). 'Autism and convictions for violent crimes: Population-based cohort study in Sweden.' *Journal of the American Academy of Child and Adolescent Psychiatry 56*, 491–497.

Heilbrun, K. & Griffin, P. A. (1998). 'Community-Based Forensic Treatment.' In R. M. Wettstein (ed.) *Treatment of Offenders with Mental Disorders* (pp.168–210). New York, NY: Guilford.

Heilbrun, K. & King, C. (2017). 'Forced medication and competency to stand trial: Clinical, legal, and ethical issues.' *Psychiatric Times 34* (4), 1–5.

Hellemans, H., Colson, K., Verbraeken, C., Vermeiren, R., & Deboutte, D. (2007). 'Sexual behavior in high-functioning male adolescents and young adults with autism spectrum disorder.' *Journal of Autism and Developmental Disorders 37* (2), 260–269.

Hénault, I. (2006). *Asperger's Syndrome and Sexuality: From Adolescence through Adulthood.* London: Jessica Kingsley Publishers.

Hénault, I. & Attwood, T. (2002). 'The sexual profile of adults with Asperger's syndrome: The need for understanding, support and sex education.' *Inaugural World Autism Congress, Melbourne, Australia.*

Henderson v. Morgan [1976]. 426 U.S. 637, 96 S. Ct. 2253, 49 L. Ed. 2d 108.

Hendricks, D. (2010). 'Employment and adults with autism spectrum disorders: Challenges and strategies for success.' *Journal of Vocational Rehabilitation 32* (2), 125–134.

Henry Ford Health System (2017). 'Autism and puberty: A parent's guide.' *Henry Ford Health System.* Accessed on 23/11/2020 at www.henryford.com/blog/2017/04/autism-puberty-parents-guide.

Henry, L., Messer, D., Wilcock, R., Nash, G., Kirke-Smith, M., & Hobson, Z. (2017). 'Do measures of memory, language and attention predict eyewitness memory in children with and without autism?' *Autism and Developmental Language Impairments 2*, 1–17.

Henshaw, M. and Thomas, S. (2012). 'Police encounters with people with intellectual disability: Prevalence, characteristics and challenges.' *Journal of Intellectual Disability Research 56*, 620–631.

Hewitt, L. E. (2011). 'Perspectives on support needs of individuals with autism spectrum disorders: Transition to college.' *Topics in Language Disorders 31* (3), 273–285.

Higgs, T. & Carter, A. J. (2015). 'Autism spectrum disorder and sexual offending: Responsivity in forensic interventions.' *Aggression and Violent Behavior 22*, 112–119.

Hill, E. L., Berthoz, S., & Frith, U. (2004). 'Cognitive processing of own emotions in individuals with autistic spectrum disorder and their relatives.' *Journal of Autism and Developmental Disorders 34*, 229–292.

Hingsburger, D. (1992). 'Erotophobic behavior in people with developmental disabilities.' *The Habilitative Mental Healthcare Newsletter 11*, 31–34.

Hingsburger, D., Griffiths, D., & Quinsey, V. (1991). 'Detecting counterfeit deviance: Differentiating sexual deviance from sexual inappropriateness.' *The Habilitative Mental Healthcare Newsletter 10* (9), 51–54.

Hippler, K., Viding, E., Klicpera, C., & Happé, F. (2010). 'Brief report: No increase in criminal convictions in Hans Asperger's original cohort.' *Journal of Autism and Developmental Disorders 40* (6), 774–780.

Hirstein, W., Iversen, P., & Ramachandran, V. S. (2001). 'Autonomic responses of autistic children to people and objects.' *Proceedings of the Royal Society of London. Series B: Biological Sciences 268* (1479), 1883–1888.

Hnatow, D. (2015). 'Working with law enforcement to provide health care for the acute mentally ill.' *Psychiatric Times* (November), 11–14.

Hoechstetter, M. (2020). 'Can a prosecutor be progressive and take sex crimes seriously?' *The Appeal*. Accessed on 23/11/2020 at https://theappeal.org/progressive-prosecutors-metoo.

Hoffmann, N. P. (2018). *When Law Enforcement and Individuals with Autism Spectrum Disorder Meet: ASD Knowledge and Confidence in Law Enforcement Officers in the Commonwealth of Kentucky* (Honors Thesis, 537).

Hofvander, B., Bering, S., Tärnhäll, A., Wallinius, M., & Billstedt, E. (2019). 'Few differences in the externalizing and criminal history of young violent offenders with and without autism spectrum disorders.' *Frontiers in Psychiatry 10* (911), 1–8.

Hofvander, B., Delorme, R., Chaste, P., Nyden, A., *et al.* (2009). 'Psychiatric and psychosocial problems in adults with normal-intelligence autism spectrum disorders.' *BMC Psychiatry 9* (1).

Höing, M. A. (2015). *Empowering Circles: Circles of Support and Accountability.* (Doctoral Dissertation, Tilberg University.) Oosterhout: OCC De Hoog B.V. Accessed on 23/11/2020 at https://research.tilburguniversity.edu/en/publications/empowering-circles-circles-of-support-and-accountability.

Holt, R., Upadhyay, J., Smith, P., Allison, C., Baron-Cohen, S., & Chakrabarti, B. (2018). 'The Cambridge Sympathy Test: Self-reported sympathy and distress in autism.' *PLOS ONE 13* (7).

Howard-Barr, E. M., Rienzo, B. A., Pigg, R. M., Jr., & James, D. (2005). 'Teacher beliefs, professional preparation, and practices regarding exceptional students and sexuality education.' *Journal of School Health 75*, 99–104.

Howlin, P. (1997). *Autism: Preparing for Adulthood.* London: Routledge.

Howlin, P. (2004). *Autism and Asperger Syndrome: Preparing for Adulthood.* London: Routledge.

Howlin, P. (2007). 'The Outcome in Adult Life for People with ASD.' In F. Volkmar (ed.) *Autism and Pervasive Developmental Disorders (Cambridge Child and Adolescent Psychiatry, pp.269–306).* Cambridge: Cambridge University Press.

Howlin, P. & Moss, P. (2012). 'Adults with autism spectrum disorders.' *The Canadian Journal of Psychiatry 57* (5), 275–283.

Howlin, P., Goode, S., Hutton, J., & Rutter, M. (2004). 'Adult outcome for children with autism.' *Journal of Child Psychology and Psychiatry 45* (2), 212–229.

Hughes, K., Bellis, M. A., Jones, L., Wood, S., *et al.* (2012). 'Prevalence and risk of violence against adults with disabilities: A systematic review and meta-analysis of observational studies.' *The Lancet 379* (9826), 1621–1629.

Hughes, R. B., Lund, E. M., Gabrielli, J., Powers, L. E., & Curry, M. A. (2011). 'Prevalence of interpersonal violence against community-living adults with disabilities: A literature review.' *Rehabilitation Psychology 56* (4), 302–319.

Hughes, S. & Peak, T. (2012). 'Evaluating mental health courts as an ideal mental health intervention.' *Best Practices in Mental Health 8* (2), 20–37.

Iacono, W. G. (2009). 'Psychophysiological Detection of Deception and Guilty Knowledge.' In J. L. Skeem, K. S. Douglas, & S. O. Lilienfeld (eds) *Psychological Science in the Courtroom: Consensus and Controversy* (pp.224–241). New York, NY: Guilford.

Imhoff, R., Schmidt, A. F., Wei, S., Young, A. W., & Banse, R. (2012). 'Vicarious viewing time: Prolonged response latencies for sexually attractive targets as a function of task—Or stimulus specific processing.' *Archives of Sexual Behavior 41*, 1389–1401.

Inbau, F. E., Reid, J. E., Buckley, J. P., & Jayne, B. C. (2013). *Criminal Interrogation and Confessions* (5th ed.). Burlington, MA: Jones & Bartlett Learning.

Ireland, J. (2000). '"Bullying" among prisoners: A review of the research.' *Aggression and Violent Behavior 5* (2), 201–215.

Ireland, J. & Archer, J. (1996). 'Descriptive analysis of bullying in male and female adult prisoners.' *Journal of Community and Applied Social Psychology 6*, 37–47.

Jefferis, D. C. & Godfrey, N. B. (2018). 'Chapman v. Bureau of Prisons: Stopping the venue merry-go-round.' *Denver Law Review.* Accessed on 24/11/2020 at www.denverlawreview.org/dlr-online-article/2018/8/2/chapman-v-bureau-of-prisons-stopping-the-venue-merry-go-roun.html.

Jennings, J. L. & Sawyer, S. (2003). 'Principles and techniques for maximizing the effectiveness of group therapy with sex offenders.' *Sexual Abuse: A Journal of Research and Treatment 15* (4), 251–267.

Johnson, S., Blume, J. H., & Hritz, A. (2018). 'Convictions of innocent people with intellectual disability.' *Albany Law Review 82* (3), 1031–1062.

Johnson, S. A., Yechiam, E., Murphy, R. R., Queller, S., & Stout, J. C. (2006). 'Motivational processes and autonomic responsivity in Asperger's disorder: Evidence from the Iowa Gambling Task.' *Journal of the International Neuropsychological Society 12* (5), 668–676.

Jones, A. P., Happé, F. G., Gilbert, F., Burnett, S., & Viding, E. (2010). 'Feeling, caring, knowing: Different types of empathy deficit in boys with psychopathic tendencies and autism spectrum disorder.' *Journal of Child Psychology and Psychiatry 51* (11), 1188–1197.

Jones, A. P., Larsson, H., Ronald, A., Rijsdijk, F., *et al.* (2009). 'Phenotypic and aetiological associations between psychopathic tendencies, autistic traits, and emotion attribution.' *Criminal Justice and Behavior 36* (11), 1198–1212.

Jones, R. S. P., Huws, J. C., & Beck, G. (2013). '"I'm not the only person out there": Insider and outsider understandings of autism.' *International Journal of Developmental Disabilities 59*, 134–144.

Jones, W. & Klin, A. (2013). 'Attention to eyes is present but in decline in 2–6-month-old infants later diagnosed with autism.' *Nature 504* (7480), 427–431.

Judd, S. & Parker, G. F. (2018). 'Court-ordered evaluations from a mental health court.' *The Journal of the American Academy of Psychiatry and the Law 46* (1), 52–62.

Kaartinen, M., Puura, K., Helminen, M., Salmelin, R., Pelkonen, E., & Juujärvi, P. (2014). 'Reactive aggression among children with and without autism spectrum disorder.' *Journal of Autism and Developmental Disorders 44* (10), 2383–2391.

Kamio, Y., Inada, N., Moriwaki, A., Kuroda, M., *et al.* (2013). 'Quantitative autistic traits ascertained in a national survey of 22 529 Japanese schoolchildren.' *Acta Psychiatrica Scandinavica 128* (1), 45–53.

Kamisar, Y. (2017). 'The Miranda case fifty years later.' *Boston University Law Review 97* (3), 1293–1307.

Kanne, S. M. & Mazurek, M. O. (2011). 'Aggression in children and adolescents with ASD: Prevalence and risk factors.' *Journal of Autism and Developmental Disorders 41* (7), 926–937.

Kanne, S. M., Gerber, A. J., Quirmbach, L. M., Sparrow, S. S., Cicchetti, D. V., & Saulnier, C. A. (2011). 'The role of adaptive behavior in autism spectrum disorders: Implications for functional outcome.' *Journal of Autism and Developmental Disorders 41* (8), 1007–1018.

Kanner, L. (1943/1973). 'Autistic Disturbances of Affective Contact.' In *Childhood Psychosis: Initial Studies and New Insights* (pp.1–43). Washington, DC: Winston & Sons. [Reprint of: 'Autistic disturbances of affective contact.' *Nervous Child 2*, 217–250.]

Kanner, L. (1949). *Feeblemindedness: Absolute, Relative and Apparent. Child Care Monographs.* New York, NY: Child Care Publications.

Kassin, S. M. (2014). 'False confessions: Causes, consequences, and implications for reform.' *Policy Insights from the Behavioral and Brain Sciences 1* (1), 112–121.

Katz, N. & Hartman-Maeir, A. H. (2005). 'Higher-Level Cognitive Functions: Awareness and Executive Functions Enabling Engagement in Occupation.' In N. Katz (ed.) *Cognition and Occupation Across the Life Span* (2nd ed., pp.3–25). Bethesda, MD: AOTA Press.

Keatley, D. A., Marono, A., & Clarke, D. (2018). 'Unmaking a murderer: Behaviour sequence analysis of false confessions.' *Psychiatry, Psychology and Law 25* (3), 425–436.

Keilty, J. & Connelly, G. (2010). 'Making a statement: An exploratory study of barriers facing women with intellectual disability when making a statement about sexual assault to police.' *Disability & Society 16* (2), 273–291.

Kelbrick, M. & Radley, J. (2013). 'Forensic rehabilitation in Asperger syndrome: A case report.' *Journal of Intellectual Disabilities and Offending Behaviour 4* (1), 60–64.

Kelch, D. (2011). 'Help me help you: An answer to the circuit split over the delegation of post-sentence judicial authority to probation officers.' *Penn State Law Review 116*, 553–575.

Kellaher, D. C. (2015). 'Sexual behavior and autism spectrum disorders: An update and discussion.' *Current Psychiatry Reports 17* (4), 1–8.

Kelley, E. (2020). *Representing People with Autism Spectrum Disorders: A Practical Guide for Criminal Defense Lawyers.* Chicago, IL: American Bar Association.

Kelly, E. & Hassett-Walker, C. (2016). 'The training of New Jersey emergency service first responders in autism awareness.' *Police Practice and Research 17* (6), 543–554.

Kendregan, C. P. (1966). 'Sixty years of compulsory eugenic sterilization: Three generations of imbeciles and the constitution of the United States.' *Chicago-Kent Law Review 43*, 123.

Kenworthy, L. E., Black, D. O., Wallace, G. L., Ahluvalia, T., Wagner, A. E., & Sirian, L. M. (2005). 'Disorganization: The forgotten executive dysfunction in high-functioning autism (HFA) spectrum disorders.' *Developmental Neuropsychology 28* (3), 809–827.

Kettleborough, D. & Merdian, H. (2013). 'The development of the children, internet, and sex cognitions scale (CISC): Understanding the cognitions of child pornography offenders.' *Presentation at the NOTA Conference, Cardiff.*

Kevles, D. J. (1999). 'Eugenics and human rights.' *BMJ 319* (7207), 435–438.

KFOR-TV & Querry, K. (2015). 'New ordinance requires sex offenders to post yard signs in Texas town.' *KFOR-TV.* Accessed on 24/11/2020 at https://kfor.com/news/new-ordinance-requires-sex-offenders-to-post-yard-signs-in-texas-town.

Khalil, R., Tindle, R., Boraud, T., Moustafa, A. A., & Karim, A. A. (2018). 'Social decision making in autism: On the impact of mirror neurons, motor control, and imitative behaviors.' *CNS Neuroscience and Therapeutics 24* (8), 669–676.

Kim, J. A., Szatmari, P., Bryson, S. E., Streiner, D. L., & Wilson, F. J. (2000). 'The prevalence of anxiety and mood problems among children with autism and Asperger syndrome.' *Autism 4* (2), 117–132.

Kim, S. H., Paul, R., Taser-Flusberg, H., & Lord, C. (2014). 'Language and Communication in Autism.' In F. R. Volkmar, R. Paul, S. J. Rogers, & K. A. Pelphrey (eds) *Handbook of Autism and Pervasive Developmental Disorders* (4th ed.) (pp.263–278). Hoboken, NJ: John Wiley & Sons.

King, R. (2010). 'Complex post-traumatic stress disorder: Implications for individuals with autism spectrum disorders: Part I.' *Journal on Developmental Disabilities 16* (3), 91–100.

Kirby, D., Laris, B. A., & Rolleri, L. (2007). 'Sex and HIV education programs: Their impact on sexual behaviors of young people throughout the world.' *Journal of Adolescent Health 40*, 206–217.

Kliemann, D., Dziobek, I., Hatri, A., Steimke, R., & Heekeren, H. R. (2010). 'Atypical reflexive gaze patterns on emotional faces in autism spectrum disorders.' *Journal of Neuroscience 30*, 12281–12287.

Klin, A., Saulnier, C. A., Sparrow, S. S., Cicchetti, D. V., Volkmar, F. R., & Lord, C. (2007). 'Social and communication abilities and disabilities in higher functioning individuals with autism spectrum disorders: The Vineland and the ADOS.' *Journal of Autism and Developmental Disorders 37*, 748–759.

Klin, A., Volkmar, F. R., Sparrow, S. S., Cicchetti, D. V., & Rourke, B. P. (1995). 'Validity and neuropsychological characterization of Asperger syndrome: Convergence with nonverbal learning disabilities syndrome.' *Journal of Child Psychology and Psychiatry 36* (7), 1127–1140.

Kluth, P. (2003). *"You're Going to Love this Kid": Teaching Students with Autism in the Inclusive Classroom.* Baltimore, MD: Paul H. Brookes.

Knapp, K. A. & Hauptly, D. J. (1991). 'State and federal sentencing guidelines: Apples and oranges.' *Journal of Neuroscience 25*, 679–694.

Kois, L., Wellbeloved-Stone, J. M., Chauhan, P., & Warren, J. I. (2017). 'Combined evaluations of competency to stand trial and mental state at the time of the offense: An overlooked methodological consideration?' *Law and Human Behavior 41* (3), 1–17.

Konstantareas, M. M. & Lunsky, Y. J. (1997). 'Sociosexual knowledge, experience, attitudes, and interests of individuals with autistic disorder and developmental delay.' *Journal of Autism and Developmental Disorders 27* (4), 397–413.

Kose, L. K., Fox, L., & Storch, E. A. (2018). 'Effectiveness of cognitive behavioral therapy for individuals with autism spectrum disorders and comorbid obsessive-compulsive disorder: A review of the research.' *Journal of Developmental and Physical Disabilities 30* (1), 69–87.

Kozéki, B. & Berghammer, R. (1992). 'The role of empathy in the motivational structure of school children.' *Personality and Individual Differences 13* (2), 191–203.

Krafka, C., Dunn, M. A., Johnson, M. T., Cecil, J. S., & Miletich, D. (2002). 'Judge and attorney experiences, practices, and concerns regarding expert testimony in federal civil trials.' *Psychology, Public Policy, and Law 8*, 1–25.

Kraper, C. K., Kenworthy, L., Popal, H., Martin, A., & Wallace, G. L. (2017). 'The gap between adaptive behavior and intelligence in autism persists into young adulthood and is linked to psychiatric co-morbidities.' *Journal of Autism and Developmental Disorders 47* (10), 3007–3017.

Kreek, M. J., Nielsen, D. A., Butelman, E. R., & LaForge, K. S. (2005). 'Genetic influences on impulsivity, risk taking, stress responsivity and vulnerability to drug abuse and addiction.' *Nature Neuroscience 8* (11), 1450–1457.

Kristensen, H. (2000). 'Selective mutism and comorbidity with developmental disorder/delay, anxiety disorder, and elimination disorder.' *Journal of the American Academy of Child and Adolescent Psychiatry 39* (2), 249–256.

Kugler, K. A. (2016). 'A prosecutor's comment on mental health court—realizing the goal of long-term public safety.' *Mitchell Hamline Law Review 42*, 523–536.

Kunstler, N. & Tsai, J. (2020). 'Understanding landlord perspectives on applicants with sex offenses.' *Housing, Care and Support 23* (1), 27–34.

Kushki, A., Drumm, E., Mobarak, M. P., Tanel, N., *et al.* (2013). 'Investigating the autonomic nervous system response to anxiety in children with autism spectrum disorders.' *PLOS ONE 8* (4).

Kwok, E. Y., Brown, H. M., Smyth, R. E., & Cardy, J. O. (2015). 'Meta-analysis of receptive and expressive language skills in autism spectrum disorder.' *Research in Autism Spectrum Disorders 9*, 202–222.

Kyle Cook, A. (2014). 'Presentence investigation report.' *The Encyclopedia of Criminology and Criminal Justice*, 1–5.

Laan, J., Ingram, R., & Glidden, M. (2013). 'Law enforcement training of mental disorders and autism spectrum disorders in the southeastern United States.' *Journal of Global Intelligence and Policy 6* (10), 51–67.

Lacombe, D. (2007). 'Consumed with sex: The treatment of sex offenders in risk society.' *The British Journal of Criminology 48* (1), 55–74.

Lai, M. C., Kassee, C., Besney, R., Bonato, S., *et al.* (2019). 'Prevalence of co-occurring mental health diagnoses in the autism population: A systematic review and meta-analysis.' *The Lancet Psychiatry 6* (10), 819–829.

Langan, P. A., Schmitt, E. L., & Durose, M. R. (2009). *Recidivism of Sex Offenders Released from Prison in 1994*. Washington, DC: Bureau of Justice Statistics (BJS), US Dept of Justice Office of Justice Programs, United States of America.

Larsen, B. Ø. (2017). 'Educational outcomes after serving with electronic monitoring: Results from a natural experiment.' *Journal of Quantitative Criminology 33* (1), 157–178.

Lartey, J. (2015). 'Risk of being killed by police is 16 times greater for those with mental illness.' *The Guardian*. Accessed on 24/11/2020 at www.theguardian.com/us-news/2015/dec/10/risk-of-being-killed-by-police-16-times-greater-mental-illness.

Latimer, J., Dowden, C., & Muise, D. (2001). *The Effectiveness of Restorative Justice Practices: A Meta-Analysis*. Ottawa: Research and Statistics Division.

Laugeson, E. A. & Frankel, F. (2010). *Social Skills for Teenagers with Developmental and Autism Spectrum Disorders: The PEERS Treatment Manual*. New York, NY: Routledge.

LaVigne, M. & Miles, S. (2018). 'Under the hood: Brandan Dassey, language impairments and judicial ignorance.' *Albany Law Review*, 873–947.

Law, B. M. (2017). 'When autism grows up—and encounters cops.' *Ashawire 22* (8), 54–57.

Laws, D. R. & Gress, C. L. Z. (2004). 'Seeing things differently: The viewing time alternative to penile plethysmography.' *Legal and Criminological Psychology 9*, 183–196.

Lee, H. J. & Park, H. R. (2007). 'An integrated literature review on the adaptive behavior of individuals with Asperger syndrome.' *Remedial and Special Education 28* (3), 132–139.

Lefkowitz, R. (2018). 'What are you en(title)d two: Protecting individuals with disabilities during interactions with law enforcement under Title II of the ADA.' *University of Memphis Law Review 49*, 707–757.

Lehmann, R. J. B., Goodwill, A. M., Hanson, R. K., & Dahle, K.-P. (2014). 'Crime scene behaviors indicate risk-relevant propensities of child molesters.' *Criminal Justice and Behavior 41* (8), 1008–1028.

Leonetti, C. (2012). 'When the emperor has no clothes III: Personnel policies and conflicts of interest in prosecutors' offices.' *Cornell Journal of Law and Public Policy 22*, 53–92.

Lerner, M. D., Haque, O. S., Northrup, E. C., Lawer, L., & Bursztajn, H. J. (2012). 'Emerging perspectives on adolescents and young adults with high-functioning autism spectrum disorders, violence, and criminal law.' *Journal of the American Academy of Psychiatry and the Law Online 40* (2), 177–190.

Levenson, J. S. (2018). 'Hidden challenges: Sex offenders legislated into homelessness.' *Journal of Social Work 18* (3), 348–363.

Levenson, J. S. & Cotter, L. P. (2005). 'The effect of Megan's Law on sex offender reintegration.' *Journal of Contemporary Criminal Justice 21* (1), 49–66.

Levenson, J. S. & Macgowan, M. J. (2002). 'Engagement, denial, and treatment progress among sex offenders in group therapy.' *Sexual Abuse: A Journal of Research and Treatment 16* (1), 49–63.

Levenson, J. S. & Tewksbury, R. (2009). 'Collateral damage: Family members of registered sex offenders.' *American Journal of Criminal Justice 34* (1), 54–68.

Levenson, J. S., D'Amora, D., & Hern, A. (2007). 'Megan's Law and its impact on community re-entry for sex offenders.' *Behavioral Sciences and the Law 25* (4), 587–602.

Levy, K. (2019). 'Normative ignorance: A critical connection between the insanity and mistake of law defenses.' *Florida State University Law Review*, 1–27.

Lewis v. Truitt [1997]. 960 F. Supp. 175, S.D. Ind., Judgment, Law, CaseMine (2017). Accessed on 24/11/2020 at www.casemine.com/judgement/us/59148214add7b0493448fc28.

Lewis, A., Pritchett, R., Hughes, C., & Turner, K. (2015). 'Development and implementation of autism standards for prisons.' *Journal of Intellectual Disabilities and Offending Behaviour 6* (2), 68–80.

Lewis, B. (2019). 'Autism FYI offers free training, app and more to law enforcement.' *Police1.* Accessed on 24/11/2020 at www.policeone.com/patrol-issues/articles/483418006-Autism-FYI-offers-free-training-app-and-more-to-law-enforcement.

Lezak, M. D. (1982). 'The problem of assessing executive functions.' *International Journal of Psychology 17,* 281–297.

Lilienfeld, S., Lynn, S. J., & Lohr, J. (2002). *Science and Pseudoscience in Clinical Psychology.* New York, NY: Guilford Press.

Lima, R. C., Feldman, C., Evans, C., & Block, P. (2018). 'Autism Policy and Advocacy in Brazil and the USA.' In *Autism in Translation* (pp.17–52). London: Palgrave Macmillan.

Limmer, M. (2014). 'The pressure to perform: Understanding the impact of masculinities and social exclusion on young men's sexual risk taking.' *International Journal of Men's Health 13* (3), 184–202.

Liss, M., Harel, B., Fein, D., Allen, D., *et al.* (2001). 'Predictors and correlates of adaptive functioning in children with developmental disorders.' *Journal of Autism and Developmental Disorders 31* (2), 219–230.

Litwack, T. R. (2003). 'The competency of criminal defendants to refuse, for delusional reasons, a viable insanity defense recommended by counsel.' *Behavioral Sciences and the Law 21* (2), 135–156.

Lloyd, C. D., Clark, H. J., & Forth, A. E. (2010). 'Psychopathy, expert testimony and indeterminate sentences: Exploring the relationship between Psychopathy Checklist-Revised testimony and trial outcome in Canada.' *Legal and Criminological Psychology 15,* 323–339.

Loftin, R. L. & Hartlage, S. A. (2015). 'Sex education, sexual health, and autism spectrum disorder.' *Pediatrics and Therapeutics 5,* 230.

Lohmann, A. J. (2017). 'Arrests and title ii of the ADA: Framework of claims for monetary damages.' *Washburn Law Journal 56* (3), 559–598.

Lombardo, P. A. (2008). *Three Generations, no Imbeciles: Eugenics, the Supreme Court, and Buck v. Bell.* Baltimore, MD: JHU Press.

Loureiro, D., Machado, A., Silva, T., Veigas, T., Ramalheira, C., & Cerejeira, J. (2018). 'Higher autistic traits among criminals, but no link to psychopathy: Findings from a high-security prison in Portugal.' *Journal of Autism and Developmental Disorders 48* (9), 1–11.

Luby, J. L., Belden, A. C., Pautsch, J., Si, X., & Spitznagel, E. (2009). 'The clinical significance of preschool depression: Impairment in functioning and clinical markers of the disorder.' *Journal of Affective Disorders 112* (1–3), 111–119.

Luke, L. (2011). *Decision-Making in Autism Spectrum Conditions* (Doctoral Dissertation, University of Cambridge).

Luke, L., Clare, I. C., Ring, H., Redley, M., & Watson, P. (2012). 'Decision-making difficulties experienced by adults with autism spectrum conditions.' *Autism 16* (6), 612–621.

Lund, E. M. & Thomas, K. B. (2017). 'Interpersonal Violence Survivors with Disabilities: Considerations for Faith-Based Organizations.' In *Religion, Disability, and Interpersonal Violence* (pp.3–9). Cham: Springer.

Lussier, P. & Mathesius, J. (2019). 'Not in my backyard: Public sex offender registries and public notification laws.' *Canadian Journal of Criminology and Criminal Justice 61* (1), 105–116.

Lynn, G. T. & Lynn, J. B. (2007). *The Asperger Plus Child: How to Identify and Help Children with Asperger Syndrome and Seven Common Co-Existing Conditions.* Shawnee, KS: AAPC Publishing.

Mackin, M. L., Loew, N., Gonzalez, A., Tykol, H., & Christensen, T. (2016). 'Parent perceptions of sexual education needs for their children with autism.' *Journal of Pediatric Nursing 31* (6), 608–618.

Macleod, A. (2010). '"Welcome to my first rant!" Report on a participatory pilot project to develop the "AS Portal", an online peer support network for higher education students on the autism spectrum.' *Journal of Assistive Technologies 4* (1), 14–24.

MacMullin, J. A., Lunsky, Y., & Weiss, J. A. (2015). 'Plugged in: Electronics use in youth and young adults with autism spectrum disorder.' *Autism, 20* (1), 1–10.

Mador, J. (2010). 'A public defender's day: 12 minutes per client.' *MPR News.* Accessed on 24/11/2020 at www.mprnews.org/story/2010/11/29/public-defenders.

Magiati, I., Ong, C., Lim, X. Y., Tan, J., *et al.* (2016). 'Anxiety symptoms in young people with autism spectrum disorder attending special schools: Associations with gender, adaptive functioning and autism symptomatology.' *Autism 20* (3), 306–320.

Mahoney, M. (2009). Asperger's syndrome and the criminal law: The special case of child pornography. *Harrington & Mahoney.* Accessed on 24/11/2020 at www.harringtonmahoney.com/content/Publications/AspergersSyndromeandtheCriminalLawv26.pdf.

Mahoney, M. (2017). 'Autism Spectrum Disorder and Online Sexual Offenses: Surviving the "Perfect Storm".' To Kill a Sex Crime Seminar, December 7–8, 2017. Texas Criminal Defense Lawyers Association, Wyndham Conference Center, Austin, TX.

Mahoney, M. (2019). 'Autism Spectrum Disorder and Online Sexual Offenses: Surviving the "Perfect Storm".' Law and All That Jazz Seminar, April 25-27, 2019. Louisiana Association of Criminal Defense Lawyers. Hyatt French Quarter, New Orleans, LA.

Mahoney, M. (2020). 'Defending Autistic People: Sex Offenses.' Texas Criminal Defense Lawyers Association. Hilton Houston Post Oak by The Galleria. December 3-4, 2020. 1-106 [email correspondence].

Maier, S. L. (2008). '"I have heard horrible stories..." Rape victim advocates' perceptions of the revictimization of rape victims by the police and medical system.' Violence Against Women 14 (7), 786-808.

Malzberg, B. (1952). 'Some statistical aspects of first admissions to the New York State Schools for mental defectives.' American Journal of Mental Deficiency 57, 27-37.

Manninen, M., Therman, S., Suvisaari, J., Ebeling, H., et al. (2011). 'Alexithymia is common among adolescents with severe disruptive behavior.' The Journal of Nervous and Mental Disease 199 (7), 506-509.

Maras, K. & Bowler, D. M. (2014). 'Eyewitness testimony in autism spectrum disorder: A review.' Journal of Autism and Developmental Disorders 44 (11), 2682-2697.

Maras, K., Marshall, I., & Sands, C. (2019). 'Mock juror perceptions of credibility and culpability in an autistic defendant.' Journal of Autism and Developmental Disorders 49 (3), 996-1010.

Maras, K., Mulcahy, S., Crane, L., Hawken, T., & Memon, A. (2018). 'Obtaining best evidence from the autistic interviewee: Police-reported challenges, legal requirements and psychological research-based recommendations.' Investigative Interviewing: Research and Practice (II-RP) 9 (1), 52-60.

Marin, G. (2008). 'Possession of child pornography: Should you be convicted when the computer cache does the saving for you?' Florida Law Review 60, 1205-1235.

Marino, K. M. (2009). 'Probation management of sex offenders: An analysis of co-facilitators' perceptions of offender progress in treatment.' Criminal Justice Review 34 (3), 382-403.

Marshall Independent (2019). 'Attorney speaks of dangers of sexting.' Marshall Independent. Accessed on 6/12/2020 at www.marshallindependent.com/news/local-news/2019/09/attorney-speaks-of-dangers-of-sexting.

Martínez-Sanchis, S. (2014). 'Neurobiological foundations of multisensory integration in people with autism spectrum disorders: The role of the medial prefrontal cortex.' Frontiers in Human Neuroscience 8, 970.

Masi, A., DeMayo, M. M., Glozier, N., & Guastella, A. J. (2017). 'An overview of autism spectrum disorder, heterogeneity and treatment options.' Neuroscience Bulletin 33 (2), 183-193.

Matson, J. L., Dempsey, T., & Fodstad, J. C. (2009). 'The effect of autism spectrum disorders on adaptive independent living skills in adults with severe intellectual disability.' Research in Developmental Disabilities 30 (6), 1203-1211.

Matson, J. L., Terlonge, C., González, M. L., & Rivet, T. (2006). 'An evaluation of social and adaptive skills in adults with bipolar disorder and severe/profound intellectual disability.' Research in Developmental Disabilities 27 (6), 681-687.

Mattison, M. L. A., Dando, C. J., & Ormerod, T. (2016). 'Drawing the answers: Sketching to support free and probed recall by child witnesses and victims with autism spectrum disorder.' Autism: International Journal of Research and Practice 22 (2), 181-194.

May, J. M. (1958). A Physician Looks at Psychiatry. New York, NY: John Day.

Mazefsky, C. A., Herrington, J., Siegel, M., Scarpa, A., et al. (2013). 'The role of emotion regulation in autism spectrum disorder.' Journal of the American Academy of Child and Adolescent Psychiatry 52 (7), 679-688.

Mazurek, M. O. (2013). 'Social media use among adults with autism spectrum disorders.' Computers in Human Behavior 29 (4), 1709-1714.

Mazurek, M. O. & Wenstrup, C. (2013). 'Television, video game and social media use among children with ASD and typically developing siblings.' Journal of Autism and Developmental Disorders 43 (6), 1258-1271.

Mazurek, M. O., Shattuck, P. T., Wagner, M., & Cooper, B. P. (2012). 'Prevalence and correlates of screen-based media use among youths with autism spectrum disorders.' Journal of Autism and Developmental Disorders 42 (8), 1757-1767.

McBarnet, D. (1983). 'Victim in the witness box: Confronting victimology's stereotype.' Crime, Law and Social Change 7 (3), 293-393.

McCabe, M. P. (1993). 'Sex education programs for people with mental retardation.' Mental Retardation 31, 377-387.

McCauley, E. J. (2017). 'The cumulative probability of arrest by age 28 years in the United States by disability status, race/ethnicity, and gender.' American Journal of Public Health 107 (12), 1977-1981.

McConkie, D. S. (2015). 'Judges as framers of plea bargaining.' Stanford Law and Policy Review 26, 61-117.

McCoy, K. B. (2014). 'The growing need for third-party special needs trust reform.' Case Western Reserve Law Review 65, 461-485.

McCrory, E., Henry, L. A., & Happé, F. (2007). 'Eye-witness memory and suggestibility in children with Asperger syndrome.' Journal of Child Psychology and Psychiatry 48, 482-489.

McEwan, T. & Freckelton, I. (2011). 'Assessment, treatment and sentencing of arson offenders: An overview.' *Psychiatry, Psychology and Law 18* (3), 319–328.

McGonigle, J., Migyanka, J., Glor-Scheib, S., Cramer, R., *et al.* (2014). 'Development and evaluation of educational materials for pre-hospital and emergency department personnel on the care of patients with autism spectrum disorders.' *Journal of Autism and Developmental Disorders 5*, 1252–1259.

McGowan, K. (2013). 'Exploring Temple Grandin's brain.' *Discover Magazine.* Accessed on 24/11/2020 at www.discovermagazine.com/mind/exploring-temple-grandins-brain.

McKeen, P. (2013). 'The impact of motor skill training on balance, hand-eye coordination and reaction in a group of adults with autism and an intellectual disability.' *Electronic Theses and Dissertations 4986.* Accessed on 24/11/2020 at https://scholar.uwindsor.ca/etd/4986.

McKenzie, K., Michie, A., Murray, A., & Hales, C. (2012). 'Screening for offenders with an intellectual disability: The validity of the Learning Disability Screening Questionnaire.' *Research in Developmental Disabilities 33* (3), 791–795.

McNaughton, H. (2017). *Self-Reported Understanding of Romantic Relationships: High School Students with ASD Compared to Neurotypical High School Students* (Doctoral Dissertation).

McPherson, L. (2016). 'The Sex Offender Registration and Notification Act (SORNA) at 10 years: History, implementation, and the future.' *Drake Law Review 64*, 741–796.

Mechling, L. C. & Gustafson, M. R. (2008). 'Comparison of static picture and video prompting on the performance of cooking-related tasks by students with autism.' *Journal of Special Education Technology 23* (3), 31–45.

Medina, D. A. (2019). 'The progressive prosecutors blazing a new path for the US justice system.' *The Guardian.* Accessed on 24/11/2020 at www.theguardian.com/us-news/2019/jul/23/us-justice-system-progressive-prosecutors-mass-incarceration-death-penalty.

Mehzabin, P. & Stokes, M. A. (2011). 'Self-assessed sexuality in young adults with high-functioning autism.' *Research in Autism Spectrum Disorders 5* (1), 614–621.

Meister, C., Norlock, D., Honeyman, S., & Pierce, K. (1994). 'Sexuality and autism: A parenting skills enhancement group.' *Canadian Journal of Human Sexuality 3* (3), 283–289.

Melvin, C. L., Langdon, P. E., & Murphy, G. H. (2017). 'Treatment effectiveness for offenders with autism spectrum conditions: A systematic review.' *Psychology, Crime and Law 23* (8), 748–776.

Mentoring and Befriending Foundation (2010). *Peer Mentoring in Schools: A Review of the Evidence Base of the Benefits of Peer Mentoring in Schools Including Findings from the MBF Outcomes Measurement Programme.* Manchester: Mentoring and Befriending Foundation.

Mercado, C. C., Alvarez, S., & Levenson, J. (2008). 'The impact of specialized sex offender legislation on community reentry.' *Sexual Abuse 20* (2), 188–205.

Mesibov, G. & Sreckovic, M. (2017). 'Child and Juvenile Pornography and Autism Spectrum Disorder.' In L. A. Dubin & E. Horowitz, *Caught in the Web of the Criminal Justice System: Autism, Developmental Disabilities, and Sex Offenses* (pp.69–94). London: Jessica Kingsley Publishers.

Michels, S. (2009). 'Sex offender dies in cold after being denied from shelter.' *ABC News.* Accessed on 12/2/2021 at https://abcnews.go.com/TheLaw/story?id=6769453&page=1.

Michna, I. & Trestman, R. (2016). 'Correctional management and treatment of autism spectrum disorder.' *Journal of the American Academy of Psychiatry and the Law Online 44* (2), 253–258.

Miliora, M. T. (2001). 'Creativity, "twinning," and self-destruction in the life and work of Tennessee Williams.' *Journal of Applied Psychoanalytic Studies 3* (2), 127–148.

Millward, C., Powell, S., Messer, D., & Jordan, R. (2000). 'Recall for self and other in autism: Children's memory for events experienced by themselves and their peers.' *Journal of Autism and Developmental Disorders 30*, 15–28.

Milosavljevic, B., Leno, V. C., Simonoff, E., Baird, G., *et al.* (2016). 'Alexithymia in adolescents with autism spectrum disorder: Its relationship to internalising difficulties, sensory modulation and social cognition.' *Journal of Autism and Developmental Disorders 46* (4), 1354–1367.

Milton, D. E. (2014). 'So what exactly are autism interventions intervening with?' *Good Autism Practice (GAP) 15* (2), 6–14.

Ming, X., Julu, P. O., Brimacombe, M., Connor, S., & Daniels, M. L. (2005). 'Reduced cardiac parasympathetic activity in children with autism.' *Brain and Development 27* (7), 509–516.

Minix, L. C. (2017). 'Examining Rule 11 (b)(1)(n) error: Guilty pleas, appellate waiver, and Dominguez Benitez.' *Washington and Lee Law Review 74*, 551–606.

Mitchell, K. L. (2017). 'State sentencing guidelines: A garden full of variety.' *Federal Probation 81* (2), 28–36.

Modell, S. J. & Cropp, D. (2007). 'Police officers and disability: Perceptions and attitudes.' *Intellectual and Developmental Disabilities 45* (1), 60–63.

Modell, S. J. & Mak, S. (2008). 'A preliminary assessment of police officer knowledge and perceptions of persons with disabilities.' *Intellectual and Developmental Disabilities 46*, 183–189.

Mogavero, M. C. (2016). 'Autism, sexual offending, and the criminal justice system.' *Journal of Intellectual Disabilities and Offending Behaviour 7* (3), 116–126.

Mogavero, M. C. (2018). 'What do criminal justice students know about autism? An exploratory study among future professionals.' *Journal of Police and Criminal Psychology 34* (4), 1–14.

Mooney, C. (2017). *Everything You Need to Know About Sexual Consent.* New York, NY: The Rosen Publishing Group, Inc.

Moran, J. (2017). 'Officials: City of Portsmouth can't ban sex offender from using public pool.' *WMUR.* Accessed on 24/11/2020 at www.wmur.com/article/officials-city-of-portsmouth-cant-ban-sex-offender-from-using-public-pool/14376626.

Morgan, L., Leatzow, A., Clark, S., & Siller, M. (2014). 'Interview skills for adults with autism spectrum disorder: A pilot randomized controlled trial.' *Journal of Autism and Developmental Disorders 44* (9), 2290–2300.

Mottron, L., Bouvet, L., Bonnel, A., Samson, F., *et al.* (2013). 'Veridical mapping in the development of exceptional autistic abilities.' *Neuroscience and Biobehavioral Reviews 37* (2), 209–228.

Mouridsen, S. E., Rich, B., Isager, T., & Nedergaard, N. J. (2008). 'Pervasive developmental disorders and criminal behaviour: A case control study.' *International Journal of Offender Therapy and Comparative Criminology 52* (2), 196–205.

Mueller, C. O., Forber-Pratt, A. J., & Sriken, J. (2019). 'Disability: Missing from the conversation of violence.' *Journal of Social Issues 75* (3), 707–725.

Mulder, E., Brand, E., Bullens, R., & Van Marle, H. (2010). 'A classification of risk factors in serious juvenile offenders and the relation between patterns of risk factors and recidivism.' *Criminal Behaviour and Mental Health 20* (1), 23–38.

Mullen, P., Pathé, M., Purcell, R., & Stuart, G. W. (1999). 'Study of stalkers.' *American Journal of Psychiatry 156,* 1244–1249.

Müller, E., Schuler, A., Burton, B. A., & Yates, G. B. (2003). 'Meeting the vocational support needs of individuals with Asperger syndrome and other autism spectrum disabilities.' *Journal of Vocational Rehabilitation 18* (3), 163–175.

Murphy, L., Mufti, E., & Kossem, D. (2009). *Education Studies: An Introduction.* Maidenhead: Open University Press.

Murrie, D. C. & Zelle, H. (2015). 'Criminal Competencies.' In *APA Handbook of Forensic Psychology, Vol. 1: Individual and Situational Influences in Criminal and Civil Contexts* (pp.115–157). Washington, DC: American Psychological Association.

Murrie, D. C., Boccaccini, M. T., Guarnera, L. A., & Rufino, K. A. (2013). 'Are forensic experts biased by the side that retained them?' *Psychological Science, 24* (10), 1889–1897.

Murrie, D. C., Boccaccini, M. T., Johnson, J., & Janke, C. (2008). 'Does interrater (dis)agreement on Psychopathy Checklist scores in sexually violent predator trials suggest partisan allegiance in forensic evaluations?' *Law and Human Behavior 32,* 352–362.

Murrie, D. C., Boccaccini, M. T., Turner, D. B., Meeks, M., Woods, C., & Tussey, C. (2009). 'Rater (dis)agreement on risk assessment measures in sexually violent predator proceedings: Evidence of adversarial allegiance in forensic evaluation?' *Psychology, Public Policy, and Law 15,* 19–53.

Murrie, D. C., Warren, J. I., Kristiansson, M., & Dietz, P. E. (2002). 'Asperger's syndrome in forensic settings.' *International Journal of Forensic Mental Health 1* (1), 59–70.

Myers, C. A. (2017). 'Police violence against people with mental disabilities: The immutable duty under the ADA to reasonably accommodate during arrest.' *Vanderbilt Law Review 70* (4), 1393–1426.

Myles, B. S. & Simpson, R. L. (2001). 'Understanding the hidden curriculum: An essential social skill for children and youth with Asperger syndrome.' *Intervention in School and Clinic 36* (5), 279–286.

Myles, B. S. & Simpson, R. L. (2002). 'Students with Asperger syndrome: Implications for counselors.' *Counseling and Human Development 34,* 1–16.

Myles, B. S., Trautman, M., & Schelvan, R. (2004). *The Hidden Curriculum: Practical Solutions for Understanding Unstated Rules in Social Situations.* Shawnee, KS: Autism Asperger Publishing.

Nagel, I. & Schulhofer, S. J. (1992). 'A tale of three cities: An empirical study of charging and bargaining practices under the federal sentencing guidelines.' *Southern California Law Review 66,* 501–579.

Nagel, S. S. (1962). 'Judicial backgrounds and criminal cases.' *Journal of Criminal Law and Criminology 53* (3), 333–339.

Nagi, C., Browne, K., & Blake, J. (2006). 'A descriptive analysis of the nature and extent of bullying at a category C prison.' *British Journal of Forensic Practice 8,* 4–9.

National Association of Pretrial Services Agencies (2019). 'Pretrial diversion.' *NAPSA.* Accessed on 24/11/2020 at https://napsa.org/eweb/DynamicPage.aspx?Site=NAPSA&WebCode=Diversion.

Neely, B. & Hunter, S. (2014). 'In a discussion on invisible disabilities, let us not lose sight of employees on the autism spectrum.' *Industrial and Organizational Psychology 7* (2), 274–277.

Neily, C. (2019). 'Are a disproportionate number of federal judges former government advocates?' *Cato Institute*. Accessed on 24/11/2020 at www.cato.org/publications/studies/are-disproportionate-number-federal-judges-former-government-advocates.

Newman, C., Cashin, A., & Waters, C. (2015). 'A hermeneutic phenomenological examination of the lived experience of incarceration for those with autism.' *Issues in Mental Health Nursing 36* (8), 632–640.

Newstrom, N. P., Miner, M., Hoefer, C., Hanson, R. K., & Robinson, B. B. E. (2018). 'Sex offender supervision: Communication, training, and mutual respect are necessary for effective collaboration between probation officers and therapists.' *Sexual Abuse*, 1079063218775970.

Nibert, D. (1995). 'The political economy of development disability.' *Critical Sociology 21* (1), 59–80.

Niles, M. C. (2017). 'A new balance of evils: Prosecutorial misconduct, Iqbal, and the end of absolute immunity.' *Stanford Journal of Civil Rights and Civil Liberties 13*, 137–188.

Nora, G. E. (2007). 'Prosecutor as "Nurse Ratched": Misusing criminal justice as alternative medicine.' *Criminal Justice 22*, 18.

Norbury, C. F., Brock, J., Cragg, L., Einav, S., Griffiths, H., & Nation, K. (2009). 'Eye-movement patterns are associated with communicative competence in autistic spectrum disorders.' *Journal of Child Psychology and Psychiatry 50* (7), 834–842.

Nordahl, C. W., Lange, N., Li, D. D., Barnett, L. A., *et al.* (2011). 'Brain enlargement is associated with regression in preschool-age boys with autism spectrum disorders.' *Proceedings of the National Academy of Sciences 108* (50), 20195–20200.

North, A. S., Russell, A. J., & Gudjonsson, G. H. (2008). 'High functioning autism-spectrum disorders: An investigation of psychological vulnerabilities during interrogative interview.' *The Journal of Forensic Psychiatry and Psychology 19*, 323–334.

Nyrenius, J. & Billstedt, E. (2019). 'The functional impact of cognition in adults with autism spectrum disorders.' *Nordic Journal of Psychiatry 74* (3), 1–6.

O'Brien, G. (2004). 'Rosemary Kennedy: The importance of a historical footnote.' *Journal of Family History 29* (3), 225–236.

O'Donnell, I. & Edgar, K. (1998). 'Routine victimisation in prisons.' *Howard Journal 37*, 266–279.

O'Mahony, M. B. (2009). 'The emerging role of the Registered Intermediary with the vulnerable witness and offender: Facilitating communication with the police and members of the judiciary.' *British Journal of Learning Disabilities 38*, 232–237.

Oh, P. B. (1997). 'The proper test for assessing the admissibility of nonscientific expert evidence under federal Rule of Evidence 702.' *Cleveland State Law Review 45*, 437–467.

Oppel Jr., R. & Patel, J. (2019). 'One lawyer, 194 felony cases, and no time.' *The New York Times*. Accessed on 24/11/2020 at www.nytimes.com/interactive/2019/01/31/us/public-defender-case-loads.html.

Orsmond, G. I., Shattuck, P. T., Cooper, B. P., Sterzing, P. R., & Anderson, K. A. (2013). 'Social participation among young adults with an autism spectrum disorder.' *Journal of Autism and Developmental Disorders 43* (11), 2710–2719.

Ortiz, L. (2018). 'Student stigma: Teens with disabilities being labeled after Parkland school shooting.' *CBS 12*. Accessed on 24/11/2020 at https://cbs12.com/news/local/student-stigma-teens-with-disabilities-being-labeled-after-parkland-school-shooting.

Ortoleva, S. (2010). 'Inaccessible justice: Human rights, persons with disabilities and the legal system.' *ILSA Journal of International and Comparative Law 17* (2), 283–320.

Osborn, C., Abel, G. G., & Warberg, B. W. (1995). 'The Abel Assessment: Its comparison to plethysmography and resistance to falsification.' Annual Conference of the Association for the Treatment of Sexual Abusers, New Orleans, LA, October 1995.

Oschwald, M., Curry, M. A., Hughes, R. B., Arthur, A., & Powers, L. (2011). 'Law enforcement's response to crime reporting by people with disabilities.' *Police Practice and Research 12* (6), 527–542.

Ousley, O. & Cermak, T. (2014). 'Autism spectrum disorder: Defining dimensions and subgroups.' *Current Developmental Disorders Reports 1* (1), 20–28.

Owen v. City of Independence [1980]. 445 U.S. 622, 638. *Justia*. Accessed on 24/11/2020 at https://supreme.justia.com/cases/federal/us/445/622.

Ozonoff, S., Iosif, A. M., Baguio, F., Cook, I. C., *et al.* (2010). 'A prospective study of the emergence of early behavioral signs of autism.' *Journal of the American Academy of Child and Adolescent Psychiatry 49* (3), 256–266.

Palermo, M. T. (2013). 'Developmental disorders and political extremism: A case study of Asperger syndrome and the neo-nazi subculture.' *Journal of Forensic Psychology Practice 13*, 341–354.

Panju, S., Brian, J., Dupuis, A., Anagnostou, E., & Kushki, A. (2015). 'Atypical sympathetic arousal in children with autism spectrum disorder and its association with anxiety symptomatology.' *Molecular Autism 6* (1), 64.

Parker, L. R, Monteith, M. J., & South, S. C. (2018). 'Dehumanization, prejudice, and social policy beliefs concerning people with developmental disabilities.' *Group Processes and Intergroup Relations*, 1–23.

Pasha, S. (2017). 'The U.S. justice system has an autism problem.' *The Dallas Morning News*. Accessed on 24/11/2020 at www.dallasnews.com/opinion/commentary/2017/08/15/the-u-s-justice-system-has-an-autism-problem.

Payne, K. L., Maras, K., Russell, A., & Brosnan, M. (2019a). 'Self-reported motivations for offending by autistic sexual offenders.' *Autism*. DOI: 10.1177/1362361319858860.

Payne, K. L., Russell, A., Mills, R., Maras, K., Rai, D., & Brosnan, M. (2019b). 'Is there a relationship between cyber-dependent crime, autistic-like traits and autism?' *Journal of Autism and Developmental Disorders 49* (10), 4159–4169.

Penrose, L. & Penrose, R. (1958). 'Impossible objects: A special type of visual illusion.' *British Journal of Psychology 49*, 31–33.

Pepler, E. F. & Barber, C. G. (2021). 'Mental health and policing: Picking up the pieces in a broken system.' *Healthcare Management Forum 34* (2), 93–99.

Peppé, S., McCann, J., Gibbon, F., O'Hare, A., & Rutherford, M. (2006). 'Assessing prosodic and pragmatic ability in children with high-functioning autism.' *QMU Speech Science Research Centre Working Papers*, WP-4.

Perlin, M. L. (1996). 'The borderline which separated you from me: The insanity defense, the authoritarian spirit, the fear of faking, and the culture of punishment.' *Iowa Law Review 82*, 1375–1426.

Perlin, M. L. (2016). 'Representing clients with mental health and/or cognitive impairments in treatment courts.' *NYLS Legal Studies Research Paper*, 2816892. Accessed on 24/11/2020 at www.american.edu/spa/jpo/initiatives/drug-court/upload/perlin-mental-impairments-7-8-16.pdf.

Perry, D. M. (2017). 'Disabled people dead in another week of police brutality.' *The Nation*. Accessed on 24/11/2020 at www.thenation.com/article/four-disabled-dead-in-another-week-of-police-brutality.

Perry, D. M. & Carter-Long, L. (2016). *The Ruderman White Paper on Media Coverage of Law Enforcement Use of Force and Disability*. Boston, MA: Ruderman Foundation.

Perske, R. (2008). 'False confessions from 53 persons with intellectual disabilities: The list keeps growing.' *Intellectual and Developmental Disabilities 46* (6), 468–479.

Pesce, L. N. (2019). 'Most college grads with autism can't find jobs. This group is fixing that.' *Market Watch*. Accessed on 24/11/2020 at www.marketwatch.com/story/most-college-grads-with-autism-cant-find-jobs-this-group-is-fixing-that-2017-04-10-5881421.

Phoenix, L. (2017). 'When you're on the autistic spectrum, consent is complicated.' *The Establishment*. Accessed on 24/11/2020 at https://theestablishment.co/when-youre-on-the-autistic-spectrum-consent-is-complicated-81b16663a43d/index.html.

Piehl, A. & Bushway, S. (2007). 'Measuring and explaining charge bargaining.' *Journal of Quantitative Criminology 23* (2), 105–125.

Plaisted, K. C. (2001). 'Reduced Generalization in Autism: An Alternative to Weak Central Coherence.' In J. A. Burack, T. Charman, N. Yirmiya, & P. R. Zelazo (eds) *The Development of Autism: Perspectives from Theory and Research* (pp.149–169). Mahwah, NJ: Lawrence Erlbaum Associates.

Płatos, M. & Wojaczek, K. (2018). 'Broadening the scope of peer-mediated intervention for individuals with autism spectrum disorders.' *Journal of Autism and Developmental Disorders 48* (3), 747–750.

Pollock, J. M. (2014). *Ethical Dilemmas and Decisions in Criminal Justice*. Scarborough, Ontario: Nelson Education.

Post, M., Storey, K., Haymes, L., Campbell, C., & Loughrey, T. (2014). 'Stalking behaviors by individuals with autism spectrum disorders in employment settings: Understanding stalking behavior and developing appropriate supports.' *Education and Training in Autism and Developmental Disabilities*, 102–110.

Postorino, V., Siracusano, M., Giovagnoli, G., & Mazzone, L. (2018). 'Aspects of Sexuality During Development in Autism Spectrum Disorder.' In E. Jannini & A. Siracusano (eds) *Sexual Dysfunctions in Mentally Ill Patients. Trends in Andrology and Sexual Medicine* (pp.63–75). Cham: Springer.

Potter, G. (2013). 'The history of policing in the United States.' *Eastern Kentucky University Online*. Accessed on 24/11/2020 at https://plsonline.eku.edu/sites/plsonline.eku.edu/files/the-history-of-policing-in-us.pdf.

Power, A. (2016). *Landscapes of Care: Comparative Perspectives on Family Caregiving*. Abingdon-on-Thames: Routledge.

Pratley, J. & Goodman-Delahunty, J. (2011). 'Increased self-disclosure of offending by intrafamilial child sex offenders.' *Sexual Abuse in Australia and New Zealand: An Interdisciplinary Journal 3* (1), 44–52.

Prins, S. J. (2014). 'Prevalence of mental illnesses in US state prisons: A systematic review.' *Psychiatric Services 65* (7), 862–872.

Pua, E. P., Malpas, C., Bowden, S., & Seal, M. (2017). 'Different brain networks underlying intelligence in autism spectrum disorders and typically developing children.' *bioRxiv 143891*.

Public Law 93-112 (1973), § 504, 87 Stat. 355 (codified at 29 U.S.C. § 794 (2006)). Accessed on 24/11/2020 at www.govinfo.gov/app/details/STATUTE-87/STATUTE-87-Pg355.

Pugliese, C. E., Anthony, L. G., Strang, J. F., Dudley, K., et al. (2016). 'Longitudinal examination of adaptive behavior in autism spectrum disorders: Influence of executive function.' *Journal of Autism and Developmental Disorders 46* (2), 467–477.

Pugliese, C. E., Anthony, L. G., Strang, J. F., Dudley, K., Wallace, G. L., & Kenworthy, L. (2015). 'Increasing adaptive behavior skill deficits from childhood to adolescence in autism spectrum disorder: Role of executive function.' *Journal of Autism and Developmental Disorders 45* (6), 1579–1587.

Pugliese, T. (2017). 'Dangerous intersection: Protecting people with mental disabilities from police brutality during arrests using the Americans with Disabilities Act.' *Hofstra Law Review 46*, 765–798.

Putnam, J. (2019). 'Lansing police chief, autism advocate join forces to train officers in a softer approach.' *Lansing State Journal*. Accessed on 24/11/2020 at www.lansingstatejournal.com/story/opinion/columnists/judy-putnam/2019/03/29/lansing-police-yankowski-autism/3308858002.

Quarmby, K. (2011). *Scapegoat: Why We Are Failing Disabled People*. London: Portobello Books.

Quinsey, V. L. (1986). 'Men Who Have Sex With Children.' In D. N. Weisstub (ed.) *Law and Mental Health: International Perspectives* (pp.140–172). New York, NY: Pergamon.

Rackmill, S. J. (1996). 'Printzlien's legacy, the Brooklyn plan, AKA deferred prosecution.' *Federal Probation Journal 60*, 8–15.

Radley, J. & Shaherbano, Z. (2011). 'Asperger syndrome and arson: A case study.' *Advances in Mental Health and Intellectual Disabilities 5* (6), 32–36.

Radonovich, K. J., Fournier, K. A., & Hass, C. J. (2013). 'Relationship between postural control and restricted, repetitive behaviors in autism spectrum disorders.' *Frontiers in Integrative Neuroscience 7*, 28.

Raggio, D. J., Massingale, T. W., & Bass, J. D. (1994). 'Comparison of Vineland adaptive behavior scales-survey form age equivalent and standard score with the Bayley Mental Development Index.' *Perceptual and Motor Skills 79* (1), 203–206.

Ramage, J. (2019). 'Reframing the punishment test through modern sex offender legislation.' *Fordham Law Review 88*, 1099–1131.

Rankin, E. (2017). 'Creep busters ambush of man with mental disability called "vigilantism."' *CBC website*. Accessed on 24/11/2020 at www.cbc.ca/news/canada/british-columbia/creep-busters-ambush-of-man-with-mental-disability-called-vigilantism-1.4009147.

Ray, F., Marks, C., & Bray-Garretson, H. (2004). 'Challenges to treating adolescents with Asperger's syndrome who are sexually abusive.' *Sexual Addiction and Compulsivity 11* (4), 265–285.

Realmuto, G. M. & Ruble, L. A. (1999). 'Sexual behaviors in autism: Problems of definition and management.' *Journal of Autism and Developmental Disorders 29* (2), 121–127.

Redford, R. C. (2010). *Crazy: My Seven Years at Bruno Bettelheim's Orthogenic School*. Bloomington, IN: Trafford Publishing.

Redlich, A. D., Bibas, S., Edkins, V. A., & Madon, S. (2017). 'The psychology of defendant plea decision making.' *American Psychologist 72* (4), 339–352.

Reed, P. (2017). 'Punishment beyond incarceration: The negative effects of sex offender registration and restrictions.' *Journal of Law and Criminal Justice 5* (2), 16–30.

Reese, C. S., Suhr, J. A., & Riddle, T. L. (2012). 'Exploration of malingering indices in the Wechsler Adult Intelligence Scale-digit span subtest.' *Archives of Clinical Neuropsychology 27* (2), 176–181.

Reid, D. (2020). '"Flash crash" trader sentenced to one year of home detention.' *CNBC*. Accessed on 23/11/2020 at www.cnbc.com/2020/01/29/flash-crash-trader-navinder-singh-sarao-sentenced-to-home-detention.html.

Reisner, A., Piel, J., & Makey, M. (2013). 'Competency to stand trial and defendants who lack insight into their mental illness.' *Journal of the American Academy of Psychiatry and the Law Online 41* (1), 85–91.

Reiss, A. J. (1974). 'Discretionary justice in the United States.' *International Journal of Criminology and Penology 2* (2), 181–205.

Respond (2020). 'Case Study: Circle of Support & Accountability (COSA): Gary.' *Respond*. Accessed on 26/03/2021 at https://respond.org.uk/wp-content/uploads/2020/05/COSA-Case-Study.pdf.

Rhee, N. (2019). 'For people with disabilities, Chicago police consent decree takes first steps toward reform.' *Chicago Reporter*. Accessed on 24/11/2020 at www.chicagoreporter.com/for-people-with-disabilities-chicago-police-consent-decree-is-just-a-first-step-toward-reform.

Rice, E., Gibbs, J., Winetrobe, H., Rhoades, H., et al. (2014). 'Sexting and sexual behavior among middle school students.' *American Academy of Pediatrics 134*, e21–e28.

Rifkin, S. (2016). 'Safeguarding the ADA's antidiscrimination mandate: Subjecting arrests to Title II coverage.' *Duke Law Journal 66*, 913.

Rivoli, D. (2016). 'The story of Darius McCollum, NYC's notorious transit thief, to screen at Lower East Side's Metrograph theater.' *NY Daily News*. Accessed on 10/12/2020 at www.nydailynews.com/new-york/documentary-transit-thief-darius-mccollum-screening-nyc-article-1.2871440.

Robic, S., Sonié, S., Fonlupt, P., Henaff, M. A., *et al.* (2015). 'Decision-making in a changing world: A study in autism spectrum disorders.' *Journal of Autism and Developmental Disorders 45* (6), 1603–1613.

Robinson, L., Spencer, M. D., Thomson, L. D., Stanfield, A. C., *et al.* (2012). 'Evaluation of a screening instrument for autism spectrum disorders in prisoners.' *PLOS ONE 7* (5), e36078.

Robinson, R. (2011). 'Does prosecutorial experience "balance out" a judge's liberal tendencies?' *Justice System Journal 32* (2), 143–166.

Robison, J. (2013). 'Autism and porn: A problem no one talks about.' *Psychology Today*. Accessed on 24/11/2020 at www.psychologytoday.com/us/blog/my-life-aspergers/201308/autism-and-porn-problem-no-one-talks-about.

Rogers, K., Dziobek, I., Hassenstab, J., Wolf, O. T., & Convit, A. (2007). 'Who cares? Revisiting empathy in Asperger syndrome.' *Journal of Autism and Developmental Disorders 37* (4), 709–715.

Rogers, S. J., Wehner, D. E., & Hagerman, R. (2001). 'The behavioral phenotype in fragile X: Symptoms of autism in very young children with fragile X syndrome, idiopathic autism, and other developmental disorders.' *Journal of Developmental and Behavioral Pediatrics 22* (6), 409–417.

Rolfe, S. M. (2019). 'When a sex offender comes to visit: A national assessment of travel restrictions.' *Criminal Justice Policy Review 30* (6), 885–905.

Rolfe, S. M., Tewksbury, R., & Schroeder, R. D. (2017). 'Homeless shelters' policies on sex offenders: Is this another collateral consequence?' *International Journal of Offender Therapy and Comparative Criminology 61* (16), 1833–1849.

Romano, M., Truzoli, R., Osborne, L. A., & Reed, P. (2014). 'The relationship between autism quotient, anxiety, and internet addiction.' *Research in Autism Spectrum Disorders 8* (11), 1521–1526.

Rosin, H. (2014). 'Why kids sext.' *The Atlantic*. Accessed on 24/11/2020 at www.theatlantic.com/magazine/archive/2014/11/why-kids-sext/380798.

Ross, D. L. (2015). 'Plumhoff v. Rickard: Clarifying the use of deadly force and qualified immunity.' *Criminal Justice Review 40* (2), 244–257.

Roth, M. E. & Gillis, J. M. (2015). '"Convenience with the click of a mouse": A survey of adults with autism spectrum disorder on online dating.' *Sexuality and Disability 33* (1), 133–150.

Roux, A. M., Rast, J. E., & Shattuck, P. T. (2018). 'State-level variation in vocational rehabilitation service use and related outcomes among transition-age youth on the autism spectrum.' *Journal of Autism and Developmental Disorders, 50* (7), 1–13.

Rozema, R. (2015). 'Manga and the autistic mind.' *English Journal*, 60–68.

Rubin, A. (2017). 'Downloading a nightmare.' *The Marshall Project*. Accessed on 24/11/2020 at www.themarshallproject.org/2017/05/31/downloading-a-nightmare.

Russo, N., Flanagan, T., Iarocci, G., Berringer, D., Zelazo, P. D., & Burack, J. A. (2007). 'Deconstructing executive deficits among persons with autism: Implications for cognitive neuroscience.' *Brain and Cognition 65* (1), 77–86.

Rydberg, J. (2018). 'Employment and housing challenges experienced by sex offenders during reentry on parole.' *Corrections 3* (1), 15–37.

Sample, L. L., Evans, M. K., & Anderson, A. L. (2011). 'Sex offender community notification laws: Are their effects symbolic or instrumental in nature?' *Criminal Justice Policy Review 22* (1), 27–49.

Samson, A. C., Huber, O., & Gross, J. J. (2012). 'Emotion regulation in Asperger's syndrome and high-functioning autism.' *Emotion 12* (4), 659.

Santos, M. G. (2007). *Inside: Life Behind Bars in America*. New York, NY: Macmillan.

Santos, M. G. (2012). *Earning Freedom: Conquering a 45-Year Prison Term*. Petaluma, CA: APS Publishing.

Santos, M. G. (2018). 'How to prepare for presentence investigation: Sentencing and prison guidance.' *Prison Professors*. Accessed on 24/11/2020 at https://prisonprofessors.com/prepare-presentence-investigation.

Sasikumar, K. & Adalarasu, K. (2015). 'Analysis of physiological signal variation between autism and control group in South Indian population.' *Biomedical Research 26* (3), 525–529.

Scarpa, A., White, S. W., & Attwood, T. (eds) (2013). *CBT for Children and Adolescents with High-Functioning Autism Spectrum Disorders*. New York, NY: Guilford Press.

Schatz, S. J. (2018). 'Interrogated with intellectual disabilities: The risks of false confession.' *Stanford Law Review 70* (2), 643–690.

Schlieder, M., Maldonado, N., & Baltes, B. (2014). 'An investigation of "Circle of Friends" peer-mediated intervention for students with autism.' *Journal of Social Change 6* (1), 27–40.

Schoneman, T. (2018). 'Overworked and underpaid: America's public defender crisis.' *Fordham Political Review*.

Schutte, J. W. & Schutte, C. W. (2018). 'Soldiers, savants, and sexual crimes: An examination of two groups of child pornography offenders.' *Forensic Psychology*. Accessed on 24/11/2020 at www.forensicpsychology. org/SchutteHandout2018.pdf.

Schwartz, J. C. (2017). 'How qualified immunity fails.' *Yale Law Journal 127* (1), 1–77.

Schwenck, C., Mergenthaler, J., Keller, K., Zech, J., *et al.* (2012). 'Empathy in children with autism and conduct disorder: Group-specific profiles and developmental aspects.' *Journal of Child Psychology and Psychiatry 53*, 651–659.

Scott, M., Milbourn, B., Falkmer, M., Black, M., *et al.* (2019). 'Factors impacting employment for people with autism spectrum disorder: A scoping review.' *Autism 23* (4), 869–901.

Serena, K. (2019). 'Meet Stephen Wiltshire: An autistic artist who can draw entire cities from memory.' *All That's Interesting*. Accessed on 24/11/2020 at https://allthatsinteresting.com/stephen-wiltshire.

Seto, M. C. (2008). *Pedophilia and Sexual Offending Against Children: Theory, Assessment, and Intervention*. Washington, DC: American Psychological Association.

Seto, M. C. (2013). *Internet Sex Offenders*. Washington, DC: American Psychological Association.

Seto, M. C. & Eke, A. W. (2015). 'Predicting recidivism among adult male child pornography offenders: Development of the Child Pornography Offender Risk Tool (CPORT).' *Law and Human Behavior 39* (4), 416.

Seto, M. C., Karl Hanson, R., & Babchishin, K. M. (2011). 'Contact sexual offending by men with online sexual offenses.' *Sexual Abuse 23* (1), 124–145.

Sevlever, M., Roth, M. E., & Gillis, J. M. (2013). 'Sexual abuse and offending in autism spectrum disorders.' *Sexuality and Disability 31* (2), 189–200.

Shafritz, K. M., Bregman, J. D., Ikuta, T., & Szeszko, P. R. (2015). 'Neural systems mediating decision-making and response inhibition for social and nonsocial stimuli in autism.' *Progress in Neuro-Psychopharmacology and Biological Psychiatry 60*, 112–120.

Shalom, D. B. (2003). 'Memory in autism: Review and synthesis.' *Cortex 39* (4–5), 1129–1138.

Shalom, D. B. (2009). 'The medial prefrontal cortex and integration in autism.' *The Neuroscientist 15* (6), 589–598.

Shanahan, M. J. (2000). 'Pathways to adulthood in changing societies: Variability and mechanisms in life course perspective.' *Annual Review of Sociology 26* (1), 667–692.

Shane-Simpson, C., Brooks, P. J., Obeid, R., Denton, E. G., & Gillespie-Lynch, K. (2016). 'Associations between compulsive internet use and the autism spectrum.' *Research in Autism Spectrum Disorders 23*, 152–165.

Shattuck, P. T., Roux, A. M., Hudson, L. E., Taylor, J. L., Maenner, M. J., & Trani, J.-F. (2012). 'Services for adults with an autism spectrum disorder.' *The Canadian Journal of Psychiatry 57* (5), 284–291.

Shechtman, P. & Cohn, D. J. (2014). *In the Supreme Court of West Virginia, Joseph A. Buffey v. David Ballard, Warden: Brief of Amici Curiae Former State and Federal Prosecutors in Support of Petitioner*. Accessed on 24/11/2020 at www.courtswv.gov/supreme-court/calendar/2015/briefs/oct15/14-0642amicus.pdf.

Shen, M. D., Kim, S. H., McKinstry, R. C., Gu, H., *et al.* (2017). 'Increased extra-axial cerebrospinal fluid in high-risk infants who later develop autism.' *Biological Psychiatry 82* (3), 186–193.

Shenson, D., Dubler, N., & Michaels, D. (1990). 'Jails and prisons, the new asylums?' *American Journal of Public Health 80*, 655–656.

Shic, F., Macari, S., & Chawarska, K. (2014). 'Speech disturbs face scanning in 6-month-old infants who develop autism spectrum disorder.' *Biological Psychiatry 75* (3), 231–237.

Shively, R. (2004). 'Treating offenders with mental retardation and developmental disabilities.' *Corrections Today 66* (6), 84–87.

Shuman, D. W., Whitaker, E., & Champagne, A. (1994). 'An empirical examination of the use of expert witnesses in the courts—part II: A three city study.' *Jurimetrics 34*, 193–208.

Siebers, T. (2008). *Disability Theory*. Ann Arbor, MI: University of Michigan Press.

Silberman, S. (2017). 'Opinion: The police need to understand autism.' *The New York Times*. Accessed on 24/11/2020 at www.nytimes.com/2017/09/19/opinion/police-autism-understanding.html.

Silk, T. J., Rinehart, N., Bradshaw, J. L., Tonge, B., *et al.* (2006). 'Visuospatial processing and the function of prefrontal-parietal networks in autism spectrum disorders: A functional MRI study.' *American Journal of Psychiatry 163* (8), 1440–1443.

Simard, I., Luck, D., Mottron, L., Zeffiro, T. A., & Soulières, I. (2015). 'Autistic fluid intelligence: Increased reliance on visual functional connectivity with diminished modulation of coupling by task difficulty.' *NeuroImage: Clinical 9*, 467–478.

Sims, T., Milton, D., Martin, N., & Dawkins, G. (2016). 'Developing a user-informed training package for a mentoring programme for people on the autism spectrum.' *Journal of Inclusive Practice in Further and Higher Education 7*, 49–52.

Singer, T. (2006). 'The neuronal basis and ontogeny of empathy and mind reading: Review of literature and implications for future research.' *Neuroscience and Biobehavioral Reviews 30*, 855–863.

Siponmaa, L., Kristiansson, M., Jonsson, C., Nydén, A., & Gillberg, C. (2001). 'Juvenile and young adult mentally disordered offenders: The role of child neuropsychiatric disorders.' *Journal of American Academy of Psychiatry and the Law 29*, 420–426.

Slisco, A. (2019). 'School officials deny that autistic 5-year-old was labelled "sexual predator" after hugging classmate.' *Newsweek*. Accessed on 24/11/2020 at www.newsweek.com/school-officials-deny-that-autistic-5-year-old-was-labelled-sexual-predator-after-hugging-1461424.

Smith, I. (2017). 'Mental age theory hurts people with intellectual disabilities.' *NOS Magazine*. Accessed on 24/11/2020 at http://nosmag.org/mental-age-theory-hurts-people-with-intellectual-disabilities.

Smith, L. E., Greenberg, J. S., & Mailick, M. R. (2012). 'Adults with autism: Outcomes, family effects, and the multi-family group psychoeducation model.' *Current Psychiatry Reports 14* (6), 732–738.

Smith, P. S. (2006). 'The effects of solitary confinement on prison inmates: A brief history and review of the literature.' *Crime and Justice 34* (1), 441–528.

Sobsey, D. (1994). *Violence and Abuse in the Lives of Persons with Disabilities: The End of Silent Acceptance?* Baltimore, MD: Paul H. Brookes.

Søndenaa, E., Helverschou, S. B., Steindal, K., Rasmussen, K., Nilson, B., & Nøttestad, J. A. (2014). 'Violence and sexual offending behavior in people with autism spectrum disorder who have undergone a psychiatric forensic examination.' *Psychological Reports 115* (1), 32–43.

South, C. R. & Wood, J. (2006). 'Bullying in prisons: The importance of perceived social status, prisonization, and moral disengagement.' *Aggressive Behavior 32*, 490–501.

South, M. & Rodgers, J. (2017). 'Sensory, emotional and cognitive contributions to anxiety in autism spectrum disorders.' *Frontiers in Human Neuroscience 11*, 20.

Sperry v. Maes [2013]. Civil Action No. 10-cv-03171-RPM, *Casetext*. Accessed on 24/11/2020 at https://casetext.com/case/sperry-v-maes-3.

Spezio, M. L., Adolphs, R., Hurley, R. S. E., & Piven, J. (2007). 'Abnormal use of facial information in high-functioning autism.' *Journal of Autism and Developmental Disorders 37*, 929–939.

Spitzer, S. & Scull, A. (1977). 'Privatization and capitalist development: The case of the private police.' *Social Problems 25* (1), 18–29.

Stabenow, T. (2011). 'A method for careful study: A proposal for reforming the child pornography guidelines.' *Federal Sentencing Reporter 24* (2), 108–136.

State of Nebraska v. Getzfred [2010]. Platte County Neb.

State v. Dassey [2007]. No. 06-CF-88 (Wis. Cir. Ct., Manitowoc Cty. Apr. 25) Evaluation Report for Determination of Eligibility for Special Education from Mishicot Sch. Dist. for Brendan Dassey, Mishicot, Wis. (Sept. 29, 2005).

Stavropolous, K. (2019). 'Trying to predict the future: Trajectories in autism.' *Psychology Today*. Accessed on 24/11/2020 at www.psychologytoday.com/us/blog/neuroscience-in-translation/201909/trying-predict-the-future-trajectories-in-autism.

Steadman, H. J. (2007). 'Treatment not jails: New leadership and promising practices.' Annual convention of the National Alliance on Mental Illness, San Diego, CA.

Steadman, H. J., Davidson, S., & Brown, C. (2001). 'Mental health courts: Their promise and unanswered questions.' *Psychiatric Services 52*, 457–458.

Steffenburg, H., Steffenburg, S., Gillberg, C., & Billstedt, E. (2018). 'Children with autism spectrum disorders and selective mutism.' *Neuropsychiatric Disease and Treatment 14*, 1163–1169.

Stein, M. A. & Lord, J. (2009). 'The Committee on the Rights of Persons with Disabilities.' In P. Alston & F. Mégret (eds) *The United Nations and Human Rights: A Critical Appraisal*. (pp.547–579). Oxford: Oxford University Press.

Steutel, J. & Spiecker, B. (2004). 'Sex education, state policy and the principle of mutual consent.' *Sex Education 4*, 49–62.

Stevenson, J. L., Harp, B., & Gernsbacher, M. A. (2011). 'Infantilizing autism.' *Disability Studies Quarterly 31* (3).

Stevenson, K., Cornell, K., & Hinchcliffe, V. (2016). '"Let's talk autism": A school-based project for students to explore and share their experiences of being autistic.' *Support for Learning 31* (3), 208–234.

Stewart, M. E., Barnard, L., Pearson, J., Hasan, R., & O'Brien, G. (2006). 'Presentation of depression in autism and Asperger syndrome: A review.' *Autism 10* (1), 103–116.

Stokes, M. & Newton, N. (2004). 'Autistic spectrum disorders and stalking.' *Autism 8*, 337–338.

Stokes, M., Newton, N., & Kaur, A. (2007). 'Stalking, and social and romantic functioning among adolescents and adults with autism spectrum disorder.' *Journal of Autism and Developmental Disorders 37* (10), 1969–1986.

Stokes, M. A. & Kaur, A. (2005). 'High-functioning autism and sexuality: A parental perspective.' *Autism 9*, 266–289.

Storbeck, J. & Clore, G. L. (2007). 'On the interdependence of cognition and emotion.' *Cognition and Emotion 21* (6), 1212–1237.

Stout, N. (2016). 'Reasons-responsiveness and moral responsibility: The case of autism.' *The Journal of Ethics 20* (4), 401–418.

Strang, J. (2018). 'Why we need to respect sexual orientation, gender diversity in autism.' *Spectrum*. Accessed on 24/11/2020 at www.spectrumnews.org/opinion/viewpoint/need-respect-sexual-orientation-gender-diversity-autism.

Strang, J. F., Powers, M. D., Knauss, M., Sibarium, E., *et al.* (2018). '"They thought it was an obsession": Trajectories and perspectives of autistic transgender and gender-diverse adolescents.' *Journal of Autism and Developmental Disorders 48* (12), 4039–4055.

Strang, H. & Sherman, L. W. (2003). 'Repairing the harm: Victims and restorative justice.' *Utah Law Review 15*, 15–42.

Strickland, J., Parry, C. L., Allan, M. M., & Allan, A. (2017). 'Alexithymia among perpetrators of violent offences in Australia: Implications for rehabilitation.' *Australian Psychologist 52* (3), 230–237.

Sugrue, D. P. (2017). 'Forensic Assessment of Individuals with Autism Spectrum Charged with Child Pornography Violations.' In L. A. Dubin & E. Horowitz, *Caught in the Web of the Criminal Justice System: Autism, Developmental Disabilities, and Sex Offenses* (pp.112–140). London: Jessica Kingsley Publishers.

Suler, J. (2004). 'The online disinhibition effect.' *Cyberpsychology and Behavior 7* (3), 321–326.

Sunderland, M. (2017). 'The autistic children who are labeled as sex offenders.' *Vice*. Accessed on 24/11/2020 at www.vice.com/en_us/article/kz7zxa/the-autistic-children-who-are-labeled-as-sex-offenders.

Suresh, G., Mustaine, E. E., Tewksbury, R., & Higgins, G. E. (2010). 'Social disorganization and registered sex offenders: An exploratory spatial analysis.' *Southwest Journal of Criminal Justice 7* (2), 180–213.

Sutton, L. R., Hughes, T. L., Huang, A., Lehman, C., *et al.* (2013). 'Identifying individuals with autism in a state facility for adolescents adjudicated as sexual offenders: A pilot study.' *Focus on Autism and Other Developmental Disabilities 28* (3), 175–183.

Swann, A. C., Lijffijt, M., Lane, S. D., Kjome, K. L., Steinberg, J. L., & Moeller, F. G. (2011). 'Criminal conviction, impulsivity, and course of illness in bipolar disorder.' *Bipolar Disorders 13* (2), 173–181.

Swanson, M. R., Shen, M. D., Wolff, J. J., Elison, J. T., *et al.* (2017). 'Subcortical brain and behavior phenotypes differentiate infants with autism versus language delay.' *Biological Psychiatry: Cognitive Neuroscience and Neuroimaging 2* (8), 664–672.

Szilagyi, J. (2019). 'Evans Co. schools turns special needs child over to court system for documented medical issue.' *All On Georgia*. Accessed on 24/11/2020 at https://allongeorgia.com/evans-board-of-education/evans-co-schools-turns-special-needs-child-over-to-court-system-for-documented-medical-issue.

Tager-Flusberg, H., Joseph, R., & Folstein, S. (2001). 'Current directions in research on autism.' *Mental Retardation and Developmental Disabilities Research Reviews 7*, 21–29.

Takara, K. & Kondo, T. (2014). 'Comorbid atypical autistic traits as a potential risk factor for suicide attempts among adult depressed patients: A case-control study.' *Annals of General Psychiatry 13* (1), 33.

Tantam, D. (2000). 'Adolescence and Adulthood of Individuals with Asperger Syndrome.' In A. Klin, F. R. Volkmar, & S. S. Sparrow (eds) *Asperger Syndrome*. (pp.367–403). New York, NY: The Guilford Press.

Tarm, M. (2020a). 'Autistic futures trader who triggered crash spared prison.' *AP News*. Accessed on 24/11/2020 at https://apnews.com/55632b678a8a172f485685caodbf2b98.

Tarm, M. (2020b). 'Autistic futures trader who triggered crash spared prison.' *Yahoo! Finance*. Accessed on 24/11/2020 at https://finance.yahoo.com/news/autistic-futures-trader-triggered-crash-003121499.html.

Taylor, J. L. & Seltzer, M. M. (2010). 'Changes in the autism behavioral phenotype during the transition to adulthood.' *Journal of Autism and Developmental Disorders 40* (12), 1431–1446.

Taylor, J. L. & Seltzer, M. M. (2011). 'Employment and post-secondary educational activities for young adults with autism spectrum disorders during the transition to adulthood.' *Journal of Autism and Developmental Disorders 41* (5), 566–574.

Teplin, L. A. & Pruett, N. S. (1992). 'Police as streetcorner psychiatrist: Managing the mentally ill.' *International Journal of Law and Psychiatry 15*, 139–258.

Tewksbury, R. (2005). 'Collateral consequences of sex offender registration.' *Journal of Contemporary Criminal Justice 21* (1), 67–82.

The Arc (2016). 'Mislabeled a sex offender: The Kelmar family's fight for justice.' *The Arc*. Accessed on 23/11/2020 at https://thearc.org/mislabeled-sex-offender-kelmar-familys-fight-justice-2.

The University of Manchester (2019). *Susceptibility to Radicalisation in those with Autism Spectrum Disorder*. Accessed on 24/11/2020 at www.research.manchester.ac.uk/portal/en/projects/susceptibility-to-radicalisation-in-those-with-autism-spectrum-disorder(00113b1e-6b96-4044-87e2-6c8bfdeo208d).html.

Think Inclusive (2017). '12 myths about autism.' *Think Inclusive*.

Thompkins, R. & Deloney, P. (1995). 'Inclusion pros and cons.' *Southwest Educational Development Laboratory 4* (1), 1–19.

Thompson, R., Valenti, E., Siette, J., & Priebe, S. (2016). 'To befriend or to be a friend: A systematic review of the meaning and practice of "befriending" in mental health care.' *Journal of Mental Health 25* (1), 71–77.

Tick, B., Colvert, E., McEwen, F., Stewart, C., *et al.* (2016). 'Autism spectrum disorders and other mental health problems: Exploring etiological overlaps and phenotypic causal associations.' *Journal of the American Academy of Child and Adolescent Psychiatry 55* (2), 106–113.

Tillmann, J., San José Cáceres, A., Chatham, C. H., Crawley, D., *et al.* (2019). 'Investigating the factors underlying adaptive functioning in autism in the EU-AIMS Longitudinal European Autism Project.' *Autism Research 12* (4), 645–657.

Tobin, T. C. (2019). 'Policing and Special Populations: Strategies to Overcome Policing Challenges Encountered with Mentally Ill Individuals.' In J. Albrecht, G. den Heyer, & P. Stanislas (eds) *Policing and Minority Communities* (pp.75–93). New York, NY: Springer.

Todd, J., Mills, C., Wilson, A. D., Plumb, M. S., & Mon-Williams, M. A. (2009). 'Slow motor responses to visual stimuli of low salience in autism.' *Journal of Motor Behavior 41* (5), 419–426.

Tonge, B. & Brereton, A. (2011). 'Autism spectrum disorders.' *Australian Family Physician 40* (9), 672–677.

Tonry, M. (1996). *Sentencing Matters.* New York, NY: Oxford University Press.

Torisky, C. (1985). 'Sex education and sexual awareness building for autistic children and youth: Some viewpoints and considerations.' *Journal of Autism and Developmental Disorders 15* (2), 213–227.

Torrado, J. C., Montoro, G., & Gomez, J. (2016). 'The potential of Smartwatches for emotional self-regulation of people with autism spectrum disorder.' *Proceedings of the 9th International Joint Conference on Biomedical Engineering Systems and Technologies (BIOSTEC 2016) 5: HEALTHINF*, 444–449.

Torrey, E. F. (1997). *Out of the Shadows: Confronting America's Mental Illness Crisis.* New York, NY: John Wiley & Sons.

Torrey, E. F., Kennard, A. D., Eslinger, D. F., Biasotti, M. C., & Fuller, D. A. (2013). *Justifiable Homicides by Law Enforcement Officers: What is the Role of Mental Illness?* Arlington, VA: Treatment Advocacy Center and National Sheriffs' Association. Accessed on 24/11/2020 at www.treatmentadvocacycenter.org/storage/documents/2013-justifiable-homicides.pdf.

Torrey, E. F., Zdanowicz, M. T., Kennard, A. D., Lamb, H. R., *et al.* (2014). *The Treatment of Persons with Mental Illness in Prisons and Jails: A State Survey.* Arlington, VA: Treatment Advocacy Center. Accessed on 24/11/2020 at www.treatmentadvocacycenter.org/storage/documents/treatment-behind-bars/treatment-behind-bars.pdf.

Townsend, J., Harris, N. S., & Courchesne, E. (1996). 'Visual attention abnormalities in autism: Delayed orienting to location.' *Journal of the International Neuropsychological Society 2* (6), 541–550.

Trainum, J. (2016). *How the Police Generate False Confessions.* Lanham, MD: Rowan & Littlefield.

Travers, B. G., Bigler, E. D., Duffield, T. C., Prigge, M. D., *et al.* (2017). 'Longitudinal development of manual motor ability in autism spectrum disorder from childhood to mid-adulthood relates to adaptive daily living skills.' *Developmental Science 20* (4), e12401.

Turner, D., Briken, P., & Schöttle, D. (2019). 'Sexual dysfunctions and their association with the dual control model of sexual response in men and women with high-functioning autism.' *Journal of Clinical Medicine 8* (4), 425.

Turygin, N. C. & Matson, J. L. (2014). 'Adaptive Behavior, Life Skills, and Leisure Skills Training for Adolescents and Adults with Autism Spectrum Disorders.' In *Adolescents and Adults with Autism Spectrum Disorders* (pp.131–160). New York, NY: Springer.

UCLA Law (2018). 'Philadelphia DA Larry Krasner spends the day at UCLA Law.' *UCLA Law.* Accessed on 22/12/2020 at https://escholarship.org/content/qt91g5q8j2/qt91g5q8j2.pdf?t=psvpkx.

Uher, R. (2009). 'The role of genetic variation in the causation of mental illness: An evolution-informed framework.' *Molecular Psychiatry 14* (12), 1072–1082.

Ulrich, T. E. (2002). 'Pretrial diversion in the federal court system.' *Federal Probation Journal 66*, 30–37.

United Nations (2019). *Article 13: Access to Justice.* Accessed on 24/11/2020 at www.un.org/development/desa/disabilities/convention-on-the-rights-of-persons-with-disabilities/article-13-access-to-justice.html.

United States v. Blattner [2008]. 2:07-CR-00281-GD-1 (W.D. Pa.).

United States v. Carlsson [2016]. 15-CR-200-B (M.D. Fla.).

United States v. Carpenter [2009]. 6:08-CR-06256-001 (W.D.N.Y.).

United States v. Danaher [2010]. CR-10-150- CAS (C.D. Ca.).

United States v. DeHaven [2009]. 08-CR-00031-LRR (N.D. Iowa).

United States v. Dolehide [2011]. No. 10-CR-92-LRR (N.D. Iowa, May 5).

United States v. Joy [2008]. 1:07-CR-000187-001 (N.D.N.Y.).

United States v. Keskin [2017]. 6:17-CR-0077-RBD-DCI (M.D. Fla.).

United States v. Meiller [2009]. 650 F.Supp.2d 887, 07-CR-0158.

United States v. Munson [2009]. 07-CR-443 (D. Md.).

United States v. Peterson [2016]. 2:14-CR-00505 (D. Utah).

United States v. Richardson [2001]. 238 F.3d 837 (7th Cir).

United States v. Rodriguez [2014]. No. 14-20877-CR-UU (S.D. Fla.).

United States v. Rubino [2008]. WD NY No. 4:08-CR-00114.

United States v. Wilson [2012]. No. 12-CR-5220-H (S.D. Cal.).

U.S. Department of Justice (2015a). *63: Standards for Determining Competency and for Conducting a Hearing.* Accessed on 24/11/2020 at www.justice.gov/jm/criminal-resource-manual-63-standards-determining-competency-and-conducting-hearing.

U.S. Department of Justice (2015b). *9-22.000: Pretrial Diversion Program.* Accessed on 24/11/2020 at www.justice.gov/jm/jm-9-22000-pretrial-diversion-program.

U.S. Department of Justice Archives (2015). *712: Pretrial Diversion.* Accessed on 24/11/2020 at www.justice.gov/archives/jm/criminal-resource-manual-712-pretrial-diversion.

U.S. Department of Justice, Civil Rights Division, Disability Rights Section (2019). *Commonly Asked Questions about the Americans with Disabilities Act and Law Enforcement.* Accessed on 24/11/2020 at www.ada.gov/q%26a_law.htm.

van Camp, T. & Wemmers, J. A. (2013). 'Victim satisfaction with restorative justice: More than simply procedural justice.' *International Review of Victimology 19* (2), 117–143.

van der Aa, C., Pollmann, M. M. H., Plaat, A., & Van der Gaag, R. (2016). 'Computer-mediated communication in adults with high-functioning autism spectrum disorders and controls.' *Research in Autism Spectrum Disorders 23*, 15–27.

van Elst, L. T., Riedel, A., & Maier, S. (2016). 'Autism as a disorder of altered global functional and structural connectivity.' *Biological Psychiatry 79* (8), 626–627.

van Impelen, A., Merckelbach, H., Jelicic, M., Niesten, I. J., & à Campo, J. (2017). 'Differentiating factitious from malingered symptomatology: The development of a psychometric approach.' *Psychological Injury and Law 10* (4), 341–357.

Vance, S. E. (2017). 'Conditions of supervision in federal criminal sentencing: A review of recent changes.' *Federal Probation Journal 81*, 3–14.

Verity, A. (2020). 'Hound of Hounslow: Who is Navinder Sarao, the "flash crash trader"?' *BBC News.* Accessed on 23/11/2020 at www.bbc.com/news/explainers-51265169.

Victorian Equal Opportunity and Human Rights Commission (2014). *Beyond Doubt: The Experience of People with Disabilities Reporting Crime – Research Findings.* Accessed on 24/11/2020 at www.humanrights.vic.gov.au/resources/beyond-doubt-the-experiences-of-people-with-disabilities-reporting-crime-jul-2014.

Viljoen, E. (2019). *Statement Taking by Police Officers from Persons with Complex Communication Needs Who Report Being a Victim of Crime* (Doctoral Dissertation, University of Pretoria).

Virginia's Legislative Information System (2020a). *LIS > Bill Tracking > SB133 > 2020 Session.* Accessed on 24/11/2020 at http://lis.virginia.gov/cgi-bin/legp604.exe?201+sum+SB133.

Virginia's Legislative Information System (2020b). *Bill Tracking > 2020 Session > Legislation.* Accessed on 24/11/2020 at http://lis.virginia.gov/cgi-bin/legp604.exe?201+ful+SB133.

Volkmar, F. R. & McPartland, J. C. (2014). 'From Kanner to DSM-5: Autism as an evolving diagnostic concept.' *Annual Review of Clinical Psychology 10*, 193–212.

Volkmar, F. R., Paul, R., Klin, A., & Cohen, D. J. (2005). 'Chapter 51: Temple Grandin. A Personal Perspective of Autism.' In *Handbook of Autism and Pervasive Developmental Disorders, Volume 1* (p.1283). Hoboken, NJ: John Wiley & Sons.

Volkmar, F. R., Sparrow, S. S., Goudreau, D., Cicchetti, D. V., Paul, R., & Cohen, D. J. (1987). 'Social deficits in autism: An operational approach using the Vineland Adaptive Behavior Scales.' *Journal of the American Academy of Child and Adolescent Psychiatry 26* (2), 156–161.

Vrij, A. (2008). *Detecting Lies and Deceit: Pitfalls and Opportunities.* Chichester: John Wiley.

Vrij, A., Granhag, P. A., & Mann, S. (2010). 'Good liars.' *Journal of Psychiatry and Law 38*, 77–98.

Vrij, A., Granhag, P. A., & Porter, S. (2010). 'Pitfalls and opportunities in nonverbal and verbal lie detection.' *Psychological Science in the Public Interest 11*, 89–121.

Wainwright-Sharp, J. A. & Bryson, S. E. (1993). 'Visual orienting deficits in high-functioning people with autism.' *Journal of Autism and Developmental Disorders 23* (1), 1–13.

Wallace, G. L., Kenworthy, L., Pugliese, C. E., Popal, H. S., et al. (2016). 'Real-world executive functions in adults with autism spectrum disorder: Profiles of impairment and associations with adaptive functioning and co-morbid anxiety and depression.' *Journal of Autism and Developmental Disorders 46* (3), 1071–1083.

Wallace, S. (2018). 'Judge rules notorious NYC Transit thief dangerously mentally ill, to be committed to lock-down facility.' *NBC New York.* Accessed on 24/11/2020 at www.nbcnewyork.com/news/local/judge-rules-notorious-nyc-transit-thief-dangerously-mentally-ill-committed-lock-down-facility-new-york-city/1820913.

Walsh, J. & Holt, D. (1999). 'Jail diversion for people with psychiatric disabilities: The sheriffs' perspective.' *Psychiatric Rehabilitation Journal 23* (2), 153–160.

Ward, T., Yates, P. M., & Long, C. A. (2006). *The Self Regulation Model of the Offence and Relapse Process, Volume II: Treatment.* Victoria, BC: Pacific Psychological Assessment Corporation.

Watanabe, T., Yahata, N., Abe, O., Kuwabara, H., *et al.* (2012). 'Diminished medial prefrontal activity behind autistic social judgments of incongruent information.' *PLOS ONE 7* (6), 1–11.

Weaver, J. (2016). 'Feds plan to drop child-porn charges against autistic Miami man.' *Miami Herald.* Accessed on 24/11/2020 at www.miamiherald.com/news/local/article76019472.html.

Wehmeyer, M. L. (2002). *Self-Determination and the Education of Students with Disabilities.* Arlington, VA: ERIC Clearinghouse on Disabilities and Gifted Education.

Weill-Greenberg, E. (2019). 'The push to end "punishment fever" against people with HIV.' *The Appeal.* Accessed on 24/11/2020 at https://theappeal.org/the-push-to-end-punishment-fever-against-people-with-hiv.

Weiss, K. J. (2011). 'Autism spectrum disorder and criminal justice: Square peg in a round hole?' *American Journal of Forensic Psychiatry 32* (3), 1–19.

Weissman, P. & Hendrick, J. (2014). *The Whole Child: Developmental Education for the Early Years.* Boston, MA: Pearson.

Wertlieb, E. C. (1991). 'Individuals with disabilities in the criminal justice system: A review of the literature.' *Criminal Justice and Behavior 18* (3), 332–350.

Wexler, D. B. & Winick, B. (eds) (1996). *Law in a Therapeutic Key: Developments in Therapeutic Jurisprudence.* Durham, NC: Carolina Academic Press.

Whitehouse, A., Watt, H., Line, E., & Bishop, D. (2009). 'Adult psychosocial outcomes of children with specific language impairment, pragmatic language impairment and autism.' *International Journal of Language and Communication Disorders 44* (4), 511–528.

Wigmore, J. (1923). *A Treatise on the Anglo-American System of Evidence in Trials at Common Law: Including the Statutes and Judicial Decisions of All Jurisdictions of the United States and Canada.* Boston, MA: Little, Brown.

Wilcock, R., Crane, L., Hobson, Z., Nash, G., & Kirke-Smith, H. (2019). 'Eyewitness identification in child witnesses on the autism spectrum.' *Research in Autism Spectrum Disorders 66*, 101407.

Wilson, C. & Saunders, R. (2003). 'COSA: Questions and answers: The theoretical framework.' *NOTA News 45*, 6–8.

Wilson, R. & Miner, M. H. (2016). 'Measurement of Male Sexual Arousal and Interest Using Penile Plethysmography and Viewing Time.' In *Treatment of Sex Offenders* (pp.107–131). Cham: Springer.

Wilson, R., McWhinnie, A., Picheca, J. E., Prinzo, M., & Cortoni, F. (2007). 'Circles of support and accountability: Engaging community volunteers in the management of high-risk sexual offenders.' *The Howard Journal of Criminal Justice 46* (1), 1–15.

Wilson, R., Picheca, J., & Prinzo, M. (2007). 'Evaluating the effectiveness of professionally-facilitated volunteerism in the community-based management of high-risk sex offenders: Part one – effects on participants and stakeholders.' *The Howard Journal of Criminal Justice 46* (3), 289–302.

Wing, L. (1981). 'Asperger's syndrome: A clinical account.' *Psychological Medicine 11*, 115–129.

Winter-Messiers, M. A., Herr, C. M., Wood, C. E., Brooks, A. P., *et al.* (2007). 'How far can Brian ride the Daylight 4449 Express? A strength-based model of Asperger syndrome based on special interest areas.' *Focus on Autism and Other Developmental Disabilities 22* (2), 67–79.

Winters, G. M., Jeglic, E. L., Calkins, C., & Blasko, B. L. (2017). 'Sex offender legislation and social control: An examination of sex offenders' expectations prior to release.' *Criminal Justice Studies 30*, 2, 202–222.

Wirral Autistic Society (2015). *Mate Crime in Merseyside.* Accessed on 24/11/2020 at www.autismtogether. co.uk/wp-content/uploads/2020/07/AT-mate-crime-report-June-2015.pdf.

Wlodarski, R. (2015). 'The relationship between cognitive and affective empathy and human mating strategies.' *Evolutionary Psychological Science 1* (4), 232–240.

Wolff, J. J., Gu, H., Gerig, G., Elison, J. T., *et al.* (2012). 'Differences in white matter fiber tract development present from 6 to 24 months in infants with autism.' *American Journal of Psychiatry 169* (6), 589–600.

Wolff, N. & Shi, J. (2009). 'Type, source and patterns of physical victimization: A comparison of male and female inmates.' *Prison Journal 89*, 172–191.

Wong, C., Odom, S. L., Hume, K. A., Cox, A. W., *et al.* (2015). 'Evidence-based practices for children, youth, and young adults with autism spectrum disorder: A comprehensive review.' *Journal of Autism and Developmental Disorders 45* (7), 1951–1966.

Woodbury-Smith, M. R., Clare, I. C. H., Holland, A. J., & Kearns, A. (2006). 'High functioning autistic spectrum disorders, offending and other law-breaking: Findings from a community sample.' *The Journal of Forensic Psychiatry and Psychology 17* (1), 108–120.

Woodbury-Smith, M. R., Clare, I. C. H., Holland, A. J., Kearns, A., Staufenberg, E., & Watson, P. (2005). 'A case-control study of offenders with high functioning autistic spectrum disorders.' *The Journal of Forensic Psychiatry and Psychology 16*, 747–763.

World Health Organization (2004). *ICD-10: International Statistical Classification of Diseases and Related Health Problems, Tenth Edition, Fourth Version* (2nd ed.). Geneva: World Health Organization.

Wright, R. (ed.) (2014). *Sex Offender Laws: Failed Policies, New Directions*. New York, NY: Springer Publishing Company.

Wrong Planet (2010). 'Did your parents ever talk to you about sex?' *Wrong Planet*. Accessed on 24/11/2020 at https://wrongplanet.net/forums/viewtopic.php?f=3&t=137836&start=60.

Wrong Planet (2012). 'Should high schools teach how to date?' *Wrong Planet*. Accessed on 24/11/2020 at https://wrongplanet.net/forums/viewtopic.php?f=6&t=210841.

Wszalek, J. A. & Turkstra, L. S. (2019). 'Comprehension of legal language by adults with and without traumatic brain injury.' *The Journal of Head Trauma Rehabilitation 34* (3), E55–E63.

Wupperman, P., Cohen, M. G., Haller, D. L., Flom, P., Litt, L. C., & Rounsaville, B. J. (2015). 'Mindfulness and modification therapy for behavioral dysregulation: A comparison trial focused on substance use and aggression.' *Journal of Clinical Psychology 71* (10), 964–978.

Xiang, A. H., Wang, X., Martinez, M. P., Walthall, J. C., *et al.* (2015). 'Association of maternal diabetes with autism in offspring.' *JAMA 313* (14), 1425–1434.

Yang, C. S. (2014). 'Have interjudge sentencing disparities increased in an advisory guidelines regime—evidence from Booker.' *New York University Law Review 89*, 1268–1328.

Yang, C. S. (2015). 'Free at last? Judicial discretion and racial disparities in federal sentencing.' *The Journal of Legal Studies 44* (1), 75–111.

Yasuda, Y., Hashimoto, R., Nakae, A., Kang, H., *et al.* (2016). 'Sensory cognitive abnormalities of pain in autism spectrum disorder: A case-control study.' *Annals of General Psychiatry 1* (15), 1–8.

Yates, P. M. & Ward, T. (2008). 'Good lives, self-regulation, and risk management: An integrated model of sexual offender assessment and treatment.' *Sexual Abuse in Australia and New Zealand: An Interdisciplinary Journal 1*, 3–20.

Yates, P. M., Prescott, D. S., & Ward, T. (2010). *Applying the Good Lives and Self Regulation Models to Sex Offender Treatment: A Practical Guide for Clinicians*. Brandon, VT: Safer Society Press.

Yi, L., Pan, J., Fan, Y., Xiaobing, Z., Wang, X., & Lee, K. (2013). 'Children with autism spectrum disorder are more trusting than typically developing peers.' *Journal of Experimental Psychology 116* (3), 755–761.

Zaboski, B. A. & Storch, E. A. (2018). 'Comorbid autism spectrum disorder and anxiety disorders: A brief review.' *Future Neurology 13* (1), 31–37.

Zaki, J. & Ochsner, K. N. (2012). 'The neuroscience of empathy: Progress, pitfalls and promise.' *Nature Neuroscience 15* (5), 675–680.

Zamanski, H. (1956). 'A technique for measuring homosexual tendencies.' *Journal of Personality 24*, 436–448.

Zerbo, O., Iosif, A.-M., Walker, C., Ozonoff, S., Hansen, R. L., & Hertz-Picciotto, I. (2013). 'Is maternal influenza or fever during pregnancy associated with autism or developmental delays? Results from the CHARGE (CHildhood Autism Risks from Genetics and Environment) Study.' *Journal of Autism and Developmental Disorders 43* (1), 25–33.

Zgoba, K. & Ragbir, D. (2016). 'Sex Offender Registration and Notification Act (SORNA).' In *Sexual Violence* (pp.33–49). Cham: Springer.

Zgoba, K. M. (2011). 'Residence restriction buffer zones and the banishment of sex offenders: Have we gone one step too far?' *Criminology and Public Policy 10* (2), 391–400.

Zgoba, K. M. & Levenson, J. (2012). 'Failure to register as a predictor of sex offense recidivism: The big bad wolf or a red herring?' *Sexual Abuse 24* (4), 328–349.

Subject Index

Author Index

Abel, G.G. 180
Abramov, E. 55, 58
Abrams, D. 108
Adalarasu, K. 138
Al-Owain, M. 137
Al-Rousan, T. 102
Alisanski, S. 45
Allely, C.S. 42, 47, 70, 92, 135, 167, 178, 182
Allen, D. 129
Allen, R. 26, 27
Allen, S. 62, 63
Alvarez, S. 174
Amanullah, S. 45
Amaral, D. 124
Ambler, P.G. 68
American Psychiatric Association 41, 130
Anderson, A.L. 173
Anderson, K.A. 18, 84
Anderson, V.V. 55
Ania, F. 124
Anthony, I.G. 135
Archer, J. 167
Arnett, J.J. 84
Ashkar, P.J. 167
Asperger, H. 25
Associated Press 58
Atladóttir, H.Ó. 124
Attwood, A. 15, 18, 19, 28, 114
Aunos, M. 19
Austin, R. 162
Autistic Self Advocacy Network 83
Aviv, R. 172

Babchishin, K.M. 140
Bacon, S.L. 109

Baer, R.A. 28
Bagenstos, S. 70
Bailey, A. 82
Baker, L.J. 72
Baldwin, J.M. 140
Baldwin, S. 100
Ballaban-Gil, K. 100
Ballan, M.S. 19, 20, 114
Baltes, B. 36
Banbury, S. 167
Barbaree, H.E. 180
Barber, C.G. 68
Barnett, J.P. 34
Baron-Cohen, S. 97, 126, 127–8, 180, 181
Barron, S. 23
Barry-Walsh, J.B. 46
Baskin-Sommers, A. 128
Bass, J.D. 118
Bates, A. 187
Bath, C. 78, 79
Batson, C.D. 181
Baude, W. 85
Beck, G. 38
Becker-Weidman, A. 123
Beddows, N. 20
Bedesem, P.L. 100
Belardinelli, C. 131
Bellard, H.S. 136
Bellin, J. 104
Bellini, S. 29
Berghammer, R. 181
Berman, D.A. 157
Berry, K. 106
Berryessa, C.M. 160
Bertilsdotter-Rosqvist, H. 37–8